ST THOMAS AQUINAS
SUMMA THEOLOGIÆ

ST THOMAS AQUINAS

SUMMA
THEOLOGIÆ

Latin text and English translation,
Introductions, Notes, Appendices
and Glossaries

NON NISI TE

BLACKFRIARS

IN CONJUNCTION WITH

EYRE & SPOTTISWOODE, LONDON, AND
McGRAW-HILL BOOK COMPANY, NEW YORK

PIÆ MEMORIÆ

JOANNIS

PP. XXIII

DICATUM

1426991

PAULI

PP. VI

MCMLXIII

HIS HOLINESS POPE PAUL VI

WAS PLEASED to grant an audience, on 13 December 1963, to a group, representing the Dominican Editors and the combined Publishers of the new translation of the *Summa Theologiæ* of St Thomas, led by His Eminence Michael Cardinal Browne, of the Order of Preachers, and the Most Reverend Father Aniceto Fernandez, Master General of the same Order.

AT THIS AUDIENCE

THE HOLY FATHER made a cordial allocution in which he first welcomed the representatives of a project in which he found particular interest. He went on to laud the perennial value of St Thomas's doctrine as embodying universal truths in so cogent a fashion. This doctrine, he said, is a treasure belonging not only to the Dominican Order but to the whole Church, and indeed to the whole world; it is not merely medieval but valid for all times, not least of all for our own.

His Holiness therefore commended the enterprise of Dominicans from English-speaking Provinces of the Order and of their friends; they were undertaking a difficult task, less because the thought of St Thomas is complicated or his language subtle, than because the clarity of his thought and exactness of language is so difficult to translate. Yet the successful outcome of their efforts would undoubtedly contribute to the religious and cultural well-being of the English-speaking world.

What gave him great satisfaction was the notable evidence of interest in the spread of divine truth on the part of the eminent laymen concerned, members of different communions yet united in a common venture.

For these reasons the Holy Father wished it all success, and warmly encouraged and blessed all those engaged. He was happy to receive the first volume presented to him as a gesture of homage, and promised that he would follow with interest the progress of the work and look forward to the regular appearance of all the subsequent volumes.

VOLUMES

GENERAL PREFACE

BY OFFICIAL APPOINTMENT THE SUMMA PROVIDES THE FRAMEWORK
for Catholic studies in systematic theology and for a classical Christian
philosophy. Yet the work, which is more than a text-book for professional
training, is also the witness of developing tradition and the source of
living science about divine things. For faith seeks understanding in the
contemplation of God's Logos, his wisdom and saving providence, running through the whole universe.

The purpose, then, of this edition is not narrowly clerical, but to share
with all Christians a treasury which is part of their common heritage.
Moreover, it consults the interests of many who would not claim to be
believers, and yet appreciate the integrity which takes religion into hard
thinking.

Accordingly the editors have kept in mind the needs of the general
reader who can respond to the reasons in Christianity, as well as of
technical theologians and philosophers.

Putting the Latin text alongside the English is part of the purpose. The
reader with a smattering of Latin can be reassured when the translator,
in order to be clear and readable, renders the thought of St Thomas into
the freedom of another idiom without circumlocution or paraphrase.

There are two more reasons for the inclusion of the Latin text. First,
to help the editors themselves, for the author's thought is too lissom to be
uniformly and flatly transliterated; it rings with analogies, and its precision
cannot be reduced to a table of terms. A rigid consistency has not been
imposed on the editors of the different volumes among themselves; the
original is given, and the student can judge for himself.

Next, to help those whose native tongue is not English or whose duty it
is to study theology in Latin, of whom many are called to teach and preach
through the medium of the most widespread language of the world, now
becoming the second language of the Church.

The Latin is a sound working text, selected, paragraphed, and punc-
tuated by the responsible editor. Important variations, in manuscripts
and such major printed editions as the Piana and Leonine, are indicated.
The English corresponds paragraph by paragraph and almost always sentence by sentence. Each of the sixty volumes, so far as is possible, will be
complete in itself, to serve as a text for a special course or for private study.

THOMAS GILBY O.P.

ST THOMAS AQUINAS

SUMMA THEOLOGIÆ

VOLUME 8

CREATION, VARIETY AND EVIL

(1a.44–49)

Latin text. English translation, Introduction,
Notes, Appendices & Glossary

THOMAS GILBY O.P.
Blackfriars, Cambridge

NON NISI TE

NIHIL OBSTAT

GEORGIUS REILLY O.P.
KENELMUS FOSTER O.P.

IMPRIMI POTEST

JOANNES HISLOP O.P.
Prior Provincialis Angliæ

die 13 Junii 1967

NIHIL OBSTAT

M. W. ASHDOWNE S.T.D.
Censor

IMPRIMATUR

✠ PATRICK CASEY
Vic. Gen.

Westminster, 8 May 1967

PRINTED IN GREAT BRITAIN BY EYRE AND SPOTTISWOODE LIMITED

CONTENTS

EDITORIAL NOTES

THE TEXT AND TRANSLATION

TO MY MIND there is no sounder working text of the *Prima Pars* than that given in the 1926 edition of the Toulouse Dominicans, here referred to as Pègues. On debatable points its informed decision favours St Thomas's *continua ratio* rather than the manuscript evidence. I have followed its readings in the main, though I have introduced new paragraphs and tidied up the punctuation. All but the most petty variants from the Piana and Leonine are noted.

While matching the order of the sentences, the translation avoids some repetitions occasioned by St Thomas's habit of dictation. It will be noticed that his own technical terms are not rendered into fixed and constant English equivalents: to do so would be to impoverish his meaning and miss the analogies of his discourse.

FOOTNOTES

Those signified by a superior number are the references given by St Thomas, with the exception of no. 1 to each article, which provides the parallel texts in his writings. Footnotes signified alphabetically are editorial references or explanatory remarks.

REFERENCES

Biblical references are to the Vulgate. Patristic references are to Migne (PG, Greek Fathers; PL, Latin Fathers). 'The Gloss' always refers to the *Glossa Ordinaria*; 'a gloss' refers to others cited in the text. Abbreviations to St Thomas's works are as follows:

Summa Theologiæ, without title. Part, question, article, reply; eg. 1a. 3, 2 ad 3. 1a2æ. 17, 6. 2a2æ, 180, 10. 3a. 35, 8.

Summa Contra Gentiles, CG. Book, chapter; e.g. *CG* 1, 28.

Scriptum in IV Libros Sententiarum, *Sent.* Book, distinction, question, article, solution or *quæstiuncula*, reply; e.g. III *Sent.* 25, 2, 3, ii ad 3.

Compendium Theologiæ, *Compend. Theol.*

Commentaries of Scripture (*lecturæ, expositiones*): Job, *In Job*; Psalms, *In Psal.*; Isaiah, *In Isa.*; Jeremiah, *In Jerem.*; Lamentations, *In Thren.*; St Matthew, *In Matt.*; St John, *In Joan.*; Epistles of St Paul, e.g. *In Rom.* Chapter, verse, *lectio* as required.

Philosophical commentaries: On the *Liber de Causis, In De causis*. Aristotle: *Peri Hermeneias, In Periherm.*; Posterior Analytics. *In Poster.*; Physics, *In Physic.; De Cælo et Mundo, In De Cæl.*; *De Generatione et Corruptione, In De gen.; Meteorologica, In Meteor.*; *De Anima, In De anima; De Sensu et Sensato, In De sensu; De Memoria et Reminiscentia, In De memor*; Metaphysics, *In Meta.*; Nicomachean Ethics, *In Ethic.; Politics, In Pol.* Book, chapter, *lectio* as required, also for Expositions on Boëthius, *Liber de Hebdomadibus* and *Liber de Trinitate, In De hebd.* and *In De Trin.*, and on Dionysius, *De Divinis Nominibus, In De div. nom.* References to Aristotle give the Bekker annotation. The *lectio* reference is to St Thomas.

Quæstiones quodlibetales (de quolibet), Quodl.

Main titles are given in full for other works, including the 10 series of *Quæstiones Disputatæ.*

ACKNOWLEDGMENT

I gratefully acknowledge my debt to the Very Revd Joseph C. Taylor, O.P., S.T.M., Ph.D., late of the Dominican House of Philosophy, Dover, Mass., who prepared a preliminary translation of the treatise, together with notes on points raised by high metaphysicians of the School. I have consulted this throughout, and regret the other duties which prevented the draft from growing into the present edition, for which, faults and all, I alone am responsible.

T.G.

INTRODUCTION

1. THE FIRST HALF of the *Prima Pars* has dwelt on God himself, in the oneness of his nature paradigmatically accessible to natural reason, and in the trinity of the blessed Persons held by faith in his Revelation. Now, in accordance with the promise of the Prologue, the second half begins with this treatise, 'on the coming forth of creatures from God'.[1]

It raises two questions. First, how can an inquiry into the condition of being a creature, especially as it is going to be conducted in the present volume, be germane to theology, which is talk about God? Next, and connected, granting the need for a theology of human salvation, should it not proceed in purely Biblical terms and rule out the speculations of natural and metaphysical philosophers? A consideration of the second question may throw light on the first, over which, therefore, we shall not linger.

2. The subsumption of rational science by the doctrine of faith is discussed in the first Question of the *Summa*.[2] There the dominant interest, *ratio formalis objecti*, is stressed, and so the study looks beyond the sacraments, the works of redemption, or the whole Christ in his head and members, to God himself.[3] Yet this is not an escape to God alone, but a search for God above all, who maintains and cherishes creatures, and bids us be like him.[4] Moreover, the Father manifested in Christ is not separated from the God of Abraham, nor from the First Cause: *sacra doctrina, sacra scriptura*, and *scientia theologica* are all the same.[5] The bogy imagination of an infinite chasm between the Creator and the creature will be curtly dismissed in the present discussions.[6] And the threat of grace offering violence to the integrity of nature is never entertained.

Consequently theology, as conceived by St Thomas, is not sectarian nor even fanatical in the loftiest sense; it is open to the arts and sciences and can see its own proper implications in them all. Not that it intrudes on their independence or uses them just to grind an axe; they alone are competent to deal with their own immediate purposes, which it should respect, and without condescension, yet with the confidence that in their fulness they are enfolded by God, their first source and ultimate end.[7] Its thoughts ascend and descend, like *the angels of God upon the Son of Man* in the vision

---

[1] Ia. 2, Prologue. First half, Vols 2–7 of this series; second half, Vols 8–15
[2] cf Vol. I, Appendices 5, 6 & 7
[3] Ia. I, 7
[4] Ia. I, 3. 2a2æ. 25, 1; 26, 2, 9 & 13; 44, 4 & 7
[5] cf Ia2æ. 107, 1 & 2. Ia. 32, 1; 45, 6
[6] Ia. 45, 2 ad 4. cf Ia. 12, 1 & 12
[7] Ia. I, 7

promised to Nathanael,[8] and creatures come in at both ends of the movement. For in the discourse of discovery, *via inventionis*, 'how false it is that our reckonings about creatures are no concern of faith so long as we think aright about God, for mistakes about them lead to mistakes about him'.[9] And in the discourse of wisdom, *via judicii*, to know things in their true and dear creatureliness is to know them as they really are and with *the mind of Christ*.[10]

3. Here a Hellenism in theology which accepts the reality and goodness of things, a naturalism not crying guilt too soon, confronts another religious spirit to which the creature seems vanity and human creatures in particular worse than nothing apart from divine favour. The conflict comes to a head at various points. Are the natural decencies any affair of the Christian theologian as such? Is natural theology a help or a stumbling-block? And, to take matters arising from the present treatise, how can he engage in philosophical arguments about the first creation when all that he is called upon to deal with is the second? And how can he take a temperate view of the problem of evil and reject the notion of utter depravity when the picture of God's Judgment tells him the contrary? We can afford no more than a passing glance at the extremes of world-accepting and world-renouncing theories, often somewhat coarsely contrasted. St Thomas adopts neither.

4. Yet his *via media* is not a way of compromise, as though grace could remain paramount while ceding some territory to nature, or as though nature dwelt in an enclave grace could not enter. Nor does the *Summa* proceed by assembling bits and pieces now from here now from there, so as to form a composition of heterogeneous parts, physical, ethical, legal, political, ecclesiastical, psychological, historical, poetical, even mystical, the whole, firmly though uneasily, held together by religious faith. Consequently the present treatise is not to be regarded as a parenthesis of philosophical physics inserted between passages of meditative faith in the blessed Trinity and of metaphysical speculation on the angels and symbolism on the six days of creation.

This would be to miss the author's intention clearly announced from the beginning, or perhaps to judge it impossible of achievement, on the supposition there was a breach between the sacred and the profane, or between godly and worldly learning. He himself never adopts such a position in depth, and avoids the various manifestations of sectarianism it involves in theological thought. His hostility to the 'double-truth theory' goes very deep, and it extends to any fragmentation into disparate and unrelated

---

[8]*John* 1, 51   [9]*CG* II, 3
[10]I *Corinthians* 2, 16. 1a. 6, 6; 14, 6; 45, 3

objects of knowledge. His genuine interests were far-ranging, even eclectic, nevertheless his leading principles were singularly unified and consistent. The clue to his combination of these qualities lies in his sense of analogy,[11] and appears in his placing of theology in the hierarchy of the sciences.[12]

5. His confidence is that all truths can be gathered under the rule, civil not despotic, of wisdom, a theology of faith and reason which neither blankets the evidence nor offers itself as a substitute for the efforts of the particular sciences. All their findings can be referred without strain to their centre in God. Is bone just a compound of ossein and chemical salts, the hair so much vegetation, the eye just an optical machine, the genitals just biological organs, or the mind just the power of contriving? To deny that they have these functions would be blind to the facts, and also strange to the spirit of theology as he conceived it, indeed his moral theology will have something to say about the ungratefulness of not accepting what God has given us and the irreligiousness of flying in the face of his Providence.[13] Furthermore, the examples we have taken are not less so because they are not merely so, but lifted into a higher whole. A governing consideration is that living things do not kick away the ladders up which they have climbed. A horse is no less complete a vegetable than a daffodil, a man no less complete a vegetable and animal than either. A higher form offers no violence to the positive content of a lower,[14] except *per accidens*, as when evil makes of man no less an animal, but a more distracted one.[15]

The body of knowledge in which theology holds the primacy is then more like a confederation than a unitary State: when St Thomas speaks of subordination, in this and in other contexts, the word would have an unhappy ring if it suggested some suppression of proper inclinations. This may be required in community relationships, but not in the polity of the sciences. A humane and divine wisdom, which sees man as created by God and lifted into divine grace, should welcome the findings of optics, biology, and behaviorist psychology, and should do so unaffectedly and on their own terms: the only tutelary role required is that of checking them when they stray outside the field on which they are competent to judge.

So then the *Summa* moves in no tight little world, clamped together by a few rigid bars and armoured against forces from outside; it develops like a healthy organism with one single convergence amid great variety. This may go to explain the presence of passages from the *Physics*, *Ethics*, and *Metaphysics*: they are introduced quite smoothly, and though sometimes charged

---

[11]cf Introduction, Vol. 3
[12]The *locus classicus* is his exposition of Boëthius' *De Trinitate*. cf especially II, 2 & 3
[13]cf 2a2æ. 21, 1 & 4; 97, 1 & 3   [14]cf 1a. 76, 3 & 4. Also 18, 3
[15]On evil as an incidental intrusion, cf below 1a. 49, 1

with a wider meaning than their immediate context demands, their sense is rarely twisted, and then only because of a defective critical apparatus, which in fact St Thomas did his best to remedy. For he and his group were more exercised over the reputation of Aristotle than over that, say, of St Augustine, and the effort was to recover the authentic sense from the Greek freed from Arabic and Averroist interpolations.

6. Some who do not criticize him for turning to philosophy and the natural sciences may regret that his choice was Aristotle, not Plato, or that a wider world of nature was not in view. The main trouble over the present treatise, however, arises less from them than from the *murmurantes* who condemn a Christian theologian for going to nature at all. Their fear is that nature spoils grace, not the reverse. Then let us recall what St Thomas is about. His capital theme is the transcendence of God, and his first purpose is to fill out the meaning of the phrase, not to arouse devotion, to explain what Christians think, not to breathe their awe, and to speak the theological language of science, not of sympathy—the two are distinct, though complementary.[16] If light is given then warmth may follow. So here the primary objective is the reasonable truth, even perhaps the hard truth, and the effort is to be probative as far as may be, *doctrina est argumentativa.*[17] Accordingly most of his time is spent on what may appear to be merely outposts to Revelation.

7. Yet make no mistake, the theological movement is from, not to, the Christian assent, 'not to establish the articles of faith, but to stretch out from them to light up something else'.[18] Cleaving with his whole heart and mind to the living God who speaks to us through the prophets and apostles, St Thomas is not a philosophical theist who also happens to be a convinced believer from another part of himself. His character is not split by the distinctions he draws. Nor do they thrust divisions into single realities. *The Father of lights with whom there is no variation nor shadow of change*[19] and the *primum immobile* are one and the same, and so too, in the unity of personal response, are the *fides* and the *quærens intellectum*. The special aspects or 'formal objects' he isolates for the sake of systematic treatment are abstractions, valid so long as we are aware of what we are about, and do not transpose them back as they stand into the world of concrete things.

8. Do we need to be reassured that St Thomas is not substituting the *fons totius esse et bonitatis* for the God who reveals himself? We should remind ourselves that the area where divine transcendence can be defended and divine responsibility for evil qualified, as both need to be, is open to reasonable discourse. That is where dialogue lies, rather than in our sub-

---

[16]Vol. I, Appendix 10   [17]Ia. I, 8
[18]ibid   [19]*James* I, 17

mission to the Lord who speaks out of the whirlwind or in our acknowledgment of guilt before the Holy One. Yet we should notice, too, that the present discussion springs out of meditation on the three blessed Persons, and that its two articles which cast back to this mystery[20] are integral parts of its movement, not dutiful insertions. The *Summa* does not oscillate between two parallel systems of reference, one of faith, the other of reason, for its *sacra doctrina* knows but one world, the world God created and for which he died, the world in which grace will possess nature and the only dispossession will be from sin.

Nature and grace, we cannot rightly assess one without the other. Mankind did not fall from original justice into nothingness. How much good remained may be disputed between the bilious and sanguine humours, but a theology which retains a strain of cool and controlled thinking will accept that at least some good was there to be redeemed. Such a view of theology will not be to the agreement of those who would reserve it to the moving account of events in salvation-history conducted in a language peculiar to itself and strange to secular interests. St Thomas is not among their number.

He saw theology in the comity of the other sciences, their mistress in the most courteous sense of the term, responsive to them, and indeed depending on them. How can it be otherwise, since every truth, whoever utters it, is from God? Grace is supported by nature, theology by philosophy, philosophy by literature and the arts of life; and if this be grudgingly admitted as but merely a dependence in the order of material causality then we need ask for no more. We may reflect that St Thomas was the first—and perhaps the last—of the canonized theologians who knew what a material cause really is, not just stuff but a component of the corporeal creature, and who saw potentiality as the condition for the blessing of being created. That is why he studies how we come from God as beings before we are reborn in his grace; the first creation passes away only in the Pauline sense.[21] That also is why he is not haunted by the prospect of an engulfing evil, for it simply makes no sense. Both matters come to a head in the present treatise.

9. If there is nothing to transcend, how can we speak of God's transcendence? And so the capital theme is joined by another. One of St Thomas's original contributions to religious thought is to have developed the truth that creatures wholly dependent on God are also real in themselves. Bodily things are first substances in their very particularity and individuality, not as examples of a type or as shadows, flickering and transient, cast by some eternal world of separate Ideas. His solicitude for

---

[20]Ia. 45, 6 & 7. [21]II *Corinthians* 5, 17. *Galatians* 6, 15

the *this* rather than the *thus,* shared by Scotus with the same Aristotelean temper though a somewhat different explanation, and his refusal to reduce metaphysics to the condition of an idealist epistemology have both been overshadowed by his reputation as a systematizer.

10. Christian doctrine, keyed to the historic events and concrete realities in God's saving Providence, had never, despite a mystical fringe, dissolved the many into the one or all values into the divine essence. Though traces of Monophysitism in feeling and popular devotion and preaching long survived the theological condemnation of its theory, and though the facts of life were somewhat roughly dealt with, human nature was respected as a distinctive value. Belief in the Word made flesh was not compatible with Manichæism, nor the Apostolic preaching to the people of the resurrection of the body with an esoteric Gnosticism. In effect the Church was too down to earth for an elevated spiritism or pantheism. Then also the teaching of the Christian moralists turned on personal responsibility. All these considerations could not fail to influence the high thinking of Christian Platonists on the emanation of the created from the uncreated, and on the manifold participations of the Good.

Nevertheless St Thomas is to be regarded as a pioneer in taking the defence of pluralism into the medium in which monism lives and from it draws its strength. We are not to suppose that its adherents are any less adjusted to everyday experience than others, or that they feel themselves less answerable for their conduct. They do not deny the multiplicity of phenomena nor cede their consciousness of freedom to some impersonal force: Spinoza ground excellent lenses and was a respected figure in the community. The debate does not lie at these levels, but at the height of metaphysical speculation and mystical insight. It was there that St Thomas went.

11. On his mysticism we do not here delay, except to note that two qualities, noted by Professor Zaehner,[22] were fulfilled, as in the Dionysian tradition, namely the worship of Another in wonder and gratitude, and a tenderness, with no illusions about it, and a zeal for the things he has created, especially the lowly and outcast: neither go with the quest for absorption or extinction. The second quality is especially associated with the Gift of the Holy Ghost called Knowledge, and with the promise, *Blessed are they that mourn, for they shall be comforted;*[23] grace does not drown the bitter-sweet experience, and the metaphysics of St Thomas do nothing to teach us that we were better without it.[24]

12. For, not leaving it at the matter-form elements of natural philosophy,

---

[22]*Mysticism, Sacred and Profane,* Oxford, 1957   [23]*Matthew* 5, 5
[24]2a2æ. 9, 2 & 4

he takes the distinction between potentiality and actuality into the very heart of being.[25] Being is recognized as offering from within itself, not merely from the accidents of its corporeal manifestation, still less as somehow entangled with nothingness, the capacity of being what it is not. This, therefore, is a principle for multiplication and variety. Many beings are possible, that is to say, they are not unthinkable according to the most rarefied speculation. Hence the monist denial of pluralism, though it might be justified perhaps on other grounds, cannot expect the rigour of metaphysics, which is about what is necessary and cannot be otherwise. At this stage a metaphysical pluralist can afford to leave the facts an open question; all he claims that his is a possible position, whereas his opponent has to prove that it is impossible. The issue is similarly stated in the debate about the eternity of the universe.[26]

We should avoid any suggestion that St Thomas's metaphysics remain in the world of ideal essences.[27] He starts with an induction from what is experienced and if he goes to the possible it is only to return to the actually real. There, confirmed by the infra-metaphysical evidence already referred to, he recognizes the diversity of cause and effect—for him causality is a conclusion, not a first principle. Again observe the consonance he expects between the various levels, and the absence of a double-truth theory in any of its forms, of commonsense against science, science against morals, morals against metaphysics, and of any of them against theology.

13. All the same he is careful to safeguard the so-called right to be wrong. The faith obliges nobody to adopt any metaphysical position as such: thus those who admit contradictions are mistaken, yet not heretical,[28] that is in the technical meaning of offending directly against faith.[29] He would not charge philosophical opponents with unorthodoxy or have them censured, not commonly a characteristic of divines in the past. It is not that he agreed that Christianity was indifferent about what you thought in spheres other than that of religion, or that grace did not enter into every truth and a refusal of grace into every voluntary error. The present treatise, however, is dealing less with the imperatives of Christian belief than with its consistencies with metaphysical and natural philosophy.

14. It may be summarized as follows. The whole of reality from top to bottom directly depends on the final, exemplar, and efficient causality of God. He is transcendent and changeless and free, and could, had he chosen, have made the universe everlasting both backwards and forwards in time. Distinctiveness, inequality, and variety are determined by his

---

[25]Appendix 1
[26]1a. 46, 1 & 2   [27]Appendix 1
[28]*De æternitate mundi*. Appendix 2   [29]2a2æ. 11, 1 & 2

intention; there is no question of their being forced on him by an alien principle, or of his being caught up with what he cannot control. Not even evil can escape him. That gain for one costs loss for another presents no great problem to a mind not unduly detached so long as the exchange is kept within limits and the balance can be struck. The inherent limitation of creatureliness is not regarded as an evil. The mystery appears with voluntary fault and its consequences; it is insoluble by human thought, and scarcely tolerable without the further mystery of the Cross.[30] The matter is shelved for later treatment,[31] even so during his acute analysis he drops some precious hints. One, the impossibility of total depravity; another, the tang of good that lurks in every mistaken choice and while no excuse may leave us more conscious of our need for God's eternal patience and saving mercy. It is what St Thomas set himself to do, to help us to be more open to God and the things of God.

The earth is the Lord's, and the fulness thereof, the world and those that dwell therein.[32] The treatise is a commentary on the text, confident and generous in spirit. Its acceptance of the world, which is its strength, is the source of a certain weakness as well. For if it moves robustly to creatures without fear of losing their maker and takes them in their essential conditions, and human creatures especially in their perennial predicament, it includes also some of the ephemeral features of the period. This applies particularly to the world-picture composed by its natural science. Hence the need for discriminating between passages meant to be strictly probative and those meant to recommend a position in the contemporary climate of opinion. The distinction can be recognized fairly easily. We may be too readily disposed to dismiss some of the physics as merely quaint, for after all they belong to the history of science and, if they are no longer regarded as true, some Aristotelean and medieval hypotheses are now respected as having been useful. In general they may be taken or left as supplementary to the main discourse, adding to it by way of illustration or confirmation from the probabilities. They may have become obsolete, but their very presence is witness to St Thomas's refusal to enclose theology apart from the ordinary world of stable convictions, current opinions, and improvisations.

---

[30]3a. 1, 1 & 2; 46, 1, 2 & 3
[31]Vols 25, 26 & 27
[32]*Psalms* 23(24), 1

the coming forth of creatures

de processione creaturarum a Deo

POST PROCESSIONEM* divinarum Personarum, considerandum restat de processione creaturarum a Deo. Erit hæc consideratio tripartita:

> ut primo consideretur de productione creaturarum;
> secundo, de distinctione earum;
> tertio, de conservatione et gubernatione.

Circa primum tria sunt consideranda;

> primo quidem, quæ sit prima causa entium;
> secundo, de modo procedendi creaturarum a prima causa;
> tertio vero, de principio durationis rerum.

---

*Piana, Leonine: *considerationem,* after considering

ªComing forth, *processio*: the term has been used of the immanent activities of knowing and loving within the Godhead (1a. 27), implying relations that signify the divine Persons (1a. 28 & 29); Vol. 6 of this series: *missio* has been used for

Creation

AFTER THE COMING FORTH of the divine Persons there now remains that of creatures from God.[a] Our study will be divided into three parts:

> first, the making of creatures;
> second, their distinction (47–102);[b]
> third, their maintenance in being and governance (103–119).

Under the first heading there are three questions:

> first, on what the first cause of beings is (44);
> second, and how creatures issue from it (45);
> third, about the beginning of their duration (46).

---

comings of the Word and the Spirit into our world (1a. 43). Now *processio* refers to God's transitive action producing effects outside himself.
[b]The present volume includes the distinction of things in general (47) and the distinction between good and evil (48 & 49). Vols 9–13 take the distinction between spiritual and material creatures.

Quæstio 44. de prima causa entium

Circa primum quæruntur quatuor:

1. utrum Deus sit causa efficiens omnium entium;
2. utrum materia prima sit creata a Deo vel sit principium ex æquo coordinatum ei;
3. utrum Deus sit causa exemplaris rerum vel sint alia exemplaria præter ipsum;
4. utrum ipse sit causa finalis rerum.

articulus 1. utrum sit necessarium omne ens esse causatum a Deo

AD PRIMUM sic proceditur:[1] 1. Videtur quod non sit necessarium omne ens esse causatum† a Deo. Nihil enim prohibet inveniri rem sine eo quod non est de ratione rei, sicut hominem sine albedine. Sed habitudo causati ad causam non videtur esse de ratione entium, quia sine hac possunt aliqua entia intelligi. Ergo sine hac possunt esse. Ergo nihil prohibet esse aliqua entia non causata a Deo.

2. Præterea, ad hoc aliquid indiget causa efficiente ut sit. Ergo quod non potest non esse non indiget causa efficiente. Sed nullum necessarium potest non esse, quia quod necesse est esse non potest non esse. Cum igitur multa sint necessaria in rebus, videtur quod non omnia entia sint a Deo.

3. Præterea, quorumcumque est aliqua causa in his potest fieri demonstratio per causam illam. Sed in mathematicis non fit demonstratio *per causam agentem*, ut per Philosophum patet.[2] Non igitur omnia entia sunt a Deo sicut a causa agente.

---

†Piana & Leonine throughout article: *creatum, creata, created*
[1]cf Ia. 65, 1. II *Sent.* 1, 1, 2; 37, 1, 2. *CG* II, 15. *De potentia* III, 15. *In De div nom.* 5, *lect.* 1. *De substantiis separatis* 9. *Compend. theol.* 68
[2]*Metaphysics* III, 2. 996a29. St Thomas, *lect.* 4
[a]The Question takes the four causes traditionally enumerated after *Metaphysics* V, 2. 1013a25. The *efficient cause, agens* (art. 1), the producer of an effect. The *material cause* (art. 2), the subject out of which and in which it is made. The *formal cause*, the inner shaping principle making the effect to be what it is, which as existing in the mind of the maker is the *exemplar cause* (art. 3). The purpose at work is found in the *final cause* or *finis*, end (art. 4).
The teaching is anticipated in Ia. 3, 8; 6, 4; Vol 2 of this series. God is not the formal or the material cause of things, but their exemplar, efficient, and final cause.
[b]'To create' and 'creature' found in most editions are used in the general sense, 'to cause' and to be an 'original production'. Not until the next Question are the technical meanings introduced. The reading 'caused' in this and the following article is preferred by Pègues, though not by Piana or Leonine.

Question 44. the first cause of things

Here there are four points of inquiry:

1. whether God is the efficient cause of all beings;
2. whether primary matter is caused by God or is an equal co-ordinate principle with him;
3. whether God is the exemplar cause of things or whether there are other exemplars besides him;
4. whether he is the final cause of things.[a]

article 1. must everything that is have been caused by God?

THE FIRST POINT:[1] 1. This does not appear necessary.[b] There is nothing against our meeting with a thing lacking a non-essential, for instance a human being who is not white. Now the relationship of effect to cause does not seem of the very nature of beings, for some are conceivable without it.[c] And hence can exist without it. What then is there to stop some beings existing which are not created by God?

2. Moreover, a thing requires an efficient cause in order to be an existing fact. Hence that which cannot but exist does not require one. Now no necessary thing is able not to be, for what has to be cannot fail to be. Since there are many such in reality,[d] all beings are not from God.

3. Further, whatever has a cause can be demonstrated through that cause. Yet Aristotle brings out how mathematical demonstrations are not conducted through an efficient cause.[2e] Not all entities, therefore, come from God as an efficient cause.

The employment of the two terms 'ens' and 'res' in this article is of no great significance. They are synonyms, though in some contexts expressing purely logical distinct shades of meaning; the first refers to actually being, the second to what actual being is; cf *De veritate* I, I.

[c]Were the notion of dependence not outside that of being we could not think of God as being—that is one implication of the argument.

[d]Namely spiritual substances and heavenly bodies which carry no principle of dissolution within themselves and are above the contingencies of material things which by substantial changes come to be and pass away; cf Ia. II, 5. Elements of necessity in this world may also be included, for instance ungenerated matter (cf Ia. 46, I obj. I), also the mathematical entities of the next argument. For the 'bound to be' and the 'able to be and not to be' see the *tertia via* which points to God's existence: Ia. 2, 3; Vol. 2, Appendix 8.

[e]Efficient cause, *causa agens*, the principle of motion, *kineseos arche*, not considered in the classical mathematical abstraction from quantity of number, shape, etc.

SED CONTRA est quod dicitur *Rom.*, *Ex ipso, et per ipsum, et in ipso sunt omnia.*[3]

RESPONSIO: Dicendum quod necesse est dicere omne quod quocumque modo est a Deo est. Si enim aliquid invenitur in aliquo per participationem, necesse est quod causetur in ipso ab eo cui essentialiter convenit; sicut ferrum fit ignitum ab igne. Ostensum est autem supra,[4] cum de divina simplicitate ageretur, quod Deus est ipsum esse per se subsistens. Et iterum ostensum est[5] quod esse subsistens non potest esse nisi unum; sicut si albedo esset subsistens non posset esse nisi una, cum albedines multiplicentur secundum recipientia. Relinquitur ergo quod omnia alia a Deo non sint suum esse, sed participant esse.

Necesse est igitur quod omnia quæ diversificantur secundum diversam participationem essendi, ut sint perfectius vel minus perfecte, causari ab uno primo ente quod perfectissime est.

Unde et Plato dixit[6] quod necesse est ante omnem multitudinem ponere unitatem. Et Aristoteles dicit quod id quod est maxime ens et maxime verum est causa omnis entis et omnis veri; sicut *id quod maxime calidum est est causa omnis caliditatis.*[7]

1. Ad primum ergo dicendum quod licet habitudo ad causam non intret definitionem entis quod est causatum, tamen sequitur ad ea quæ sunt de ejus ratione; quia ex hoc quod aliquid per participationem est ens sequitur quod sit causatum ab alio. Unde hujusmodi ens non potest esse quin sit

---

[3]*Romans* 11, 36
[4]Ia. 3, 4
[5]Ia. 7, 1 ad 3; 2
[6]According to St Augustine, *De civitate Dei* VIII, 4. PL 41, 231. cf Plato, *Parmenides* 164b–166b. Plotinus, *Enneads* V, III, 12
[7]*Metaphysics* II, 1. 993b19–31. St Thomas, *lect.* 6. cf Ia. 2, 3, fourth way
[f]Vulgate, *in ipso*. The Greek, however, is better rendered, *in ipsum*. For the motion towards God as final cause see below, art. 4.
[g]The statement refers to things as existent wholes, cf Ia. 45, 1. Whether they contain uncaused elements is left open for the moment. The following article will hold that even primary matter is caused by God.
[h]An example only, and, like the concluding phrase of the article, illustrative, not probative, and to be dispensed with if found unhelpful to the argument, as with the *quarta via*, Ia. 2, 3, of which it is a development in terms of efficient causality.
[i]Sheer existence subsisting of his very nature, *ipsum esse per se subsistens*. The phrase, sometimes shortened to *esse subsistens*, often occurs. To subsist, *subsistere* (the abstract, *subsistentia*, is less common) means to exist as a substance, not as seated in another, and, properly, to be complete and rounded off as a concrete thing. The doubling, 'subsistent existence', is reserved to God, whose existence, unlike that of creatures, is identical with his essence.

Note that in this context to be by essence, *per essentiam*, is contrasted with to be

ON THE OTHER HAND in *Romans* we read, *For from him and through him and unto him* are all things.[3]

REPLY: We are bound to conclude that everything that is at all real is from God.[g] For when we encounter a subject which shares in a reality then this reality must needs be caused there by a thing which possesses it of its nature, as when, for example, iron is made red-hot by fire.[h] Now we have already shown when treating of the divine simplicity,[4] that God is sheer existence subsisting of his very nature.[i] And such being, as we have also noted,[5] cannot but be unique, rather as whiteness would be were it subsistent, for its repetition depends on there being many receiving subjects. We are left with the conclusion that all things other than God are not their own existence but share in existence.

It follows strictly that all things which are diversified by their diverse sharing in existence, so that some are fuller beings than others, are caused by one first being which simply *is* in the fullest sense of the word.[j]

On these grounds Plato held that before the many you must place the one;[6] and Aristotle that the supremely real and true is the cause of everything that is real and true, his illustration being fire, which is *hottest and the cause of heat in everything else.*[7]

Hence: 1. While a relationship to a cause does not enter into the definition of a being that is caused, nevertheless it follows from what is bound up in a being by participation, for from the fact that a thing is such it follows that it is caused by another. Such a being cannot exist without being caused, no

---

by sharing, *per participationem*: essential is not contrasted with accidental. cf Appendix 1.

[j]Actuality is not self-limiting. Limitation, and hence multiplication, derives from the potentiality which as it were receives it: be careful, however, about picturing either as concrete things.

The Platonic idea of subsistent whiteness may be found teasing. St Thomas holds there is no such thing, but he is arguing that if there were then it would be sole not that nothing else would be white. That many things in fact are white argues a principle of non-whiteness. The thought moves more freely when it leaves the comparison, though it ends with the reflection that the hotter a thing the more heat it gives off.

Existence is actuality, and existence pure and simple must therefore be single. Yet many things exist. The diversification of existence, which is the middle term of the argument, points to a real non-actual principle, the potentiality which is 'existentialized'. This conclusion will gather strength during the course of the treatise, notably from 1a. 47, 1, cf Introduction 12: St Thomas is a pluralist by his metaphysics, not only by his ethics of personal responsibility or his philosophy of commonsense.

causatum; sicut nec homo quin sit risibile. Sed quia esse causatum non est de ratione entis simpliciter, propter hoc invenitur aliquod ens non causatum.

2. Ad secundum dicendum quod ex hac ratione quidam moti fuerunt ad ponendum quod id quod est necessarium non habeat causam, ut dicitur in *Physic*.[8] Sed hoc manifeste falsum apparet in scientiis demonstrativis, in quibus principia necessaria sunt causæ conclusionum necessariarum. Et ideo dicit Aristoteles quod sunt quædam necessaria quæ habent causam suæ necessitatis.[9] Non ergo propter hoc solum requiritur causa agens, quia effectus potest non esse, sed quia effectus non esset si causa non esset. Hæc enim conditionalis est vera, sive antecedens et consequens sint possibilia sive impossibilia.

3. Ad tertium dicendum quod mathematica accipiuntur ut abstracta secundum rationem, cum tamen non sint abstracta secundum esse. Unicuique autem competit habere causam agentem secundum quod habet esse. Licet igitur ea quæ sunt mathematica habeant causam agentem, non tamen secundum habitudinem quam habent ad causam agentem cadunt sub consideratione mathematici. Et ideo in scientiis mathematicis non demonstratur aliquid per causam agentem.

articulus 2. utrum materia prima sit causata a Deo

AD SECUNDUM six proceditur:[1] 1. Videtur quod materia prima non sit causata* a Deo. Omne enim quod fit componitur ex subjecto et ex aliquo

---

*Piana, Leonine: *creata*, created

[8]*Physics* VIII, 1. 252a35. *lect*. 3

[9]*Metaphysics* V, 5. 1015b6–11. *lect*. 6

[1]cf *CG* II, 16. *De potentia* III, 5. *In Physic*. VIII, *lect*. 2. *Compend. theol*. 69

[k]The analogy lies in the necessary connection; that existence is a property of essence is not implied.

Risibile, the ability to laugh, regarded as property of human nature. Though not everybody displays a sense of humour, for essential abilities can be obstructed, cf below 1a. 48, 4.

[1]A definition of a being, namely a statement of what-it-is, is not committed to its real existence, namely that-it-is, and therefore does not include a reference to its efficient cause, though in reality or actual fact as a being 'by participation' it is caused. cf 1a. 45, 4.

1 *Sent*. 33, 1, 1 ad 1, 'To be', *esse*, is used 1. of the defined whatness, *quidditas*, of a thing; 2. of the actuality of its essence, thus for animate things to live is to be; 3. of the copula between Subject and Predicate of a proposition. But cf Appendix 1.

[m]Aristotle, *in loc*., describes necessity as that because of which a thing cannot be otherwise. A thing may be necessary in itself or because of another: that the sun will rise tomorrow may be necessary, but the source of this necessity does not lie in the sun. cf 1a. 19, 8; 22, 4: Vol. 5 of this series.

more than a human being can without a sense of the comic.[k] Yet since to be caused is not essential to the meaning of being as such we can meet with a being that is uncaused.[1]

2. This was the objection, as noticed in the *Physics*,[8] which prompted the conclusion that what is necessary has no cause. Yet the demonstrative sciences bring out how fallacious it is, for necessary premises there offer grounds for necessary conclusions. Accordingly Aristotle remarks in the *Metaphysics*[9] that there are some objects which have a cause for their necessity. The reason why an efficient cause is required is not just because the effect is such that it may or may not exist, but because it would not exist did its cause not exist. This conditional judgment is true whether the antecedent clause or the consequent clause express what is possible or impossible.[m]

3. Mathematical objects are taken as abstract concepts of reason, all the same they are not abstract where they exist in reality. Now having an efficient cause is due to having real existence. And so, although the things mathematics are about do have an efficient cause, it is not under that aspect that a mathematician studies them.[n] That is why mathematical demonstration does not work through the medium of efficient causality.

article 2. is primary matter caused by God?

THE SECOND POINT:[1] 1. No, it would seem.[a] For a thing that is made is composed of that in which it is made and of some other principle, as the

---

This reply has been criticized for ignoring the difference between the concrete and the abstract by appealing from the real to the logical order in bringing up the necessary connection in thought between premises and conclusion and between the antecedent and consequent clauses of an hypothetical proposition. Its purpose, however, is merely to show that 'caused' and 'necessary' are not incompatible ideas.

An hypothetical statement may be logically valid without being verified in reality, so likewise a correct syllogism. Either can maintain 'the impossible'. Impeccable logic may be mad. If man is a donkey—this is St Thomas's example—then etc. quite logically: 1a. 25, 3 ad 2.

[n]Mathematics considers quantity apart from its physical environment. There it exists as a property of a sensible body and as subject to efficient causality.

[a]This article does not regard matter in the concrete as the common stuff from which all bodily things are made or as the ultimate particles composing physical reality, but more abstractly and, as it were, as the potential 'substrate' actualized by form and present in all things that come to be and cease to be through substantial chnage. cf *Physics* I, 9. 192a31. *Metaphysics* VI, 3. 1029a20. St Thomas *in loc.* Also *De spiritualibus creaturis* I, 1. Primary matter, common matter, bare matter; contrasted with particular or this bit of matter, *materia signata*; 1a. 3, 3; 75, 4.

alio, ut dicitur in *Physic.*[2] Sed materiæ primæ non est aliquod subjectum. Ergo materia prima non potest esse facta a Deo.

2. Præterea, actio et passio dividuntur contra se invicem. Sed sicut primum principium activum est Deus, ita primum principium passivum est materia. Ergo Deus et materia prima sunt duo principia contra se invicem divisa, quorum neutrum est ab alio.

3. Præterea, omne agens agit sibi simile, et sic, cum omne agens agat inquantum est actu, sequitur quod omne factum aliquo modo sit in actu. Sed materia prima est tantum in potentia inquantum hujusmodi. Ergo contra rationem materiæ primæ est quod sit facta.

SED CONTRA est quod dicit Augustinus,[3] *Duo fecisti, Domine, unum prope te,* scilicet angelum, *aliud prope nihil,* scilicet materiam primam.

RESPONSIO: Dicendum quod antiqui philosophi paulatim et quasi pedetentim intraverunt in cognitionem veritatis. A principio enim quasi grossiores existentes, non existimabant esse entia nisi corpora sensibilia. Quorum qui ponebant in eis motum, non considerabant motum nisi secundum aliqua accidentia, ut puta secundum raritatem et densitatem, per congregationem et segregationem. Et, supponentes ipsam substantiam corporum incausatam,† assignabant aliquas causas hujusmodi accidentalium transmutationum, ut puta amicitiam, litem, intellectum, aut aliquid hujusmodi.

Ulterius vero procedentes distinxerunt per intellectum inter formam substantialem et materiam, quam ponebant incausatam,† et perceperunt transmutationem fieri in corporibus secundum formas essentiales. Quarum

---

†So Pègues. Piana & Leonine read *increatam,* uncreated. See note art, 1 above
[2]*Physics* I, 7. 190b1. *lect.* 12
[3]*Confessions* XII, 7. PL 32, 828.
[b]Does not have any subject: that is does not presuppose anything else out of which it is made or underlying its existence, since it is the basic potentiality in bodily substances.
[c]*Actio* and *passio,* the ninth and tenth of Aristotle's categories. *Categories* 9. 11b1. *In Physic.* III. *lect.* 5.
[d]*Inquantum hujusmodi, toiouton,* the lengthened *toion.* In fact matter never exists just so, but only as actualized by form.
[e]J. Burnet, *Early Greek Philosophy,* Edinburgh, 4th ed., 1930, includes many fragments to illustrate the following paragraph.
St Thomas is basing his account on *Metaphysics* I, 3–4. 983b6–985b22. Also *Physics* I, 4–8, 187a12 & sqq.

Physics point out.[2] Primary matter, however, does not have any subject.[b] Therefore it cannot have been made by God.

2. Besides, to act on and to be acted on[c] are divided as not overlapping. Now as the first active principle is God so the first passive principle is matter. They are two opposite principles, neither of which comes from the other.

3. Also, every agent produces its like, and, since it is because it is actual that it is productive, it follows that what it produces is also actual in some manner. But primary matter precisely as such[d] is purely potential. It is against its very meaning to be something produced.

ON THE OTHER HAND St Augustine cries,[3] *Two hast thou made, O Lord, one close to thyself,* namely angelic nature, *the other close to nothing,* namely prime matter.

REPLY: The ancient philosophers entered into the truth step by step and as it were haltingly.[e] Somewhat raw to begin with, they reckoned that the only realities were sensible bodies.[f] Those of them who maintained these were subject to change thought of this only in terms of outward modification,[g] for instance according to rarefaction and condensation,[h] or to mingling or separating out.[I] They supposed that bodily substance was unproduced, and the changes of condition which happened to it they ascribed to such causes as love and strife,[j] mind,[k] and so forth.

They advanced further when they grasped the distinction between substantial form and matter—which they held was unproduced—and gathered that it was according to their essential forms that bodily things were changed from one thing into another. Such transformations

---

[f]cf *Physics* IV, 6. 213a29. *Metaphysics* II, 5. 1002a8. *De civitate Dei* VIII, 2. PL 41,225.

[g]Change of 'accidents', here translated 'outward modification'. The Eleatics— Parmenides, Melissus, Zeno—rejected motion as illusory. For the originative sources of coming-to-be and passing-away, cf *De generatione* II, 9. 335a25 & sqq.

[h]Anaximenes regarded air as the *Urstoff* of the world, becoming fire when rarefied, wind, cloud, earth, and stones when condensed.

[I]The primary element, according to Anaximander, is *to apeiron*, substance without limits; plurality comes from an eternal motion of sifting or separating, *apokrisis*, one from another.

[j]Empedocles, according to *Metaphysics* I, 4. 985a8. Attraction and repulsion, harmony and discord are conceived as physical forces bring together or sifting out the particles of the four elements. cf *Metaphysics* I, 4. 985a5. *Physics* I, 5. 188b22.

[k]Anaxagoras, cf *Physics* VIII, 2. 250b24. Whether he conceived of *nous* as itself corporeal is controverted.

transmutationum quasdam causas universaliores ponebant, ut 'obliquum circulum' secundum Aristotelem, vel ideas secundum Platonem.[4]

Sed considerandum est quod materia per formam contrahitur ad determinatam speciem, sicut substantia alicujus speciei per accidens ei adveniens contrahitur ad determinatum modum essendi; ut homo contrahitur per album. Utrique igitur consideraverunt ens particulari quadam consideratione, vel inquantum est hoc ens vel inquantum est tale ens. Et sic rebus causas particulares assignaverunt.

Et ulterius aliqui erexerunt se ad considerandum ens inquantum est ens, et consideraverunt causam rerum, non solum secundum quod sunt hæc vel talia, sed secundum quod sunt entia. Hoc igitur quod est causa rerum inquantum sunt entia oportet esse causam rerum, non solum secundum quod sunt talia per formas accidentales, nec secundum quod sunt hæc per formas substantiales, sed etiam secundum omne illud quod pertinet ad esse illorum quocumque modo. Et sic oportet ponere etiam materiam primam causatam‡ ab universali causa entium.

1. Ad primum ergo dicendum quod Philosophus loquitur de fieri particulari, quod est de forma in formam, sive accidentalem sive substantialem; nunc autem loquimur de rebus secundum emanationem earum ab universali principio essendi. A qua quidem emanatione nec materia excluditur, licet a primo modo factionis excluditur.

2. Ad secundum dicendum quod passio est effectus actionis. Unde et rationabile est quod primum principium passivum sit effectus primi

---

‡Piana & Leonine: *creatam*, created

[4]*De generatione* II, 10. 336a32. cf Socrates' dialogue with Cebes, *Phædo* 96a–102a

[1]Aristotle is arguing *De generatione* II, 10. 336a15, that it is not the primary motion of the first heaven, *protos ouranos*, that causes the coming-to-be and passing-away of material things, but the slanting of the sun's rays as it alternates between far and near in its annual ecliptic or zodiac cycle. St Thomas is here not rejecting the physical hypothesis but merely noting its inadequacy to meet the present question. The Ideas or Forms, however, represent a greater metaphysical effort; cf *Phædo* 100b–101e. Criticized in *De generatione* II, 9. 335b10. How they are associated with matter is not worked out. St Thomas remarks that the Platonists, drawing no distinction between matter and privation, classified it as non-being, and were not on the track of a cause, since causality applies only to being. *In De div, nom*, III. lect. 1.

[m]Matter, which of itself is indeterminate, enters into the composition of a definite kind of thing when actuated by substantial form (cf 1a. 7, 1), and indeed must be included in its definition (cf 1a. 75, 4). The analogy is drawn with the qualification of substance by an 'accident' or mode of being.

[n]*Hoc ens, tale ens*; a little later, *hæc vel talia*: the first refers to what a being is, the second to how it is affected. A thing may be thus or so-and-so, and being thus may also be suchlike. An *ens* is *hoc* by its substance, *tale* by a modification of that substance.

they attributed to more universal causes, for instance Aristotle's 'inclined circle', or Plato's Ideas.[14]

Yet notice that form pins matter down to a determinate kind of thing,[m] rather as a supplementary property shapes a substance of a species to a determinate mode of being, as a human being is limited by being white. On both sides, therefore, they were still looking at being under a particular aspect, namely as this sort of being or as existing in such and such a manner.[n] That is why they remained at the particular efficient causes for things.[o]

Later others climbed higher to the prospect of being as being, and observed the cause of things inasmuch as they are beings, not merely as things of such a kind or quality.[p] To be the cause of things in that they are beings is to be the cause of all that belongs to their existence in any way whatsoever, not merely as regards what they are like by the properties which shape them or what kind they are by their substantial forms. So we have to lay down that even primary matter is caused by the all-embracing cause of beings.

Hence: 1. Aristotle is there speaking of a particular coming into existence, that is by transformation, whether with respect to substance or properties. We, however, are now speaking of things in their issuing from the universal source of being. Not even matter is left out of this, though it is not produced in the first way referred to.

2. To be the effect of action, that is what passion is.[q] Hence it is reasonable that the primary passive principle should be the effect of the first

---

[o]That is, the causes of transmutation. For a more detailed summary cf *In Meta* I, *lect.* 5–10.

[p]The article seems to be somewhat grudging about the metaphysical insight of Plato and Aristotle, and to be reserving the credit for a more total consideration to the Neo-Platonists and Avicenna and Maimonides. Here, however, St Thomas is merely showing the inadequacy of two particular explanations associated with their names; elsewhere he gives them more generous recognition, cf *De potentia* III, 5; *In Physic.* VIII, *lect.* 2. Aristotle certainly considers being as being, but does not teach the doctrine of creation, the metaphysics of which is the original work of St Thomas: as Newman observes, it takes time for conclusions to be drawn from premises.

St Thomas's view of Aristotle on ungenerated and indestructible matter will be found below, 1a. 46, 1 ad 3. That Plato held that matter was uncreated was the view of some commentators, cf Chalcidius on the *Timæus*, 148, referred to 1a. 15, 3 ad 3.

The articles on transubstantiation will be found helpful on the metaphysics of production; 3a. 75, 3, 4, 6 & 7. Vol. 58.

[q]Production in the active and in the passive sense are correlatives. '*Passio*' here means being acted on.

principii activi, nam omne imperfectum causatur a perfecto. Oportet enim primum principium esse perfectissimum, ut dicit Aristoteles.[5]

3. Ad tertium dicendum quod ratio illa non ostendit quod materia non sit causata, sed quod non sit causata sine forma. Licet enim omne causatum sit in actu, non tamen est actus purus. Unde oportet quod etiam illud quod se habet ex parte potentiæ sit causatum, si totum quod ad esse ipsius pertinet causatum est.*

articulus 3. utrum causa exemplaris sit aliquid præter Deum

AD TERTIUM sic proceditur:[1] 1. Videtur quod causa exemplaris sit aliquid præter Deum. Exemplatum enim habet similitudinem exemplaris. Sed creaturæ longe sunt a divina similitudine. Non ergo Deus est causa exemplaris earum.

2. Præterea, omne quod est per participationem reducitur ad aliquid per se existens; ut ignitum ad ignem, sicut jam dictum est.[2] Sed quæcumque sunt in sensibilibus rebus sunt solum per participationem alicujus speciei; quod ex hoc patet quod in nullo sensibilium invenitur solum id quod ad rationem speciei pertinet, sed adjungitur principiis speciei principia individuantia. Oportet ergo ponere ipsas species per se existentes; ut per se hominem et per se equum et hujusmodi. Et hæc dicuntur exemplaria. Sunt igitur exemplaria res quædam extra Deum.

3. Præterea, scientiæ et definitiones sunt de ipsis speciebus, non secundum quod sunt in particularibus, quia particularium non est scientia nec definitio. Ergo sunt quædam entia quæ sunt entia vel species non in singularibus. Et hæc dicuntur exemplaria. Ergo idem quod prius.

---

*Piana & Leonine read *creata* or *creatum* throughout the reply
[5]*Metaphysics* XI, 7. 1072b29. *lect.* 9
[1]cf Ia. 15, 1–3. I *Sent.* 36, 2, 1–3. *De veritate* III, 1 & 2. *CG* I, 54. *In De div nom.* 5, *lect.* 3. *In Meta.* I, *lect.* 15
[2]Ia. 44, 1
[r]Literally, every imperfect thing is caused by a perfect. St Thomas always charges the relation between being participatively and being essentially with a causal sense.
[s]Not in so many words. Aristotle is speaking about life, and concludes that the essential actuality of God is life most good and eternal. The reply implies the refutation of dualism.
[t]It is as a whole that a thing exists; see below Ia. 45, 4.
[a]Exemplar cause: an archetype or, less strongly a prototype, that to the likeness of which a thing is made. It is like a final cause and a formal cause, yet differs from the first because its effect is what is true rather than what is good, and from the second because it is in the mind of the maker, and extrinsic to the effect produced. For 'exemplarism' see *In Meta.* V, *lect* 2; VII, *lect.* 6.

active principle, for whatever is incomplete depends causally on what is complete.[r] And, as Aristotle says,[5] this must be the utterly complete.[s]

3. The argument shows that matter is not produced without form, not that it is not produced. For although everything that is caused in actuality is, it is not nevertheless pure actuality. Hence even what is potential in it has to be caused if all that belongs to it as an existent is caused.[t]

article 3. is an exemplar cause anything other than God?

THE THIRD POINT:[1] 1. Yes, it would seem.[a] For a copy bears the likeness of the exemplar. Yet creatures are far from being like God. Therefore he is not their exemplar cause.

2. Besides, whatever exists by sharing comes back to what is self-existing: the example has been used of a thing catching fire.[2] Now all things in the world of sense exist only as sharing in some species, as appears from the fact that in none of them do you discover only what belongs to the meaning of the species, for the specific are also conjoined there with individuating elements. Hence we cannot but suppose there are self-existing species, for instance a *per se* man or a *per se* horse and the like. These are called exemplars, and they are things outside God.

3. Moreover, sciences and definitions are about pure types themselves, not as existing in particular cases, which are beyond science and definition. Hence there are realities which are beings or species separate from individuals. These are said to be exemplars. So we are led again to the same conclusion.[b]

The inquiry, which is whether God makes the world on certain models or patterns which are other than him, recalls the Platonist teaching of the Ideas or Forms (the terms are used interchangeably) which somehow exist apart from sensible things. St Augustine's doctrine of the divine Ideas has already been discussed (1a. 15, Vol. 4 of this series), and his authority is invoked in the *sed contra*. Plato's own teaching was more delicate than some later simplifications imposed on it: the *Phædo, Timæus, Phædrus*, and *Sophist* on his theory of knowledge and the Forms should be read with the hesitations of Socrates at the beginning of the *Parmenides* in mind. Yet Aristotle's criticism (*Metaphysics* I, 5–6. 987a30–988a15. XIII, 4. 1078b30–1079b10) is informed: it is the source for the summary judgment on Plato in the second and third objections and replies.

[b]Science is here used in the strict sense of *episteme*, a deduced theoretical knowledge of necessary truth; definition also, *horismos*, indicates what a thing is. Both surpass the opinion, *doxa*, we can arrive at in the changing world of individual things; it gives us, according to Plato, images and reflections, not the true knowledge of originals and archetypes. For the simile of the Line, cf *Republic* 509d–511e: for the allegory of the Cave, ibid 514a–518d. It is the separation of 'this world' and a 'world above' that Aristotle and St Thomas criticize.

4. Præterea, hoc idem videtur per Dionysium, qui dicit quod *ipsum secundum se esse prius est eo quod est per se vitam esse, et eo quod est per se sapientiam esse.*[3]

SED CONTRA est quod exemplar est idem quod idea. Sed ideæ, secundum quod Augustinus dicit, sunt *formæ principales quæ divina intelligentia continentur.*[4] Ergo exemplaria rerum non sunt extra Deum.

RESPONSIO: Dicendum quod Deus est prima causa exemplaris omnium rerum.

Ad cujus evidentiam, considerandum est quod ad productionem alicujus rei ideo necessarium est exemplar ut effectus determinatam formam consequatur: artifex enim producit determinatam formam in materia propter exemplar ad quod inspicit, sive illud sit exemplar ad quod extra intuetur sive sit exemplar interius mente conceptum.

Manifestum est autem quod ea quæ naturaliter fiunt determinatas formas consequuntur. Hæc autem formarum determinatio oportet quod reducatur, sicut in primum principium, in divinam sapientiam, quæ ordinem universi excogitavit, qui in rerum distinctione consistit. Et ideo oportet dicere quod in divina sapientia sunt rationes omnium rerum, quas supra diximus ideas,[5] idest formas exemplares in mente divina existentes. Quæ quidem licet multiplicentur secundum respectum ad res, tamen non sunt realiter aliud a divina essentia, prout ejus similitudo a diversis participari potest diversimode. Sic igitur ipse Deus est primum exemplar omnium.

Possunt etiam in rebus creatis quædam aliorum exemplaria dici secundum quod quædam sunt ad similitudinem aliorum, vel secundum eamdem speciem vel secundum analogiam alicujus imitationis.

---

[3]*De divinis nominibus* 5. PG 3, 820. St Thomas, *lect.* 1
[4]*Lib. 83 Quæst.* 46. PL 40, 30
[5]1a. 15, 1
[c]The One behind the many ideas.
[d]Teaching drawn on by John Donne, *Sermons* I, 2, 3; II, 28, 28.
[e]Things made by nature: the argument echoes Aristotle that a nature is an innate tendency to movement and change (*Physics* II, 1. 192b8–193a10), but that this is defined or determinated by the form (193a10–b31). The 'reaching after' need not be conscious in the subject. Some sort of fixation is implied in the process, but this working to a definite term is not such as to rule out the evolution of species. The thought is that we should look to the form (the logos or meaning), not to the material, as the principle of production and reproduction. The analogy is drawn between works of art and works of nature, the conclusion being that Nature is God's art. There is this difference between divine and human art, that the form implanted by the first, but not the second, is from itself fruitful. 'Men propagate men,' Aristotle remarks (193b8), 'but bedsteads do not propagate bedsteads.'

16

4. Then this also appears from the words of Dionysius, *What is existence of itself lies behind what is* per se *life and what is* per se *wisdom.*[3c]

ON THE OTHER HAND an exemplar is the same as an idea, and Augustine speaks of the Ideas as *the master-forms held in the divine intelligence.*[4]

REPLY: It is to be held that God is the first exemplar cause of all things.[d]

To make this clear reflect that for a thing to be produced an exemplar is required so that it may achieve a determinate form: thus an artist gives a definite shape to his material because of an exemplar before him, whether this be a model he looks at from outside or a pattern interiorily conceived in his mind.

Now manifestly the things made by nature reach after determinate forms.[e] Their configuration has to be traced back to its original source in divine wisdom which contrived the world-order consisting in the distinctiveness of things.[f] Hence we should say that divine wisdom holds the originals of all things, and these we have previously called the Ideas,[5] that is the exemplar forms existing in the divine mind. And though they are many and various in the relationship of things to them, nevertheless they are not really other than the divine essence proportionably to the manifold sharing of its likeness by diverse things. In this sense, therefore, God is the original exemplar of them all.[g]

Yet even among created things some may be called exemplars of others which are made to their likeness either in their specific nature or by analogy of some resemblance.[h]

---

[f]The distinctiveness of things: the *Summa* will later take up the thought that this is chosen by God, not, as it were, thrust upon him; 1a. 47, 1 & 2. It has already appeared 1a. 19, 8; 22, 2, and is rooted in 1a. 14, 8; 19, 26; Vols 4 & 5.

[g]By one and the same act God comprehends his essence in itself and as variously 'imitable', *participabilis*, by creatures, each after its fashion, and so is to know with the 'idea' proper to each; cf 1a. 14, 6, also 15, 2 & 3. This high philosophy is taken into the dimensions of the theology of Revelation on the uncreated Word and the Image of the Father, cf 1a. 34, 3; 35, 1. The Logos expresses the Father, and both expresses and makes each creature.

[h]A cause which reproduces its specific nature is said to be 'univocal', and to be 'analogical' when the effect merely has some proportion to it. cf 1a. 4, 2; 6, 2. St Thomas constantly works with the analogies or relationships between things of different classes, with 'the one touch' of Shakespeare's, *One touch of nature makes the whole world kin*.

The distinction is elaborated below, 1a. 45, 7. Creatures are like divine footprints and bear a *representatio vestigii*. Rational creatures, however, can reflect God by knowledte and love, and are said to bear a *representatio imaginis*. Note again that the full doctrine of this article can be appreciated only in the theology of the Trinity.

1. Ad primum ergo dicendum quod licet creaturæ non pertingant ad hoc quod sint similes Deo secundum suam naturam similitudine speciei, ut homo genitus homini generanti, attingunt tamen ad ejus similitudinem secundum repræsentationem rationis intellectæ a Deo, ut domus quæ est in materia domui quæ est in mente artificis.

2. Ad secundum dicendum quod de ratione hominis est quod sit in materia, et sic non potest inveniri homo sine materia. Licet igitur hic homo sit per participationem speciei, non tamen potest reduci ad aliquid existens per si in eadem specie, sed ad speciem superexcedentem, sicut sunt substantiæ separatæ. Et eadem ratio est de aliis sensibilibus.

3. Ad tertium dicendum quod licet quælibet scientia et definitio sit solum entium, non tamen oportet quod res eumdem modum habeant in essendo quem intellectus habet in intelligendo. Nos enim per virtutem intellectus agentis abstrahimus species universales a particularibus conditionibus; non tamen oportet quod universalia præter particularia subsistant ut particularium exemplaria.

4. Ad quartum dicendum quod, sicut dicit Dionysius, *per se vitam et per se sapientiam*[6] quandoque nominat ipsum Deum, quandoque virtutes ipsis rebus datas; non autem quasdam subsistentes res, sicut antiqui posuerunt.

---

[6]*De divinis nominibus* 11. PG 3, 953. St Thomas, *lect.* 4

[i]cf 1c, 4, 3, on the likeness between God and creatures.

[j]The suggestion is not that man's exemplar cause is one of the spiritual or 'separate' substances. The reply is content to parry the objection and point out that any exemplar proposed must be above the human level.

Note that a full cause of a thing in a species is neither the species itself nor a thing of that species. cf 1a. 13, 5 ad 1; 25, 2 ad 2; 104, 1; 105, 1 ad 1.

[k]Sciences concerned with beings: all revolve round reality, but at different degrees of remove. Formal logic, for instance, is concerned with purely mental entities, sometimes called *secundæ intentiones*. cf 1 *Sent.* 23, 1, 3; 26, 1, 1 ad 3; III, 6, 1, 1, 1.

A thing in the mind is 'otherwise' than it is in fact, yet this does not mean that the mind is false as judging its object to be other than it is, cf 1a. 85, 1 ad 1. Also 1a. 16, 3 ad 1 & 3. Recall St Thomas's epistemology that species, concepts, representations, and ideas are not direct objects of human knowledge.

[l]The active intellect, *intellectus agens, nous poietikos*, the power of mind, not itself cognitive, which makes the sensible into the intelligible: cf *De Anima* III, 5.

Hence: 1. Granted that creatures are never so perfect as to be like God according to likeness of nature, namely to be of the same species as child and parents are, nevertheless they touch his likeness in representing the exemplar understood by God, rather as does the house in bricks and mortar the house in the architect's mind.[1]

2. To be in matter is of man's essential nature, and there is no man found without it. Hence although this individual man is man because he belongs to the species, he cannot be traced back to some cause that is purely subsisting human nature, but only to some superior type of being, such as are bodiless substances.[j] The same line of reasoning applies to other sensible things.

3. Though sciences and definitions, no matter what, are concerned with beings, a thing does not have to have the same way of being that the mind has in understanding.[k] For by virtue of the active intellect[l] we abstract universal natures from their particular embodiments; there is no need for these universals to subsist outside particular substances as their exemplars.

4. When Dionysius speaks of life *per se* and wisdom *per se*[6] he is sometimes naming God himself, sometimes the powers given to things themselves, but not subsisting things such as were postulated by philosophers of old.[m]

430a10. St Thomas, *lect.* 10. 1a. 85, 1. It belongs directly to the psychology of the human process of knowledge rather than to epistemology or the theory of knowledge itself, and enters into the article to counter a contemporary 'exemplarism', according to which the human mind is illuminated by the pure forms among which it dwells, or, according to St Bonaventure, by the divine Ideas: whereas for St Thomas, as for Aristotle, it must acquire knowledge by its own exertions from a material, and therefore, only potentially intelligible world. Contrasted with the *intellectus possibilis*, better rendered as the mind able to be informed by things, than as the passive mind receiving them. 'Mind is of one kind in virtue of its becoming everything, and of another by making everything as in a state like light' (430a12).

mPhilosophers of old: the *antiqui Platonici*. Realism about universals, however, was well represented in the century before the *Summa* in the School of Chartres, notably by Gilbert de la Porrée (*d.* 1154) and Clarembaud of Arras (*d.* before 1170).

articulus 4. *utrum Deus sit causa finalis omnium*

AD QUARTUM sic proceditur:[1] 1. Videtur quod Deus non sit causa finalis omnium. Agere enim propter finem videtur esse alicujus indigentis fine. Sed Deus nullo est indigens. Ergo non competit sibi agere propter finem.

2. Præterea, finis generationis et forma generati et agens non incidunt in idem numero, ut dicitur in *Physic.*,[2] quia finis generationis est forma generati. Sed Deus est primum agens omnium. Non ergo est causa finalis omnium.

3. Præterea, finem omnia appetunt. Sed Deum non omnia appetunt, quia neque omnia ipsum cognoscunt. Deus ergo non est omnium finis.

4. Præterea, finalis causa est prima causarum. Si igitur Deus sit causa agens et causa finalis, sequitur quod in eo sit prius et posterius. Quod est impossibile.

SED CONTRA est quod dicitur *Prov.*,[3] *Universa propter semetipsum operatus est Dominus.*

RESPONSIO: Dicendum quod omne agens agit propter finem; alioquin ex actione agentis non magis sequeretur hoc quam illud, nisi a casu. Est autem idem finis agentis et patientis inquantum hujusmodi, sed aliter et aliter; unum enim et idem est quod agens intendit imprimere et quod patiens intendit recipere. Sunt autem quædam quæ simul agunt et patiuntur, quæ sunt agentia imperfecta; et his convenit quod etiam in agendo intendant aliquid acquirere. Sed primo agenti, qui est agens tantum, non convenit agere propter acquisitionem alicujus finis, sed intendit solum communicare suam perfectionem, quæ est ejus bonitas. Et unaquæque creatura intendit consequi suam perfectionem, quæ est similitudo perfectionis et bonitatis divinæ. Sic ergo divina bonitas est finis rerum omnium.

---

[1]cf 1a. 65, 2; 103, 2. II *Sent.* 1, 2, 1 & 2. *CG* III, 17 & 18. *Compend. theol.* 100 & 101

[2]*Physics* II, 7. 198a24–27. *lect.* 11

[3]*Proverbs* 16, 4

[a]Final cause, *to heneka*, that for the sake of which, *cujus gratia*, something is produced or exists. *De partibus animalium* I, 1. 639b14. A cause by attraction, as setting up a 'want' deciding the action of the efficient cause; this 'intention' originates the process of causality work on the material cause to produce the form cause and so arrive at the end, which comes last in the order of execution. cf 1a2æ. 1, 2.

[b]This argument is not directly to the point of the inquiry, which is not whether God is subject to final causality.

[c]Aristotle says the opposite. 'In many cases three of these "becauses" coincide, for the essential nature of a thing and the purpose for which it is produced are often

article 4. is God the final cause of all things?

THE FOURTH POINT:[1] 1. It would seem not. For does not acting for an end mean acting from need of it?[a] But God needs nothing. Therefore it does not become him to act for an end.[b]

2. Besides, the purpose for which a thing is produced, the form of the thing produced, and the efficient cause producing it, are not numerically identical, we are told in the *Physics*;[2c] the purpose is the form. God is the first efficient cause all things. Hence he is not the final cause.

3. Also, all things want their goal. Yet all do not want God, since they do not even know him. So for all things he is not the goal.

4. Then again, the final cause is the first of the causes. Were God to be both efficient and final cause there would be in him a *before* and *after*. Which is impossible.

ON THE OTHER HAND it is said, *The Lord made all things for himself.*[3]

REPLY: Every agent acts for the sake of an end; otherwise the result of its action would not be this rather than that, unless by chance.[d] Now purpose is identical for the thing acting and for the thing acted upon when both are taken precisely as such, though the manner is different for each; the effect the one is extended to impress on the other is identical with the effect the other is open to receive.[e] There are some things which are at once acting on and acted upon; these are agents which are incomplete, and to them it belongs that even in their acting they are out to get something. However there is no question of the first agent, who is purely active, acting in order to achieve some purpose; he intends only to communicate his own completeness, which is his goodness. Each and every creature stretches out to its own completion, which is a resemblance of divine fulness and excellence. Thus, then, divine goodness is the final cause of all things.

---

identical (so that the final cause coincides with the formal), and moreover the efficient cause must bear some resemblance in "form" to the effect (so that the efficient cause also must coincide with the formal to that extent).' Yet despite the misquotation the line of argument is authentically Aristotelean: there is a distinction between the agent and the purpose of change. See earlier in the *Physics* II, 3. 194b30.

[d]Chance: cf 1a. 19, 6; 116, 1. *CG* III, 2.

[e]cf *Physics* III, 3. 202a12–20. St Thomas, *lect.* 4. 'Is extended' renders *intendit*, intends, which may suggest conscious direction. But, as here, the term may mean any tending to an end. The teleology of Aristotle and St Thomas should be read without psychological and ethical overtones. Thus the intention and appetite in gravitation: cf *In Physic.* I, 1, *lect.* 15.

The situation referred to is one of 'natural', not 'violent', action and reaction.

1. Ad primum ergo dicendum quod agere propter indigentiam non est nisi agentis imperfecti, quod natum est agere et pati. Sed hoc Deo non competit. Et ideo ipse solus est maxime liberalis, quia non agit propter suam utilitatem, sed solum propter suam bonitatem.

2. Ad secundum dicendum quod forma generati non est finis generationis nisi inquantum est similitudo formæ generantis, quod suam similitudinem communicare intendit. Alioquin forma generati esset nobilior generante, cum finis sit nobilior his quæ sunt ad finem.

3. Ad tertium dicendum quod omnia appetunt Deum ut finem appetendo quodcumque bonum, sive appetitu intelligibili sive sensibili sive naturali qui est sine cognitione; quia nihil habet rationem boni et appetibilis, nisi secundum quod participat Dei similitudinem.

4. Ad quartum dicendum quod cum Deus sit causa efficiens, exemplaris et finalis omnium rerum, et materia prima sit ab ipso, sequitur quod principium omnium rerum sit unum secundum rem. Nihil tamen prohibet in eo considerari multa secundum rationem, quorum quædam prius cadunt in intellectu nostro quam alia.

---

[f]Generous, *liberalis*: cf 2a2æ. 117. The terms 'egoism' and 'altruism' are irrelevant here, as indeed they are in the morality of acting for the Good.
[g]cf Ia. 19, 2 ad 3; 3.
[h]A knotted reply, which Cajetan, *in loc.*, slowly unties. In brief the meaning is that God as first efficient cause reproduces his varying likeness, that this in creatures is the *finis*, yet is derivative from the original exemplar (art. 3), which as ultimate final cause is God. cf Ia, 6, 1. The end of an action is the agent, not as the subject of the effect but as having the form communicated.

Hence: 1. To act from need is the mark only of an agent which is un-fulfilled and made to be both acting on and acted upon. But this is not the case with God. He alone is supremely generous,[f] because he does not act for his own benefit but simply to give of his goodness.[g]

2. The form of the thing produced is not the purpose of the production except in so far as it is the likeness of the producer's own form, a likeness which it is set to communicate. Otherwise, since an end is higher than the steps to it, we would have the anomaly of the form of the thing produced being better than the producer.[h]

3. All things want God as their goal in wanting any good whatsoever, whether by intelligent or by sensitive appetite, or by natural appetite which is unconscious, for nothing strikes the note of being good or desirable except as sharing God's likeness.[i]

4. Since God is the efficient, exemplary, and final cause of everything, and since primary matter is from him, we infer that the origin of all things in reality is single. There is nothing to stop us, however, from considering divine attributes as many from the standpoint of human reason; for some strike our minds before others do.[j]

---

[i]cf 1a2æ. 1, 8. Also 1a. 6,4. 'Whatever is desirable is any happiness whatsoever, be it true or false, all that is there pre-exists, and more highly, in the divine happiness:' 1a. 26, 4.

Intellective appetite, will; sensitive appetite, the power of feeling emotion; natural appetite, a blind tendency to good: 1a. 19, 1.

[j]cf 1a. 4, 2: the manifold perfections of God.

Quæstio 45. de modo emanationis rerum a primo principio

Deinde quæritur de modo emanationis rerum a primo principio, qui dicitur creatio. De qua quæruntur octo:

1. quid sit creatio;
2. utrum Deus possit aliquid creari;
3. utrum creatio sit aliquid ens in rerum natura;
4. cui competit creari;
5. utrum solius Dei sit creare;
6. utrum commune sit toti Trinitati aut proprium alicujus Personæ;
7. utrum vestigium aliquod Trinitatis sit in rebus creatis;
8. utrum opus creationis admisceatur in operibus naturæ et voluntatis.

articulus 1. utrum creare sit ex nihilo aliquid facere

AD PRIMUM sic proceditur:[1] 1. Videtur quod creare non sit ex nihilo aliquid facere. Dicit enim Augustinus,[2] *Facere est quod omnino non erat, creare vero est ex eo quod jam erat educendo aliquid constituere*

2. Præterea, nobilitas actionis et motus ex terminis consideratur. Nobilior igitur est actio quæ ex bono in bonum est, et ex ente in ens, quam quæ est ex nihilo in aliquid. Sed creatio videtur esse nobilissima actio, et prima inter omnes actiones. Ergo non est ex nihilo in aliquid, sed magis ex ente in ens.

3. Præterea, haec præpositio 'ex' importat habitudinem alicujus causæ, et maxime materialis; sicut cum dicimus quod statua fit ex aëre. Sed nihil non est materia entis, nec aliquo modo causa ejus. Ergo creare non est ex nihilo aliquid facere.

SED CONTRA est quod super illud *Gen.*, *In principio creavit Deus cælum*, etc., dicit Glossa[3] quod creare est aliquid ex nihilo facere.

---

[1]cf II *Sent.* 1, 1, 2   [2]*Contra adversarium Legis et Prophetarum* I, 23. PL 42, 633
[3]*Genesis* 1, 1. *Glossa ordinaria super Gen.* The Venerable Bede. PL 91, 191
[a]Nothing: *nihil*, or no being at all, *nullum ens*: a blanker term than non-being, *non-ens*, which may refer to the absence either of some due reality in a subject called a privation, or of some actuality, called a potentiality. *In Meta.* XII, lect. 2. Nothing, what in no way is, *quod nullo modo est*, pure and unqualified non-being, *non-ens omnino, purum, simpliciter.*
    From nothing: *ex nihilo*, cf below ad 3; also 1a. 46, 2 ad 2.

Question 45. creation

Next we discuss how things flow from their original source. On this, which is called creation, there are eight points of inquiry:

1. what is creation?
2. whether God can create something;
3. whether creation is something in reality;
4. what exactly is produced by creation?
5. whether God alone can create;
6. whether creating is common to the whole Trinity or proper to one Person;
7. whether it leaves any trace of the Trinity in things created;
8. whether the work of creation mingles in the operations of nature and will.

article 1. does creating mean making something from nothing?

THE FIRST POINT:[1] 1. Apparently not.[a] For according to St Augustine,[2] *Making is of a thing that did not exist at all, while creating is to fashion it by bringing it forth from what already existed.*

2. Then also, you assess the value of an action or motion from whence it comes and where it goes.[b] So an action which is from good to good or from being to being is worth more than one from nothing into something. Of all action creation would seem to be the chief and best, and consequently is not from nothing into something but rather from being into being.

3. Moreover, the preposition 'from' implies a causal relation, especially that of a material cause, as when we say that a statue is cast from bronze. But 'nothing' is neither the material of being nor its cause in any way at all. Therefore to create is not to make something from nothing.

ON THE OTHER HAND, on *Genesis, In the beginning God created the heavens and earth,* the Gloss comments that to create is *to make something out of nothing.*[3c]

---

[b]Motion or change, conceived as transferring a subject from one term to another, each being taken as a point of reference for estimating its value.

[c]The Gloss: the *Glossa ordinaria,* the work of Anselm of Laon (*d.* 1117) and his school, though parts derive from Walafrid Strabo (*d.* 849), monk of Fulda, to whom the work is ascribed by St Thomas (cf 1a. 66, 3). Referred to in this edition as 'the Gloss'. The text given in PL 113 is not the one used in the *Summa.* 'A gloss' refers to other glosses, such as the *Glossa interlinearis* or the *Glossa Lombardi.*

ERSPONSIO: Dicendum quod, sicut supra dictum est,[4] non solum oportet considerare emanationem alicujus entis particularis ab aliquo particulari agente, sed etiam emanationem totius entis a causa universali, quæ est Deus; et hanc quidem emanationem designamus nomine creationis.

Quod autem procedit secundum emanationem particularem non præsupponitur emanationi, sicut si generatur homo non fuit prius homo, sed homo fit ex non homine, et album ex non albo. Unde, si consideretur emanatio totius entis universalis a primo principio, impossibile est quod aliquod ens præsupponatur huic emanationi. Idem autem est nihil quod nullum ens. Sicut igitur generatio hominis est ex non ente quod est non homo, ita creatio, quæ est emanatio totius esse, est ex non ente quod est nihil.

1. Ad primum ergo dicendum quod Augustinus æquivoce utitur nomine creationis secundum quod creari dicuntur ea quæ in melius reformantur, ut cum dicitur aliquis creari in episcopum. Sic autem non loquimur hic de creatione, sed sicut dictum est.[5]

2. Ad secundum dicendum quod mutationes accipiunt speciem et dignitatem non a termino a quo, sed a termino ad quem. Tanto ergo perfectior et prior est aliqua mutatio quanto terminus ad quem illius mutationis est nobilior et prior; licet terminus a quo, qui opponitur termino ad quem, sit imperfectior. Sicut generatio simpliciter est nobilior et prior quam alteratio propter hoc quod forma substantialis est nobilior quam forma accidentalis; tamen privatio substantialis formæ, quæ est terminus a quo in generatione, est imperfectior quam contrarium, quod est terminus a quo in alteratione. Et similiter creatio est perfectior et prior quam generatio et alteratio, quia terminus ad quem est tota substantia rei; id autem quod intelligitur ut terminus a quo, est simpliciter non ens.

3. Ad tertium dicendum quod cum dicitur 'aliquid ex nihilo fieri,' hæc præpositio 'ex' non designat causam materialem, sed ordinem tantum; sicut cum dicitur, 'ex mane fit meridies', idest 'post mane fit meridies'. Sed intelligendum est quod hæc præpositio 'ex' potest includere negationem

---

[4]Ia. 44, 2
[5]In the body of the article
[d]Any being, or some being, *aliquod ens*, which God is not: cf Ia. 3, 5.
[e]*Terminus ad quem*, the term whereto; *terminus a quo*, the term wherefrom. Creation, as will be seen, is not the type of change in which a subject exchanges one state or condition for another, or what is called a *mutatio physica*. It is defined as the production of a thing *ex nihilo sui et subjecti*: from its own nothingness (which is the case with any fresh production) and from the nothingness of not presupposing a material cause or subject.
[f]The plain coming to be, *generatio simpliciter, genesis* (opposed to ceasing to be, *corruptio, phthora*) of a substance in matter. The being altered, *alteratio, alloiosis,*

REPLY: As already remarked,[4] it is not enough to consider how some particular being issues from some particular cause, for we should also attend to the issuing of the whole of being from the universal cause, which is God; it is this springing forth that we designate by the term 'creation'.

Now when a thing makes its first appearance according to a particular system of reference you do not presume its presence there already; a man does not exist before he is begotten, but becomes a man out of what was not a man, like a thing becoming white from a being not white. So then if we consider the coming forth of the whole of all being from its first origins we cannot presuppose to it any being.[d] But no-being and nothing are synonymous. As therefore the begetting of a human being is out of that non-being which is non-human being, so creation, the introduction of being entirely, is out of the non-being which is nothing at all.

Hence: 1. St Augustine is using the word 'creation' in an equivocal sense, not as we have explained it.[5] He speaks of things being created when promoted to a higher position; so we speak of someone being created a bishop.

2. Changes get their meaning and value from their point of arrival, not from their point of departure.[e] The better and more important the stage they reach, so also are the changes themselves, whatever the incompleteness of the stage they start from. For instance the plain coming to be of a thing is a greater achievement than its becoming altered, since the shaping principle of a thing's substance is more capital than a shaping principle which modifies it, despite the fact that the opening condition of the first change, namely the privation of the substantial form in question, is emptier than that of the second, namely the contrary of the property in question.[f] And, to deepen the comparison, creation is more complete and comes before either, for it achieves a thing's entire substance, although its starting-point is conceived as non-being utterly.

3. When he speak of something being made from nothing, the preposition 'from' signifies a sequence, not a material cause; as when we say that noon comes from the dawn we mean that it follows after.[g] Yet appreciate that the preposition 'from' can inflect or be inflected by the

---

any change in the modifications ('accidents') of substance, but more strictly a change of quality. Shaping principle which makes a thing what it is, *forma substantialis*; which modifies it, *forma accidentalis*. Substantial change starts from a lack, *privatio*, of the form produced, e.g. man from non-man; qualitative change from a contrary, e.g. green from blue.

[g]The sequence is merely in our minds. We conceive 'nothing' as the term 'where-from' of creative production, whereas in reality there is nothing there at all: cf below art. 2 ad 2.

importatam in hoc quod dico 'nihil', vel includi ab ea. Si primo modo, tunc ordo remanet affirmatus, et ostenditur ordo ejus quod est ad non ens præcedens. Si vero negatio includit præpositionem, tunc ordo negatur, et est sensus, 'fit ex nihilo', idest 'non fit ex aliquo'; sicut dicatur, 'iste loquitur de nihilo', quia non loquitur de aliquo. Et utroque modo verificatur cum dicitur 'ex nihilo aliquid fieri'. Sed primo modo hæc præpositio 'ex' importat ordinem, ut dictum est; secundo modo importat habitudinem causæ materialis quæ negatur.

articulus 2. utrum Deus possit aliquid creare

AD SECUNDUM sic proceditur:[1] 1. Videtur quod Deus non possit aliquid creare. Quia secundum Philosophum antiqui philosophi acceperunt ut communem conceptionem animi, *ex nihilo nihil fieri*.[2] Sed potentia Dei non se extendit ad contraria primorum principiorum, utpote quod Deus faciat quod totum non sit majus sua parte, vel quod affirmatio et negatio sint simul vera. Ergo Deus non potest aliquid ex nihilo facere, vel creare.

2. Præterea, si creare est aliquid ex nihilo facere, ergo creari est aliquid fieri. Sed omne fieri est mutari. Ergo creatio est mutatio. Sed omnis mutatio est ex aliquo subjecto, ut patet per definitionem motus, nam motus est actus existentis in potentia. Ergo est impossibile aliquid a Deo ex nihilo fieri.

3. Præterea, quod factum est necesse est aliquando fieri. Sed non potest dici quod illud quod creatur simul fiat et factum sit, quia in permanentibus quod fit non est, quod autem factum est jam est; simul ergo aliquid esset et non esset. Ergo si aliquid fit, fieri eius præcedit factum esse. Sed hoc non potest esse nisi præexistat subjectum in quo sustentetur ipsum fieri. Ergo impossibile est aliquid fieri ex nihilo.

4. Præterea, infinitam distantiam non est pertransire. Sed infinita distantia est inter ens et nihil. Ergo non contingit ex nihilo aliquid fieri.

---

[1]cf *CG* II, 16. *De potentia* III, 1. *Compound. theol.* 69. II *Sent.* I, 1, 2. *In Physic.* VIII, *lect.* 2

[2]*Physics* I, 4. 187a26

[h]Creation, though not working on material causes, covers material causes: cf 1a. 44, 2; 45, 4 & 5.

[a]A contradiction in terms sets a quasi-limit to omnipotence. But it is less because God cannot make it than that it cannot be made: 1a. 25, 3.

[b]The classical Aristotelean 'definition' of *kinesis*. *Physics* III, 1. 201a10.

[c]*In permanentibus*, not to be translated as 'among permanent things', with its distracting suggestion of 'incorruptible bodies'. *Permanens* is synonymous with

negation the term 'nothing' expresses. In the first case the sequence is stated by showing the relationship of what is now to the preceding non-being. In the second case, where the negation governs the preposition, the sequence is denied, and being made from nothing means not being made from anything, as when we remark of somebody that he speaks of nothing, because he does not speak of anything. 'From' has both senses when we say that something is made from nothing; the first expresses sequence, as we have noted, while the second expresses and denies relationship to a material cause.[h]

article 2. can God create anything?

THE SECOND POINT:[1] 1. It seems he cannot. For Aristotle notes that to the ancient philosophers it was a commonplace that nothing comes from nothing.[2] Now God's power does not stretch to what is contrary to first principles, as though, for instance, he could make a whole to be less than its part, or the affirmation and negation of the same to be simultaneously true.[a] Therefore he cannot make something out of nothing, in other words, create.

2. Again, if to create is to make something from nothing then to be created is to become something. Now every becoming is a changing. Therefore creation is a change. But all change is of a subject, as appears from its definition, namely an actualization of what exists in potentiality.[b] Hence for God to make something out of nothing is impossible.

3. Furthermore, what has been made must at some time have been in process of being made. You cannot contend that what is created is at one and the same time both becoming made and already made, for looking at things within themselves[c] then what is becoming made is not yet finished, and what has become is already finished. Say that it is both and you are maintaining that it both is and is not simultaneously. So then when anything is made its becoming made precedes its having been made. This, however, cannot be except given a subject on which the change is based.[d] Therefore it is impossible to become something out of nothing.

4. Then also, an infinite distance cannot be crossed. This is what lies between being and nothing. Hence the making of something from nothing does not come about.

---

manens, and is contrasted with *pertransiens, transiens, transitivus*. A thing is *manens* in itself, *transiens* to something else. The verb's sense is here to stay, remain, stop, rather than to await, expect.

[d]Neglecting the transient character of change or motion, the objection rests its case on there being two fixed terms, one before and the other after, linked together in a common subject.

SED CONTRA est quod dicitur *Gen.*,[3] *In principio creavit Deus cælum et terram.*[*]

RESPONSIO: Dicendum quod non solum non est impossibile a Deo aliquid creari, sed necesse est ponere a Deo omnia creata esse, ut ex præmissis habetur.

Quicumque enim facit aliquid ex aliquo, illud ex quo facit præsupponitur actioni ejus et non producitur per ipsam actionem; sicut artifex operatur ex rebus naturalibus, ut ex ligno et aëre, quæ per artis actionem non causantur sed causantur per actionem naturæ. Sed et ipsa natura causat res naturales quantum ad formam, sed præsupponit materiam. Si ergo Deus non ageret nisi ex aliquo præsupposito, sequeretur quod illud præsuppositum non esset causatum ab ipso. Ostensum est autem supra[4] quod nihil potest esse in entibus quod non sit a Deo, qui est causa universalis totius esse. Unde necesse est dicere quod Deus ex nihilo res in esse producit.

1. Ad primum ergo dicendum quod antiqui philosophi, sicut supra dictum est,[5] non consideraverunt nisi emanationem effectuum particularium a causis particularibus, quas necesse est præsupponere aliquid in sua actione; et secundum hoc erat eorum communis opinio, *ex nihilo nihil fit.* Sed tamen hoc locum non habet in prima emanatione ab universali rerum principio.

2. Ad secundum dicendum quod creatio non est mutatio nisi secundum modum intelligendi tantum. Nam de ratione mutationis est quod aliquid idem se habeat aliter nunc et prius: nam quandoque est idem ens actu,[†] aliter se habens nunc et prius, sicut in motibus secundem quantitatem et qualitatem et ubi;[‡] quandoque vero est idem ens in potentia tantum, sicut in mutatione secundum substantiam, cujus subjectum est materia. Sed in creatione, per quam producitur tota substantia rerum, non potest accipi aliquid idem aliter se habens nunc et prius, nisi secundum intellectum tantum, sicut si intelligatur aliqua res prius non fuisse totaliter, et postea esse. Sed cum actio et passio conveniant in substantia motus et differant

---

[*]Piana adds: *ubi dicit Glossa quod creare est aliquid ex nihilo facere,* on which the Gloss says that to create is to make something out of nothing. A repetition of art. 1 *sed contra*

[†]Piana: *actualiter se habens,* the identical being actually (such) now and (otherwise) earlier, by changes etc.

[‡]Piana: omits *et ubi*

[3]*Genesis* 1, 1   [4]Ia. 44, 1 & 2   [5]Ia. 44, 2
[6]A new note is introduced into the discussion. Creation is not only possible, but, given the existence of things, the alternative is impossible. See Appendix 2.

ON THE OTHER HAND *Genesis* opens,[3] *In the beginning the Lord created the heavens and earth,* on which the Gloss says that to create is *to make out of nothing.*

REPLY: Not only is it not impossible for God to create something, but from what has been established we cannot but hold that all things are created by him.[e]

For whenever you make something from something else that something else is presupposed to the action and is not produced by it; thus a craftsman works in natural materials, such as wood or metal, but these the working of nature, not his art, produces. Even nature itself causes natural things as to their form, yet presupposes their matter.[f] Were God to work only on something presupposed, the implication would be that it was not caused by him. We have already shown[4] that there is naught in being that is not from God, who is the all-embracing cause of existence entire.[g] That is why we are bound to infer that God brings things into existence from nothing.

Hence: 1. We have remarked[5] how the ancient philosophers concentrated their attention on the issuing of particular effects from particular causes. These, of course, presuppose something to act on, and in this context the general reckoning was that nothing comes from nothing.[h] The axiom, however does not apply to the original flowing out from the universal source of things.

2. Creation is not a change, except merely according to our way of understanding. For change means that a constant is now otherwise than what it was before: sometimes this is the same actual being which varies by changes of quantity or quality or place; sometimes it is the same potential being, as in the case of substantial change where matter is the subject. But creation, whereby the entire substance of things is produced, does not allow of some common subject now different from what it was before, except according to our way of understanding, which conceives an object as first not existing at all and afterwards as existing.[i] Now since

---

[f]Matter, for Aristotle, is not a product of nature, for nature is the principle of motion and therefore requires a subject upon which to work.

[g]*Causa universalis totius esse*: a fully 'extensive' and 'intensive' concept, to be taken in breadth and in depth. The cause of all things and in all that they have. God is the proper cause of existence, 1a. 8, 1, and what exist are 'wholes', 1a. 45, 4.

[h]Aristotle uses the axiom to show that potentiality is real. In creation there is antecedent possibility and creative power, but not potentiality.

[i]Our understanding is limited by its dependence on the senses, which are familiar with a world in which we perceive change and consider its implications. It is

Footnote i continued on page 32.

solum secundum habitudines diversas, ut dicitur in *Physic.*,[6] oportet quod subtracto motu non remaneant nisi diversæ habitudines in creante et creato.

Sed quia modus significandi sequitur modum intelligendi, ut dictum est,[7] creatio significatur per modum mutationis; et propter hoc dicitur quod creare est ex nihilo aliquid facere. Quamvis 'facere' et 'fieri' magis in hoc conveniant quam 'mutare' et 'mutari', quia 'facere' et 'fieri' important habitudinem causæ ad effectum et effectus ad causam, sed mutationem ex consequenti.

3. Ad tertium dicendum quod in his quæ fiunt sine motu simul* est fieri et factum esse, sive talis factio sit terminus motus, sicut illuminatio (nam simul aliquid illuminatur et illuminatum est), sive non sit terminus motus, sicut simul formatur verbum in corde et formatum est. Et in his quod fit est; sed cum dicitur 'fieri' significatur† ab alio esse, et prius non fuisse. Unde, cum creatio sit sine motu, simul aliquid creatur et creatum est.

---

*Piana: *similiter*, are like

†Piana: *sed significatur*, the phrase but signifies that, etc.

[6]*Physics* III, 3. 202a20

[7]Ia. 13, 1

natural then that we should imagine and speak of creation as though it were a change or process. We can do this without error, on this and other matters that lie beyond our experience, if, as St Thomas observes *passim*, we recognize the limitations under which our thought is working and qualify our conclusions: e.g. Ia. 13, 1.

Change requires a contrast between what was and what is, and a subject persisting throughout. This subject is a thing's substance—the being in actuality—when the change is of modes of existing (accidents); when the change is of a thing's substance then its subject, ensuring continuity, is primary or substantial matter. This bare matter is not itself a being, but *ens in potentia*: cf *In Physic. I, lect.* 6 & 13. Ia. 76, 4. 3a. 85, 3 & 4.

Every product is new and fresh, and in this sense comes from its own non-being, *ex nihilo sui*; only a created product comes from the complete non-being of not even a real potentiality or matter, *ex nihilo subjecti*.

If it is said that they come from their 'possibility', note (1) that this is not a 'real potentiality' (called by later Scholastics a 'subjective potentiality', who also speak of 'possibility' as 'objective potentiality'); and (2) that this does not belong to material causality, but to the exemplar causality of divine Ideas and God's simple understanding of himself. cf Ia. 14, 2–4; 15, 2. Vol. 4.

The succession of being to pure non-being is a mental category only: the picture of one replacing the other is formed from our experience of relative and particular beginnings.

ᴶAristotle is arguing that there is one movement, not two movements, in actual setting-in-motion and set-in-motion: *actio* and *passio* coincide in the one reality, which, however, may be regarded from two different aspects. The ratio 1 : 2

to act and to be acted upon coincide in the change that really takes place and differ only according to the way you look at them, as remarked in the *Physics*,[6][j] it follows that when you eliminate change from the situation you are left just with the relations diverse in the creator and in the thing created. Yet because our mode of signifying corresponds to our mode of understanding, as we have noted,[7] we express creation in terms of change, and accordingly speak of creating as making something from nothing. All the same, note that making and being made are more appropriate terms here than changing and being changed, for they directly imply the relationship of cause to effect and of effect to cause, and convey the notion of a process of change only because of supervening elements in the situation.[k]

3. In the case of things produced without process of change, to become and to be are simultaneous regardless of whether the production marks the term of a change (thus there is no interval of time between becoming lit and being lit), or whether it does not, thus when a concept is at once being formed and is formed in the mind. In all such cases what is being made at that moment is; by speaking of its becoming made we signify that it comes from another and previously did not exist. Hence, since there is no process of change in creation, a thing is simultaneously being created and is created.[1]

---

is the same as the ratio 2 : 1, and the inclination of a line is the same whether you regard it as sloping up or down. cf *Physics* III, 3. 202a15–b30. 1a. 28, 3 ad 1.

[k]Not an easy reply. It shows the effort required to fit the new concept of creation into the familiar background of change, for which *mutatio* is used in the premises and conclusion and *motus* in between: there is no difference of meaning; cf 1a. 27, 1 & 2. *Actio* is the actualization of the active principle of change, the setter in motion; *passio* that of the passive principle or subject of change, the being set in motion; 1a. 25, 1. This double reference is kept in the concept of creation, though a process of change is ruled out. The relations consequent on creative action are real with regard to the things created though purely mental with regard to the creator; cf 1a. 13, 7; 28, 1 ad 3; 45, 3.

[1]How can the producing and production be instantaneous for a thing which is the term of a successive change? Go back to the objection which takes things as they are in themselves apart from extrinsic factors which may have attended their coming to be. Now it was the old theory that illumination itself was not a successive action, and that the effect was instantaneous in a transparent medium given the presence of the illuminating body. Yet it could well be the term of a change, namely the approach of that body. Optics was by no means a rudimentary science in the Middle Ages; the argument, however, does not depend on the illustration from an outmoded theory of light. It is showing that a product may follow a change and yet not in itself imply a change, namely from a condition of becoming to that of being. The 'moment' for both is identical. For the *Summa* on light and lights in the firmament see 1a. 67 & 70. Vol. 10 of this series.

Concept, *verbum in corde* or *verbum mentis*, *logos* as inward thought, cf 1a. 27, 1 & 2. Its relation to motions of sense, 1a. 84, 6–8; 85, 1–5.

4. Ad quartum dicendum quod objectio illa procedit ex falsa imaginatione, ac si sit aliquod infinitum medium inter nihilum et ens, quod patet esse falsum. Procedit autem falsa hæc imaginatio ex eo quod creatio significatur ut quædam mutatio inter duos terminos existens.

articulus 3. *utrum creatio sit aliquid in creatura*

AD TERTIUM sic proceditur:[1] 1. Videtur quod creatio non sit aliquid in creatura. Sicut enim creatio passive accepta attribuitur creaturæ, ita creatio active accepta attribuitur creatori. Sed creatio active accepta non est aliquid in creatore, quia si sic,* sequeretur quod in Deo esset aliquid temporale. Ergo creatio passive accepta non est aliquid in creatura.

2. Præterea, nihil est medium inter creatorem et creaturam. Sed creatio significatur ut medium inter utrumque; non enim est creator, cum non sit æterna, neque creatura, quia oporteret† eadem ratione aliam ponere creatiorem qua ipsa crearetur, et sic in infinitum. Creatio ergo non est aliquid.

3. Præterea, si creatio est aliquid præter substantiam creatam oportet quod sit accidens ejus. Omne autem accidens est in subjecto. Ergo res creata esset subjectum creationis. Et sic idem esset‡ subjectum creationis et terminus. Quod est impossibile, quia subjectum prius est accidente, et conservat accidens; terminus autem posterius est actione et passione cujus est terminus, et eo existente, cessat actio et passio. Igitur ipsa creatio non est aliqua res.

SED CONTRA, majus est fieri aliquid secundum totam substantiam quam secundum formam substantialem vel accidentalem. Sed generatio simpliciter vel secundum quid, qua fit aliquid secundum formam substantialem vel accidentalem, est aliquid in generato. Ergo multo magis creatio, qua fit aliquid secundum totam substantiam, est aliquid in creato.

RESPONSIO: Dicendum quod creatio¶ ponit aliquid in creato secundum relationem tantum. Quia quod creatur non fit per motum vel per muta-

---

*Leonine: *quia sic sequeretur*, for so it would follow
†Piana: *oportet*
‡Piana: *est*
¶Piana: *creatio non ponit*, creation does not put
[1]cf CG II, 18. *De potentia* III, 3. 1 *Sent.* 40, 1 ad 1; II, 1, 1, 2 ad 4 & 5
mThe idea of creation implies infinite power, cf art. 5 ad 3 below, yet the infinite cannot be represented as a real relation of distance between two terms. There is but one real term, namely finite being; the other, nothing, is entirely non-real. The relation between the two is purely nominal or conceptual. 'Between existence and non-existence, which are like the extreme terms in creation, there cannot be a

4. The objection draws a misleading picture of some infinite middle stretch between the two extremes of nothing and of being, which is plainly false. This figment of the imagination rises from taking creation as a change existing between two terms.[m]

1426991

article 3. is creation something real in the creature?

THE THIRD POINT:[1] 1. It seems not. For the verb 'to create' in its passive voice is applied to the creature as in its active voice it is to the creator. But to create is not something real in the creator, for if it were the consequence would follow of something temporal in God. No more, therefore, is creation something real in the creature.[a]

2. Moreover, no reality mediates between God and the creature. Yet creation is represented as being a kind of intermediary, since it is neither the creator, for it is not eternal, nor the creature, for if it were another creation to create it would be required, and so on *ad infinitum*. Accordingly creation is not something real.

3. Next, were creation something additional to a created substance it would have to be a modification of it.[b] Any modification is in the subject it modifies. So a created thing would be the subject of creation. And so also the subject and the result of creation would be identical. This is impossible, for a subject is prior to and sustains its modification, whereas a result is subsequent to and terminates the action exercised and undergone, which stops as soon as it exists. Therefore creation itself is not a thing.

ON THE OTHER HAND it is mightier for a thing to be made as to its entire substance than as to its substantial form or the modifications it receives. Yet in both these cases, namely the plain production of a thing's substantial form and the qualified production of forms which modify it, there is a corresponding reality in the thing produced. Much more then does creation, whereby a thing is made as its whole substance, denote a reality in the thing created.

REPLY: Creation puts a reality into a created thing only as a relation. For to be created is not to be produced through a motion or mutation which

---

middle term', *CG* II, 19. On the picture of the infinite as the 'extensive all', see 1a. 7, 1–3.
[a]An agent is designated so when it produces its effect. Likewise the creator. Now, as will be shown in 1a. 46, 1, creation as taken in this article (passively, namely, as being created) is not eternal. Hence the corresponding embarrassment of attributing the non-eternal to God.
On the use of 'time words' about God see 1a. 13, 7. Vol. 3 of this series.
[b]Modification or 'accident'.

tionem. Quod enim fit per motum vel mutationem fit ex aliquo præexistenti, quod quidem contingit in productionibus particularibus aliquorum entium; non autem potest hoc contingere in productione esse totius a causa universali omnium entium, quæ est Deus. Unde Deus creando producit res sine motu. Subtracto autem motu ab actione et passione, nihil remanet nisi relatio, ut dictum est.² Unde relinquitur quod creatio in creatura non sit nisi relatio quædam ad creatorem, ut ad principium sui esse: sicut in passione quæ est cum motu importatur relatio ad principium motus.

1. Ad primum ergo dicendum quod creatio active significata significat actionem divinam, quæ est ejus essentia cum relatione ad creaturam. Sed relatio in Deo ad creaturam non est realis, sed secundum rationem tantum. Relatio vero creaturæ ad Deum est relatio realis, ut supra dictum est, cum de divinis nominibus ageretur.³

2. Ad secundum dicendum quod quia creatio significatur ut mutatio, sicut dictum est,⁴ mutatio autem media quodammodo est inter movens et motum; ideo etiam creatio significatur ut media inter creatorem et creaturam. Tamen creatio passive accepta est in creatura et est creatura. Neque tamen oportet quod alia creatione creetur, quia relationes, cum hoc ipsum quod sunt, 'ad aliquid' dicantur, non referuntur per aliquas alias relationes, sed per seipsas; sicut etiam supra dictum est, cum de æqualitate Personarum ageretur.⁵

3. Ad tertium dicendum quod creationis, secundum quod significatur ut mutatio, creatura est terminus; sed secundum quod vere est relatio creatura est ejus subjectum, et prius ea, sicut subjectum accidente. Sed

---

²Ia. 45, 2 ad 2
³Ia. 13, 7
⁴Ia. 45, 2 ad 2
⁵Ia. 42, 1 ad 4
ᶜLiterally: the particular productions of some beings. cf above, art. 1.
ᵈPiana alone of the current editions starts off the paragraph, and with fair mss warrant, 'Creation does not put a reality into a created thing only as a relation'. Though apparently a textual error in the light of the immediate context, and a local contradiction of the Leonine reading here adopted, nevertheless it fits in with the whole sense of the article, which is that to be created represents something real and indeed substantial. Creatureliness certainly seems much more than the relation, *pros ti*, listed by Aristotle as the fourth of his categories (*Categories* 4 & 7. 1b25 & 6b27), the 'predicamental relation', as it is called by the scholastics, which is an *accidens*, the modification contracted by a given subject by its real bearing on another. Rather is it a 'transcendental relation', the reference to another included in the very nature of the subject, in this case the whole existing being of the creature. But see *ad* 3 below. A created thing is in itself but not of itself: this reflection runs throughout the *Summa*.

works on something that already exists, as is the case with the limited causality that produces some sorts of being.[c] Not, however, with the production of existence entire by the universal cause of all beings, which is God. Hence in creating he produces a thing without motion in the making. Take away motion from the acting-on acted-upon situation and only relation remains: this has been already observed.[2] Hence creation in the creature is left just as a relation to the creator as the origin of its existence; so also the category of being acted on and changed carries a relationship to the principle which sets up the change.[d]

Hence: 1. In its active sense creation means God's action, which is his essence with a relationship to the creature. But this in God is not a real relation, but only conceptual.[e] The relation of the creature to God, however, is real, as was shown in our discussions on naming God.[3]

2. It is because creation is expressed in terms of change, as we have, as we have recognized,[4] and change is a sort of intermediary between what sets in motion and what is set in motion, that it too is described as mediate between the creator and the creature. Nevertheless taken in its passive sense, creation is in the creature and is the creature. Nor does this demand a further creation for its creation, since being with reference to another, which is precisely what a relation is, explains itself without need for supervening relations: this also was shown when we were discussing the equality of the divine Persons.[5f]

3. When creation is signified as a change then a creature is its term, but taken as it truly is,[g] namely a relation, then a creature is its subject, and

---

Whether creation 'puts something real into': the same turn of phrase is used when inquiring whether God's predestinating and grace have a real creaturely effect: 1a. 23, 2 & 1a2æ. 110, 1.

A point for specialists: if St Thomas is picking his terms carefully, then notice the contrast between the particular production of beings (*entium*), which secondary causes can perform, and the universal production of existence (*esse*) proper to God. cf 1a. 105, 5.

[e]Real relation, *relatio realis*, in the nature of things; conceptual relation only, *relatio rationis tantum*, merely in the human mind collating one object with another: 1a. 28, 1. One or both objects are sometimes purely logical entities.

For St Thomas's philosophy of relation, cf 1a. 13, 7 & 28, 1–3. Vols 3 & 6 of this series. For debates on the relation of God and creatures, cf *De potentia* VII, 8, 9 & 11.

[f]The objection has been guilty of reification by treating relation as a thing (that needs another thing that needs another thing and so on). To be related is to open out to another directly and immediately without an interminable series being involved, and to be created needs no intervening relationship for its reference to the creator. Creation is a relation in a result that has been reached without process of production and no real point of departure.

[g]A relation properly speaking, not merely by a figure of speech: cf 1a. 28, 2.

habet quamdam rationem prioritatis ex parte objecti ad quod dicitur, quod est principium creaturæ. Neque tamen oportet quod quamdiu creatura sit dicatur creari, quia creatio importat habitudinem creaturæ ad creatorem cum quadam novitate seu inceptione.

articulus 4. *utrum creari sit proprium compositorum et subsistentium*

AD QUARTUM sic proceditur:[1] Videtur quod creari non sit proprium compositorum et subsistentium. Dicitur enim in libro De causis,[2] *Prima rerum creatarum est esse.* Sed esse rei creatæ non est subsistens. Ergo creatio proprie non est subsistentis et compositi.

---

[1]cf *De veritate* XXVII, 3 ad 9. *De potentia* III, 1 ad 12; 3 ad 2; 8 ad 3.*Quodl.* IX, 5, 1
[2]*De causis* 4. St Thomas, *lect.* 4
[h]At the risk of increasing the obscurity some notes should be added to this controverted reply.

First as to the text, which may be paraphrased as follows. Creation (taken passively), while not a change, may be signified as such (art. 2 ad 2); the creature is then taken as the *terminus ad quem*, the terminal point of arrival (art. 1 ad 1), though there has been no real point of departure. Signified as a relation then creation has a subject, that which is related; this must be at least thought of as being before being related. More than that, if the categories of Aristotle are severely applied, as by many commentators, it must be a being before being so qualified, as substance by its modification or *accidens*: 'before', of course, refers to a priority of nature, not of time. There is no question of the creature being separable from a relation which necessarily invests it. Nevertheless, as in any relation, there is also that to which the subject is related, usually called the 'term' (*terminus* in a relation should be distinguished from *terminus* in a change), though here the 'object', is the active creative principle. On this count creation comes before the thing created.

Second as to the translation. The specialist reader will notice the easing of the sense. Thus, 'is prior to it in existence as is any subject to a modification' is preferred to 'is prior to as substance to accident'. Again, for *ex parte objecti ad quod dicitur* the '*dicitur*' has been loaded with the sense of a relation *secundum dici* (1a. 13, 7 ad 1) to prevent the relation being isolated as an 'accident', to bring in its substantial foundation, the whole creaturely being of a thing, and to allow for the entrance of a transcendental relation. This is justified, the editor thinks, by the whole context of St Thomas's thought, and in particular by the preceding reply; 'taken in its passive meaning creation is in the creature and is the creature'.

Third as to the difficulty. Cajetan, who takes Scotus to task for treating *creatio passiva* as a transcendental relation (one, namely, included in the very being of a thing, unlike a predicamental relation which supervenes), says that you get from the text manifestly that creation is an *accidens*, and as such really distinct from the substance of a creature. He appeals to *De potentia* III, 3 ad 3 and with his customary surgical skill gets to work on three difficulties arising. Unless his fuller treatment of relation and the foundation for relation be consulted (in 1am. 28, 1–3), he leaves the impression of not appreciating the inner relativeness of creaturely substance, also of applying Aristotle's categories delicately, to be sure, yet also somewhat metallically. His position, which is shared by Ferrariensis (in *CG* II, 18) and Bañez—a prior to it in existence, as is any subject to a modification. All the same it gathers some measure of priority from the object which defines it, namely the source from which a creature derives.[h] This does not require us to say that so long as it continues to exist a creature is being created, since creation strikes this special note, of the creature's relation to creator marked by the freshness of starting off.[1]

article 4. to be created, is this proper to composite and subsisting things?

THE FOURTH POINT:[1] 1. It would not seem so.[a] For we read in the *De causis*,[2b] *The first of created things is existence.* The existence of a created thing, is not subsistent. Therefore it is not the subsisting and composite thing that is created.

---

formidable conjunction, at least has the merit of bringing out the 'absolute' reality of creatures in themselves: while involving no process of 'before' and 'after', creation is logically posterior to being. Sylvius, a sound witness to the tradition of the School in the Low Countries, rejects Scotus because a transcendental relation is a relation between actuality and potentiality, and there is no question of God being either with respect to the creature. Gredt, however, who can be trusted to reproduce the high Thomism of the Habsburg baroque, sums up the matter thus. Passive creation consists in a twofold predicamental relation; (a) a real relation to God as cause, (b) a conceptual relation to the non-existence preceding. The foundation of the real relation is contingent existence, or the contingent coupling of existence with essence. In this composition there is the transcendental relation of actuality and potentiality.

Distinctions such as that between the four notes in relation, namely the relationship itself, the subject related, the term or object to which it is related, and the foundation from which the relation results, are not idle refinements, but bear directly on two great mysteries for natural theology and Christian theology respectively, how a being can exist that is not God and how there can be three really distinct persons in one single nature.

[1] Creation indicates the moment of newness and originality. Its duration is considered in the next Question, and the continuance of creative activity in 1a. 104, 1 & 2, on *conservatio in esse*. The distinction between beginning and remaining in existence is nominal and conceptual. On the presence of God within each thing maintaining it in existence cf 1a. 8, 1. Vol. 2.

[a] Is the 'subject' of creation the composite and subsisting thing? The inquiry covers the composition of essence and existence found in all created substances, even non-material simple substances or pure forms, cf 1a. 3, 2 & 4. Composite, i.e. the concrete thing (1a. 3, 3 ad 1), that which subsists or exists in itself. It is this which is created. So creative activity is of the complete substance, the whole thing, the 'this', the *quod est*, unlike non-creative action which transforms a given material and directly produces part of a thing, the 'what', the *quo est*.

[b] The *Liber De causis*, an anonymous compilation of excerpts from *The Elements of Theology* of the Neo-Platonist Proclus (*d.* 485), translated from the Greek or Arabic, perhaps by Gerard of Cremona (*d.* 1187). An influential work, but St Albert the Great recognized that it was not by Aristotle.

2. Præterea, quod creatur est ex nihilo. Composita autem non sunt ex nihilo, sed ex suis componentibus. Ergo compositis non convenit creari.

3. Præterea, illud proprie producitur per primam emanationem quod supponitur in secunda, sicut res naturalis per generationem naturalem quæ supponitur in operatione artis. Sed illud quod supponitur in generatione naturali est materia. Ergo materia est quæ proprie creatur, et non compositum.

SED CONTRA est quod dicitur Gen.,[3] In principio creavit Deus cælum et terram. Cælum autem et terra sunt res compositæ subsistentes. Ergo horum proprie est creatio.

RESPONSIO: Dicendum quod creari est quoddam fieri, ut dictum est.[4] Fieri autem ordinatur ad esse rei. Unde illis proprie convenit fieri et creari quibus convenit esse. Quod quidem convenit proprie subsistentibus, sive sint simplicia, sicut substantiæ separatæ, sive sint composita, sicut substantiæ materiales. Illi enim proprie convenit esse quod habet esse, et quod est subsistens in suo esse. Formæ autem et accidentia et alia hujusmodi non dicuntur entia quasi ipsa sint, sed quia eis aliquid est; ut albedo ea ratione dicitur ens, quia ea subjectum est album. Unde, secundum Philosophum,[5] accidens magis proprie dicitur 'entis' quam 'ens'. Sicut igitur accidentia et formæ et hujusmodi quæ non subsistunt magis sunt coexistentia quam entia, ita magis debent dici concreata quam creata. Proprie vero creata sunt subsistentia.

1. Ad primum ergo dicendum quod cum dicitur, prima rerum creatarum est esse: ly[6] esse non importat subjectum creatum,* sed importat propriam rationem objecti creationis. Nam ex eo dicitur aliquid creatum quod est ens, non ex eo quod est hoc ens, cum creatio sit emanatio totius esse ab ente universali, ut dictum est.[7] Et est similis modus loquendi sicut

---

*Piana: substantiam creatam, the created substance

[3]Genesis 1, 1   [4]Ia. 45, 2 ad 2

[5]Metaphysics VII, 1. 1028a15-20. lect. 1

[6]ly, a transliteration of the Arabic article el, used like the Greek to   [7]Ia. 45, 1

cA dig at the Aristotelean doctrine of uncaused matter.

dRecall that a sed contra is often no more than a statement of position.

eA complete spiritual substance is not composed of matter and form, and therefore without the essential composition (as it is called) present in bodily natures. Yet as a creature it is composed of essence and existence, also of substance and accident: cf Ia. 3, 1–7; 50, 2; 54, 1. The objection, however, treats matter as running throughout all creation.

fSupports its own existence, literally, is subsisting in its existence. Its independence is that of not existing in another as in a subject as does a modification or

2. Besides, what is created comes out of nothing. Now composite things come out of their components, not nothing, and therefore it is not them exactly that are created.

3. Then again, to be exact, that which is produced in a primary origination is presupposed to what issues in the second place: thus a natural product underlies what is worked up by art. Now matter underlies natural production, and consequently it, and not the concrete thing composed of it, is what, properly speaking, is created.^c

ON THE OTHER HAND *Genesis* declares that *in the beginning God created the heavens and earth*.³ Both stand for composite subsisting things. To them therefore, is creation properly attributed.^d

REPLY: We have already noted that creation is one sort of coming into existence.⁴ Existence, then, is the dominant. Hence to come to be and to be created directly and immediately apply where existence applies. That is, strictly speaking, to things that subsist, whether they be simple, like unembodied substances, or compound, like material substances.^e Only that is an existent, in the proper sense of the term, which has existence and supports its own existence.^f As for forms and modifications and the like, you do not speak of them as beings as though they themselves were things, but because they affect things; for instance the reason why you call whiteness real is that by it a subject is white. Hence, to cite Aristotle,⁵ we say that a modification is more fittingly called 'of a being' than 'a being'. As, then, forms and accidents and the like, which do not subsist, are co-existents rather than beings, so they ought to be referred to as co-created rather than created. To be downright, then, it is subsisting things that are created.^g

Hence: 1. In the phrase, 'The first of created things is existence', the term⁶ 'existence' refers to the distinctive note creative action strikes, not the subject created. For because it is a being is something said to be created, not because it is being of a certain sort, since creation is the issuing of the whole of being from universal being, as we have remarked.^{7h} We use a

---

accidens, not of not depending on God as its efficient, exemplar, and final cause (1a. 44, 1, 3 & 4). Furthermore it is a complete substance, not a partial substance, like the co-principles of substantial form and primary matter: this last is implied in '*et alia hujusmodi*' of the next sentence.

^gCreative causality embraces the whole being of a thing, creaturely activity reaches to this or that sort of thing, though the whole of the effect's being is involved: the thought will be developed below, art. 5 ad 1.

The example takes a modification, or 'accidental' form, but the argument applies to any component within a thing, shaping or shaped, substantial or accessory.

^hcf art. 5 ad 1 below & Appendix 1.

si diceretur quod 'primum visibile est color', quamvis illud quod proprie videtur est coloratum.

2. Ad secundum dicendum quod creatio non dicit constitutionem rei compositæ ex principiis præexistentibus; sed compositum sic dicitur creari quod simul cum omnibus suis principibus in esse producitur.

3. Ad tertium dicendum quod ratio illa non probat quod sola materia creetur, sed quod materia non sit nisi ex creatione. Nam creatio est productio totius esse, et non solum materiæ.

articulus 5. utrum solius Dei sit creare

AD QUINTUM sic proceditur:[1] 1. Videtur quod non solius Dei sit creare. Quia secundum Philosophum,[2] perfectum est quod potest sibi simile facere. Sed creaturæ immateriales sunt perfectiores creaturis materialibus, quæ faciunt sibi simile; ignis enim generat ignem, et homo generat hominem. Ergo substantia immaterialis potest facere substantiam sibi similem. Sed substantia immaterialis non potest fieri nisi per creationem, cum non habeat materiam ex qua fiat. Ergo aliqua creatura potest creare.

2. Præterea, quanto major est resistentia ex parte facti tanto major virtus requiritur in faciente. Sed plus resistit contrarium quam nihil. Ergo majoris virtutis est aliquid facere ex contrario, quod tamen creatura facit, quam aliquid facere ex nihilo. Multo magis igitur creatura hoc facere potest.

3. Præterea, virtus facientis consideratur secundum mensuram ejus quod fit. Sed ens creatum est finitum, ut supra probatum est,[3] cum de Dei infinitate ageretur. Ergo ad producendum per creationem aliquid creatum non requiritur nisi virtus finita. Sed habere virtutem finitam non est contra rationem creaturæ. Ergo non est impossibile creaturam creare.

SED CONTRA est quod Augustinus dicit[4] quod neque boni neque mali angeli possunt esse creatores alicujus rei. Multo minus igitur aliæ creaturæ.

---

[1]cf 1a. 65, 3; 90, 3. *CG* II, 20 & 21; III, 66 & 67. *De potentia* III, 4. *De veritate* V, 9. *De substantiis separatis* 10. *Quodl.* III, 3, 1. *Compend. theol.* 70. II *Sent.* 1, 1, 3; IV, 5, 1, 3, iii   [2]*Meteorlogica* IV, 3. 380a12–15. *De Anima* II, 4. 415a26–61   [3]1a. 7, 2—4   [4]*De Trinitate* III, 8. PL 42, 876

[1]That matter was absent from spiritual beings was not generally agreed. Stemming from Avicenna (*d.* 1037) and Ibn Gabirol (*d.c.* 1058), the last in particular, there was a stream of thought, strong among the Franciscans, to which matter went far beyond the corporeal world; it was the *possibilitas essendi*, or the potentiality lying at the heart of all created being, and this spiritual hylemorphism lay at the root of the distinction between all creatures and the creator. The thought is found in Thomas of York (*d.c.* 1260) and the *Summa philosophiæ* of the Pseudo-Grosseteste; it continues with Roger Bacon (*d.* after 1292) and St Bonaventure (*d.* 1274), and is recorded by Peter Olieu (Olivi) as the common view towards the end of the cen-

similar turn of speech when we say that what is first visible is colour, although that which is seen, properly speaking, is a coloured thing.

2. Creation tells, not of a thing being constituted from pre-existing elements, but of a composite so caused as to be brought into being all together with its component principles.

3. The argument proves that matter does not exist save from creation, not that it is created alone. For creation is the production of a whole existent, not merely of its matter.[1]

article 5. is it exclusively for God to create?

THE FIFTH POINT:[1] 1. It would appear that creation is not for God alone. According to Aristotle[a2] the ability to reproduce its like is the mark of a fully developed thing. Now spiritual creatures are more achieved than material creatures who reproduce themselves, for instance the fire that kindles fire, the human being who begets another. So a spiritual substance can make another substance like itself. Such a substance cannot be made except by creation, since it has no material out of which it can be made. Hence a creature is capable of creating.

2. Moreover, the stiffer the resistance it offers the stronger the power demanded to make a thing. Now a contrary is more resistant than nothingness. It argues more power to make something from its contrary, which a creature can do, than from nothing. *A fortiori*, then, a creature can do this.[b]

3. Furthermore, the thing made supplies the measure of its maker's strength. Now a created thing is finite, as we saw when discussing God's infinity.[3] Therefore merely finite power is required to produce it through creation, and this is not inconsistent with the creature's condition. So then it is not out of the question for a creature to create.

ON THE OTHER HAND St Augustine says that *neither good angels nor bad can be the creators of anything.*[4] Much less, therefore, lesser creatures.

---

tury. St Thomas makes his own position clear in rejecting spiritual matter within the human soul, 1a. 75, 5.

[a]*Meteorlogica*: 'the process of ripening is perfect when the seeds in fruit are able to reproduce the fruit in which they are found'. *De Anima*: 'for any living creature, provided it has reached its normal development and is not maimed, and whose mode of generation is not spontaneous, the most natural act is the production of another like itself. . . . That is a goal towards which all things strive, the final cause of all its natural functions.'

[b]Contraries represent positive opposites. 'A contrary is more apart from its contrary than from its simple negation, as black is more apart from white than from merely non-white.' 1a. 79, 4. 2a2æ. 21, 3 ad 2. Contraries are diametrically opposed; *De cælo* 1, 8. 277a23. *Meteorlogica* 11, 6. 363a33.

43

RESPONSIO: Dicendum quod satis apparet in primo aspectu, secundum præmissa,[5] quod creare non potest esse propria actio nisi solius Dei. Oportet enim universaliores effectus in universaliores et priores causas reducere. Inter omnes autem effectus universalissimum est ipsum esse. Unde oportet quod sit proprius effectus primæ et universalissimæ cause, quæ est Deus. Unde etiam dicitur libro De causis,[6] quod neque intelligentia vel anima nobilis dat esse, nisi inquantum operatur operatione divina. Producere autem esse absolute, non inquantum est hoc vel tale, pertinet ad rationem creationis. Unde manifestum est quod creatio est propria actio ipsius Dei.

Contingit autem quod aliquid participet actionem propriam alicujus alterius non virtute propria, sed instrumentaliter, inquantum agit in virtute alterius; sicut aër per virtutem ignis habet calefacere et ignire. Et secundum hoc aliqui opinati sunt quod licet creatio sit propria actio universalis causæ, tamen aliqua inferiorum causarum, inquantum agit in virtute primæ causæ, potest creare. Et sic posuit Avicenna[7] quod prima substantia separata creata a Deo creat aliam post se, et substantiam orbis et animam ejus; et quod substantia orbis creat materiam inferiorum corporum. Et secundum hunc etiam modum Magister dicit,[8] quod Deus potest creaturæ communicare potentiam creandi, ut creet per ministerium non propria auctoritate.

Sed hoc esse non potest. Quia causa secunda instrumentalis non participat actionem causæ superioris nisi inquantum per aliquid proprium dispositive operatur ad effectum principalis agentis. Si igitur nihil ibi ageret secundum illud quod est sibi proprium frustra adhiberetur ad agendum, nec oporteret esse determinata instrumenta determinatarum actionum. Sic enim videmus quod securis scindendo lignum, quod habet

---

[5]Ia. 44, 1 & 2; 45, 1
[6]Liber De causis 3. St Thomas, lect. 3
[7]Metaphysics IX, 4
[8]IV Sentences 5, 3 (Quaracchi II, 575)
cProper activity: here means the activity of a principal cause, as opposed to that of an instrumental cause.
dExistence most universal: i.e. present in everything that actually is, and as the actuality of the whole.
eProper effect: in secondary causality the effect of what is conceived as a property, to idion, of an agent, which is not its nature, but which belongs to that exclusively and always: cf Topics I, 5. 102a18. Applied to the first cause, though God has no properties in this sense, and also to secondary causes as acting by their own proper form.
fNoble soul: the superior soul animating a heavenly body, participating in the knowledge possessed by bodiless substances, and accordingly communicating

REPLY: In the light of what has been established,[5] a glance is enough to show that creation is the proper activity of God alone.[c] Effects which are more universal need to be taken to more universal and original causes. Among all effects the most universal is existence itself,[d] which should accordingly be the proper effect of the first and most universal cause, which is God.[e] So then we read in the *De causis* that neither *intelligence nor the noble soul[f] gives existence except as operating with divine activity*.[6] Now to produce existence absolutely, nor merely of this thing or of that sort of thing, belongs to the meaning of creation. Manifestly creation is the proper action of God himself.

All the same the fact is that a thing can share in the action proper to another, not by its own power, but instrumentally, as acting in the power of the other; air, for example, can heat and ignite through the power of fire. Accordingly some have been of the opinion that even though creation is an action proper to the universal cause, nevertheless some lesser causes can also create as acting in the power of the first cause.[g] Avicenna,[7h] for one, held that God's creation, the first bodiless substance, after itself created another, and then the heavenly sphere and its soul, which in its turn creates the matter of inferior bodies. And in the same vein Peter Lombard[i] taught that God can communicate power to a creature so that it created ministerially, not of its own authority.[8j]

This, however, cannot be. A secondary instrumental cause does not enter into a superior cause's action unless because of something proper to itself it acts dispositively to the effect of the principal. Futile to employ it if it contributes nothing in virtue of own special quality: you would not pick this tool rather than that for a determinate job. Take the carpenter's saw which is designed in itself to cut wood, and therefore also productive

---

movement to physical bodies. St Thomas describes the theory as unconfirmed in faith, *non rata in fide*: *In De causis*, *lect.* 3.

[g]Instrumental cause: an efficient cause which acts as moved by a principal cause, which acts by its own proper form. (Note that a principal cause may also be a secondary cause.) cf 1a. 105, 5. *CG* III, 69. *De potentia* III, 7. The *locus classicus* for sacramental causality is 3a. 62, 1, 3 & 4.

[h]Avicenna, *Metaphysics* IX, 4. cf Averroes, *Destruct. destruct* III. For the Neo-Platonism; Macrobius, *In somnum Scipionis* I, 14. Chalcidius on the *Timæus* 41a. St Albert the Great, *Summa de creaturis* II, 61, 2. It was a common view that the heavens and the world were quickened by intelligences.

[i]Peter Lombard (*d.* 1169), called *Magister, the* Master, as Aristotle is called *the* Philosopher, St Paul *the* Apostle, Averroes *the* Commentator. Author of the standard theological work, the *Sentences, Libri IV Sententiarum.*

[j]Ministerially and authoritatively: used at greater depth than their juridical senses. An author was rather an originator than an authorizer. *Fontalitas et auctoritas*; 1a. 33, 4 ad 1.

ex proprietate suæ formæ, producit scamni formam, quæ est effectus proprius principalis agentis. Illud autem quod est effectus proprius Dei creantis est illud quod præsupponitur omnibus aliis, scilicet esse absolute. Unde non potest aliquid operari dispositive et instrumentaliter ad hunc effectum, cum creatio non sit ex aliquo præsupposito quod possit disponi per actionem instrumentalis agentis.

Sic igitur impossibile est quod alicui creaturæ conveniat creare, neque virtute propria neque instrumentaliter sive per ministerium. Et hoc præcipue inconveniens est dici de aliquo corpore quod creet, cum nullum corpus agat nisi tangendo vel movendo, et sic requirit in sua actione aliquid præexistens quod possit tangi et moveri; quod est contra rationem creationis.

1. Ad primum ergo dicendum quod aliquod perfectum participans aliquam naturam facit sibi simile, non quidem producendo absolute illam naturam, sed applicando eam ad aliquid. Non enim hic homo potest esse causa naturæ humanæ absolute, quia sic esset causa sui ipsius; sed est causa quod natura humana sit in hoc homine generato. Et sic præsupponit in sua actione determinatam materiam per quam est hic homo.

Sed sicut hic homo participat humanam naturam, ita quodcumque ens creatum participat, ut ita dixerim, naturam essendi; quia solus Deus est suum esse, ut supra dictum est.[9] Nullum igitur ens creatum potest producere aliquod ens absolute, nisi inquantum esse causat in hoc; et sic

---

[9]Ia. 7, 1 ad 3; 2

kAn instrument in the widest sense is any subordinate cause, but in the specific sense, as here, it means an efficient cause of which the action is lifted under the influence of a principal cause to the production of an effect higher than itself, as when a chisel is used skilfully to produce a work of art or when an image of fancy becomes an idea in the mind. Instrumental causality plays a major part in sacramental theology; the Thomist school stresses that it really reaches to the effect produced, against the opinion of some Scotists that it merely produces a disposition to this effect. The technicalities of the debate scarcely affect the course of the present argument.

lQuantity, a primary condition for *actio-passio* in bodily things.

mThe part of parents in fashioning a human soul may present a difficulty. It is created (*CG* II, 87), but do they not play an instrumental rôle? Note (*a*) the article is taking its terms exactly and abstractly. Instrumental causality is treated in terms of efficient causality; in the order of final causality there are what are known as 'moral instruments', and thus, e.g. a child may come in answer to prayer. cf Bañez *in loc*. But the creative action of the first efficient cause allows for no secondary efficient causality either to qualify the action itself or to prepare the material which will enter into its effect. (*b*) But human parents do really generate or procreate a human being, by preparing the matter, even the animal matter, that enters into its composition; they apply (see ad 1) a body to the soul created by God, and are the cause not only of the body but of the union of soul and body which makes a man.

of the bench's shape, the proper effect of the principal agent.[k] Now God's proper effect in creating is that which is presupposed to any other, namely existence *tout court*. There is not anything that can work dispositively and instrumentally to produce this, since creation is not from any pre-existing material to be rendered or prepared by an instrumental cause's action.

So then for creative action to be attributed to any creature is impossible, either by its own proper power or instrumentally as a minister. And to ascribe it to a bodily substance is particularly incongruous, for a body acts only by physical contact and setting in motion,[1] and so requires something pre-existing that can be touched and changed, which is ruled out by the very meaning of creation.[m]

Hence: 1. A complete substance of some specific nature can reproduce its like, not indeed by producing that nature as such, but by applying it to a subject.[n] For a human individual cannot be the cause of human nature itself, for in that case he would be the cause of himself; he is the cause of human nature being in human individual who is born. Hence his action presupposes the determinate matter indispensable for being an individual man.

Now as an individual man shares in human nature so, too, every created being whatever shares, if I may put it so, in the nature of existing;[o] God alone, as we have seen, is his own existence.[9] Hence no created being can produce a being purely as such, but only to the extent of causing existence

---

(c) This body is not the material out of which the rational soul is made; rather it assembles the conditions on which we can look for God's creative action, without, however, taking it for granted. (d) St Thomas faced the difficulties arising from his doctrine that the rational soul is both the substantial form of the body and a spiritual and immortal substance; 1a. 75–6. Vol. 11 of this series. His solution does not contradict the teaching of this present article.

[n]By applying: application, the putting of one to another; in its technical sense, an operation restricted to some sort of transformation or variation of what is already given. Thus the elucidation of individual cases by universal truths; 1a. 14, 11. When efficient causality is involved, then it is limited to bringing a form to its matter, 1a, 14, 16, or an intention to its execution, 1a. 93, 6 ad 4, *CG* 111, 67. This last sense is studied at length in 1a2æ. 16, 1, 3 & 4.

The argument is that although creatures are true efficient causes, cf 1a. 105, 5, their effect is not directly a being considered in its entirety. They act to make this kind of being. Later, 1a. 104, 1, it is noticed that they may cause other things to begin, but not to continue in being. The distinction is between *causa secundum fieri tantum* and *causa secundum esse directe*.

[o]If I may put it so: St Thomas is wary about *natura essendi* or treating existence as a predicate, cf Appendix 1 & art. 4 ad 1 above.

oportet quod præintelligatur id per quod aliquid est hoc actioni qua facit sibi simile.

In substantia autem immateriali non potest præintelligi aliquid per quod sit hæc; quia est hæc per suam formam, per quam habet esse, cum sint formæ subsistentes. Igitur substantia immaterialis non potest producere aliam substantiam immaterialem sibi similem quantum ad esse ejus, sed quantum ad perfectionem aliquam superadditam; sicut si dicamus quod superior angelus illuminat inferiorem, ut Dionysius dicit[10]. Secundum quem modum etiam in cælestibus est paternitas, ut ex verbis Apostoli patet, *ex quo omnis paternitas in cælo et in terra nominatur.*[11] Et ex hoc etiam evidenter apparet quod nullum ens creatum potest causare aliquid nisi præsupposito aliquo. Quod repugnat rationi creationis.

2. Ad secundum dicendum quod ex contrariis fit aliquid *per accidens,* ut dicitur in *Physic.*,[12] per se autem fit aliquid ex subjecto quod est in potentia. Contrarium igitur resistit agenti inquantum impedit potentiam ab actu in quem intendit reducere materiam* agens; sicut ignis intendit reducere aquam in actum sibi similem, sed impeditur per formam et dispositiones contrarias, quibus quasi ligatur potentia ne reducatur in actum. Et quanto magis fuerit potentia ligata tanto requiritur major virtus in agente ad reducendum materiam in actum. Unde multo magis potentia requiritur in agente si nulla potentia præexistat. Sic ergo patet quod multo majoris virtutis est facere aliquid ex nihilo quam ex contrariis.

3. Ad tertium dicendum quod virtus facientis non solum consideratur ex substantia facti sed etiam ex modo faciendi; major enim calor non solum magis sed etiam citius calefacit. Quamvis igitur creare aliquem effectum finitum non demonstret potentiam infinitam, tamen creare ipsum ex nihilo demonstrat potentiam infinitam. Quod ex prædictis patet.[13] Si enim tanto major virtus requiritur in agente quanto potentia est magis remota ab actu, oportet quod virtus agentis ex nulla præsupposita potentia, quale agens est creans, sit infinita; quia nulla proportio est nullius potentiæ ad aliquam potentiam quam præsupponit virtus agentis naturalis, sicut non entis ad ens. Et quia nulla creatura habet simpliciter potentiam infinitam,

---

*Leonine: omits *materiam*

[10]*De cælesti hierarchia* 8. PG 3, 240

[11]*Ephesians* 3, 15

[12]*Physics* I, 7. 190b23–29

[13]Above ad 2

pA spiritual being, or 'separate substance', i.e. a non-embodied thing, is simple in that its essence is without the matter-form composition of material substances. By its nature it is wholly form, so that each one stands unique as a species or kind of thing; cf Ia. 50, 2–4. Vol. 9 of this series. It cannot be numerically repeated by the individuation coming from quantified matter. cf *Metaphysics* V, 6. 1016b–331.

in this being; accordingly that because of which something is individual should be preconceived to the action whereby it reproduces its like.

In spiritual substance, however, such an individuating principle cannot be postulated, since it is individual by its form through which it has existence—for there are subsisting forms.[p] Consequently one spiritual substance cannot produce another like spiritual substance as regards its existence, but only as regards some added perfection, thus when following Dionysius we talk of a higher angel enlightening a lower.[10] In this sense there is fathering in heaven, according to the saying of St Paul, *From whom all fatherhood in heaven and earth is named.*[11q] Hence also it clearly appears that no created being can cause anything unless a subject be presupposed, which is incompatible with the meaning of creation.

2. That a thing rises from its contrary is incidental to its production, as noted in the *Physics*;[12] what is essential is that it comes from a subject which is in potentiality to it.[r] A contrary resists the agent inasmuch as it holds the potential subject from the actuality the agent seeks to induce in the material; thus the action of fire, to make water boil and hot like itself, is checked by the form and contrary dispositions of water, which, as it were, restrain the potentiality to be hot. The more the potentiality is held back the greater the power required in the agent to overcome the constraint. Much more stronger power is called for from the agent when there is not even a pre-existing potentiality. Evidently it is mightier to make something from nothing than from its contrary.

3. A cause's strength is assessed not only by the substance of the thing made but also by the manner of its making; intense heat gives heat not only more thoroughly but also more quickly. Hence, even though the creation of a finite effect does not demonstrate infinite power, its being made from nothing certainly does: this emerges from what has already been stated.[13] For if an efficient cause's power must be increased in proportion to the potentiality's distance from actuality,[s] then surely when no potentiality is present, as with creative causality, this power must be infinite; there is no proportion between no potentiality and some potentiality (which a natural cause's power presupposes) as there is none between non-being and some being. And since no creature has infinite power unreser-

---

St Thomas, *lect.* 8. cf x, 9 & xii, 8. 1058a37 & 1074a34. *In De Trin.* iv, 2 ad 4. *CG* iv, 65.

qSt Paul is introduced more for parenthesis than proof.

rA contrary is an initial condition for an existing subject of change, thus a light changes to green given a start from another colour. Yet it is not a cause of the change in the way that the subject's capacity or potentiality for receiving it may be called so.

sInfinite distance: cf above art. 2 ad 4.

sicut neque esse infinitum, ut supra, probatum est,[14] relinquitur quod nulla creatura possit creare.

articulus 6. utrum creare sit proprium alicujus Personæ

AD SEXTUM sic proceditur:[1] 1. Videtur quod creare sit proprium alicujus Personæ. Quod enim est prius est causa ejus quod est post, et perfectum imperfecti. Sed processio divinæ Personæ est prior quam processio creaturæ, et magis perfecta, quia divina Persona procedit in perfecta similitudine sui principii, creatura vero in imperfecta. Ergo processiones divinarum Personarum sunt causa processionis rerum. Et sic creare est proprium Personæ.

2. Præterea, Personæ divinæ non distinguuntur ab invicem per suas processiones et relationes. Quidquid igitur differenter attribuitur divinis Personis, hoc convenit eis secundum processiones et relationes Personarum. Sed causalitas creaturarum diversimode attribuitur divinis Personis; nam in Symbolo Fidei[2] Patri attribuitur quod sit *creator omnium visibilium et invisibilium*;* Filio autem attribuitur quod *per eum omnia facta sunt*; sed Spiritui Sancto, quod sit *Dominus et vivificator*. Causalitas ergo creaturarum convenit Personis secundum processiones et relationes.

3. Præterea, si dicatur quod causalitas creaturæ attenditur secundum aliquod attributum essentiale quod appropriatur alicui Personæ, hoc non videtur sufficiens. Quia quilibet effectus divinus causatur a quolibet attributo essentiali, scilicet potentia, bonitate et sapientia; et sic non magis pertinet ad unum quam ad aliud. Non deberet ergo aliquis determinatus modus causalitatis attribui uni Personæ quam alii, nisi distinguerentur in creando secundum relationes et processiones.

SED CONTRA est quod dicit Dionysius,[3] quod communia totius divinitatis sunt omnia causalia.†

---

*Piana: *creator omnium invisibilium et visibilium*
†Piana: *creabilia*

[14]1a. 7, 2
[1]cf *De potentia* x, 5 ad 20. II *Sent.* Prologue   [2]Denzinger-Umberg 86
[3]*De divinis nominibus* 2. PG 3, 637. *lect.* 1
[a]Is creative activity to be attributed to the divine nature, and thus common to all three Persons, or is creation peculiarly the work of one? 'Proper' in this context is used in contrast with 'common'. The Greek and Latin Fathers are in solid agreement as to the reply. One Almighty, not three Almighties, in the words of the Athanasian Creed.
[b]The causality of the original and complete: cf *quarta via*, 1a. 2, 3.
[c]Coming forth: *processio*. Divine procession, immanent, or remaining within the Godhead; procession of creatures, transitive, or going out from God: 1a. 27, 1.

vedly any more than it has infinite existence, and this we have proved,[14] we
are left with the conclusion that no creature can create.

article 6. is creation proper to any one divine Person?

THE SIXTH POINT:[1] 1. It seems so.[a] For what is original is the cause of what
comes after, and what is complete of what is incomplete.[b] Yet the coming
forth of a divine Person comes before and is more perfect than that of the
creature, for a divine Person issues as the full likeness of its principle
whereas the creature is but a partial likeness. The comings forth of the
divine Persons are therefore the cause of the coming forth of creatures,
and in this sense creation is the proper characteristic of a divine Person.

2. To pursue this line of thought, the distinction between the divine
Persons is only because of their processions and relations.[c] Each different
attribute applied to them is because of these. Now creative causality is
attributed to them in different ways, for in the Nicene Creed[d] we profess
that the Father is *the creator of all things visible and invisible*, of the Son that
through him all things were made, and of the Holy Ghost that he is *the Lord
and life-giver*.[2] The causing of creatures, then, attaches to the Persons
according to the divine processions and relations.

3. And to continue, the question is not met if you submit that the
causation which produces a creature matches an essential attribute of the
divine nature especially associated with one Person.[e] For each divine effect
is caused by each of the essential attributes, which in the present case are
power, wisdom, and goodness, and so does not belong to one more than to
another. Consequently one determinate manner of causing could not be
attributed to one of the Persons rather than to the others, unless in their very
creating they be distinguished according to the processions and relations.

ON THE OTHER HAND Dionysius teaches that all things caused are common
to the whole divinity.[3]

The term 'cause' in Latin usage is not applicable within the Trinity, cf 1a. 33, 1 ad 1.

The two processions, that of the Word called 'generation', that of the Holy
Ghost called '*spiratio*', are the foundations of the four real relations of fatherhood
and sonship, which distinguish the Father and the Son, and of active and passive
'spiration' which distinguish the Father and Son from the Holy Ghost. 1a. 27–8;
Vol. 6 of this series.

[d]Called simply the *Symbolum Fidei*. 1st Ecumenical Council, Nicea, 325.

[e]Especially associated with: the theological procedure of 'appropriation', *kollesis*,
which takes an essential attribute of the divine nature and refers it particularly,
though not exclusively, to one of the divine Persons to the benefit of our contemplation and meditation. For discussions of its validity, cf 1a. 39, 7 & 8. Vol. 6
of this series, Appendix 9.

SUMMA THEOLOGIÆ, 1a, 45, 6

RESPONSIO: Dicendum quod creare est proprie causare sive producere esse rerum. Cum autem omne agens agat sibi simile, principium actionis considerari potest ex actionis effectu; ignis enim est qui generat ignem. Et idea creare convenit Deo secundum suum esse; quod est ejus essentia, quæ est communis tribus Personis. Unde creare non est proprium alicui Personæ, sed communis toti Trinitati.

Sed tamen divinæ Personæ secundum rationem suæ processionis habent causalitatem respectu creationis rerum. Ut enim supra ostensum est,[4] cum de Dei scientia et voluntate ageretur, Deus est causa rerum per suum intellectum et voluntatem, sicut artifex rerum artificiatarum. Artifex autem per verbum in intellectu conceptum et per amorem suæ voluntatis ad aliquid relatum operatur. Unde et Deus Pater operatus est creaturam per suum Verbum, quod est Filius, et per suum Amorem, qui est Spiritus Sanctus. Et secundum hoc processiones Personarum sunt rationes productionis creaturarum, inquantum includunt essentialia attributa, quæ sunt scientia et voluntas.

1. Ad primum ergo dicendum quod processiones divinarum Personarum sunt causa creationis sicut dictum est.[5]

2. Ad secundum dicendum quod sicut natura divina, licet sit communis tribus Personis, ordine tamen quodam eis convenit, inquantum Filius accipit naturam divinam a Patre, et Spiritus Sanctus ab utroque; ita etiam et virtus creandi, licet sit communis tribus Personis, ordine tamen quodam eis convenit; nam Filius habet eam a Patre, et Spiritus Sanctus ab utroque. Unde creatorem esse attribuitur Patri, ut ei qui non habet virtutem creandi ab alio. De Filio autem dicitur *per quem omnia facta sunt*, inquantum habet eamdem virtutem, sed ab alio, nam hæc præpositio 'per' solet denotare causam mediam, sive principium de principio. Sed Spiritui Sancto, qui habet eamdem virtutem ab utroque, attribuitur quod dominando gubernet et vivificet quæ sunt creata a Patre per Filium.

Potest etiam hujus attributionis communis ratio accipi ex appropriatione essentialium attributorum. Nam, sicut supra dictum est,[6] Patri attribuitur et appropriatur potentia, quæ maxime manifestatur in creatione; et ideo attribuitur Patri creatorem esse. Filio autem appropriatur sapientia, per quam agens per intellectum operatur, et ideo dicitur de Filio *per quem omnia facta sunt*. Spiritui Sancto autem appropriatur bonitas, ad quam

---

[4]1a. 14, 8; 19, 4
[5]In the body of the article
[6]1a. 39, 8
[1]Cause known from its effect, i.e. from its direct and immediate, or 'proper' effect.
[g]cf 1a. 4, 3: essence and existence identical in God.
[h]On creatures being made through the Word, cf 1a. 34, 3.

REPLY: Properly speaking to create is to cause or produce the existence of things. Since every agent enacts its like, we can identify the originator of an action from the kind of effect it produces; it is from fire that things catch fire.[f] Hence creation is God's action by reason of his existence, which is his very nature,[g] and this is common to the three Persons. So that creative action is not peculiar to any one Person, but is common to the whole Trinity.

Still, the causality concerning the creation of things answers to the respective meaning of the coming forth each Person implies. For, as was shown when we were discussing God's knowledge and willing,[4] God is the cause of things through his mind and will, like an artist of works of art. An artist works through an idea conceived in his mind and through love in his will bent on something. In like manner God the Father wrought the creature through his Word, the Son, and through his Love, the Holy Ghost. And from this point of view, keeping in mind the essential attributes of knowing and willing, the comings forth of the divine Persons can be seen as types for the comings forth of creatures.

Hence: 1. The comings forth of the divine Persons are causes of creation in the manner indicated above.[5]

2. As the divine nature, while common to all three Persons, is theirs according to a certain precedence, in that the Son receives it from the Father, and the Holy Ghost from them both, so it is with creative power, for it is common to them all; all the same the Son has it from the Father, and the Holy Ghost from them both. Hence to be the Creator is attributed to the Father as to one not having the power from another. Of the Son we profess that through him all things were made, for while yet not having this power yet from himself, for the preposition 'through' in ordinary usage customarily denotes an intermediate cause, or a principle from a principle.[h] Then of the Holy Ghost, who possesses the power from both, we profess that he guides and quickens all things created by the Father through the Son.

There is, furthermore, a general justification for laying a special emphasis on an essentially divine perfection when we think of one of the divine Persons.[i] For, as we have noted,[6] power, which is supremely manifested in creation, is especially the Father's, and so we stress that he is Creator. Wisdom, through which an intelligent cause operates, is especially the Son's, and so we declare that through him all things were made. Goodness is especially the Holy Ghost's, and so we acknowledge that he vivifies

---

[i] All perfections are formally identical in God's singleness as pure actualities, However, in so far as they strike distinct notes for us, we draw a conceptual distinction between them and see in God a plurality of perfections; cf 1a. 4, 2. Vol. 2.

pertinet gubernatio deducens res in debitos fines, et vivificatio; nam vita in interiori quodam motu consistit, primum autem movens est finis et bonitas.

3. Ad tertium dicendum quod licet effectus Dei procedat ex quolibet attributorum, tamen reducitur unusquisque effectus ad illud attributum cum quo habet convenientiam secundum propriam rationem; sicut ordinatio rerum ad sapientiam, et justificatio impii ad misericordiam et bonitatem se superabundanter diffundentem. Creatio vero, quæ est productio ipsius substantiæ rei, reducitur ad potentiam.

articulus 7. utrum in creaturis sit necesse inveniri vestigium Trinitatis

AD SEPTIMUM sic proceditur:[1] Videtur quod in creaturis non sit necesse inveniri vestigium Trinitatis. Per sua enim vestigia unumquodque investigari potest. Sed Trinitas Personarum non potest investigari ex creaturis, ut supra dictum est.[2] Ergo vestigia Trinitatis non sunt in creatura.

2. Præterea, quidquid in creatura est creatum est. Si igitur vestigium Trinitatis invenitur in creatura secundum aliquas proprietates suas, et omne creatum habet vestigium Trinitatis, oportet in unaquaque illarum inveniri etiam vestigium Trinitatis; et sic in infinitum.

3. Præterea, effectus non repræsentat nisi suam causam. Sed causalitas creaturarum pertinet ad naturam communem, non autem ad relationes, quibus Personæ et distinguuntur et numerantur. Ergo in creatura non invenitur vestigium Trinitatis, sed solum unitatis essentiæ.

SED CONTRA est quod Augustinus dicit[3] quod *Trinitatis vestigium in creatura apparet.*

RESPONSIO: Dicendum quod omnis effectus aliqualiter repræsentat suam causam, sed diversimode. Nam aliquis effectus repræsentat solam causalitatem causæ, non autem formam eius, sicut fumus repræsentat ignem; et talis repræsentatio dicitur esse repræsentatio vestigii; vestigium enim demonstrat motum alicuius transeuntis, sed non qualis sit. Aliquis autem

---

[1]cf Ia. 93, 1, 2 & 6. *CG* IV, 26. *De potentia* IX, 9
[2]Ia. 32, 1
[3]*De Trinitate* VI, 10. PL 42, 932
[1]An echo of Abelard. *Introductio ad theologiam* I, 10. PL 178,992. The thought of Plato, the desire for the Good as giving the first impulse of motion, is found also in the Victorines. cf Ia. 5, 4; 6, 4.

and guides things to their fitting ends: life is an inner spring, and its source is the end and the good.[j]

3. Although an effect of God springs from each and all of his attributes, all the same it is ascribed to that attribute to which it corresponds by its own special character: thus the ordering of things to wisdom, the justification of sinner to mercy and an extravagantly generous goodness. As for creation indeed, the production of the very substance of a thing, that is ascribed to power.

article 7. must a trace of the Trinity be discoverable in creatures?

THE SEVENTH POINT:[1] 1. It seems not.[a] For a cause can be tracked from the traces it leaves. It has been shown that the Trinity of Persons, however, cannot be discovered from creatures,[2] consequently they disclose no traces of the Trinity.

2. Besides, all that is in a creature is created. If then a trace of the Trinity could be found there because of this trait or that, and if every created thing showed a trace, then you would find one in each, and so on indefinitely.[b]

3. Moreover, an effect reveals no more than its cause. Yet the causing of creatures is from the divine nature common to all Persons, not to the relations whereby they are distinct and threefold. Hence the trace of divinity in creatures marks the unity of nature, not the Trinity of Persons.

ON THE OTHER HAND there is St Augustine says that a trace of the Trinity is displayed by the creature.[3]

REPLY: Any effect somehow copies its cause, yet variously. For some represent the causality alone of the cause, not its form, thus smoke and fire. This is called a likeness of trace; for a trace or footprint shows that somebody has passed that way, but not what manner of person he was.[c]

---

[a]The mystery of the blessed Trinity is known only from divine Revelation. Yet are hints of it to be found in the field of philosophical experience without faith? That it can be recommended to reason is shown by the treatise on the Trinity in the *Summa*. Also that analogies can be drawn from outside explicitly Christian theology. It cannot, however, be proved from creation; cf 1a. 32, 1. On the likeness of creature to God; 1a. 4, 3. On the distinction between an image, *imago*, and a trace, *vestigium*, footprint, cf 1a. 93, 4 & 5. Vol. 13.

[b]The second objection, somewhat obscurely expressed, and possibly one that cropped up in St Thomas's teaching-course, seems to be that myriad reflections take us nowhere, never reaching to God himself, but at most going through an endless series of theophanies. cf Vol. 3, Introduction II.

[c]e.g. Man Friday.

effectus repræsentat causam quantum ad similitudinem formæ ejus, sicut ignis generatus ignem generantem, et statua Mercurii Mercurium; et hæc est repræsentatio imaginis.

Processiones autem divinarum Personarum attenduntur secundum actus intellectus et voluntatis, sicut supra dictum est;[4] nam Filius procedit ut Verbum intellectus, Spiritus Sanctus ut Amor voluntatis. In creaturis igitur rationalibus in quibus est intellectus et voluntas, invenitur repræsentatio Trinitatis per modum imaginis, inquantum invenitur in eis verbum conceptum et amor procedens.

Sed in creaturis omnibus invenitur repræsentatio Trinitatis per modum vestigii, inquantum in qualibet creatura inveniuntur aliqua quæ necesse est reducere in divinas Personas sicut in causam. Quælibet enim creatura subsistit in suo esse, et habet formam per quam determinatur ad speciem, et habet ordinem ad aliquid aliud. Secundum igitur quod est quædam substantia creata repræsentat causam et principium, et sic demonstrat Personam Patris, qui est principium non de principio. Secundum autem quod habet quamdam formam et speciem repræsentat Verbum, secundum quod forma artificiati est ex conceptione artificis. Secundum autem quod habet ordinem repræsentat Spiritum Sanctum, inquantum est Amor, quia ordo effectus ad aliquid alterum est ex voluntate creantis.

Et ideo dicit Augustinus[5] quod vestigium Trinitatis invenitur in unaquaque creatura, secundum quod unum aliquid est, et secundum quod aliqua specie formatur, et secundum quod quemdam ordinem tenet. Et ad hæc etiam reducuntur illa tria, *numerus, pondus et mensura*, quæ ponuntur *Sap.*,[6] nam mensura refert ad substantiam rei limitatam suis principibus, numerus ad speciem, pondus ad ordinem. Et ad hæc etiam reducuntur alia tria quæ ponit Augustinus,[7] *modus, species, et ordo*. Et ea quæ ponit,[8] *quod constat, quod discernitur, quod congruit*: constat enim aliquid per suam substantiam, discernitur per forma, congruit per ordinem. Et in idem de facili reduci possunt quæcumque sic dicuntur.

1. Ad primum ergo dicendum quod repræsentatio vestigii attenditur

---

[4]1a. 27, 1–5
[5]*De Trinitate* VI, 10. PL 42, 932
[6]*Wisdom* 11, 21
[7]*De natura boni* 3. PL 42, 553
[8]*Lib.* 88 *Quæst.* 18. PL 40, 15
[d]This compressed account barely renders the richness of St Augustine's thought, and a literal translation further impoverishes it. The translation is a paraphrase. Thus *ordo*; order or the 'ordering' suggests a place in a plan or obedience to a

However, there are some effects that represent their cause in the likeness of its form, thus a flame and the fire that sets it alight, or an effigy of Hermes; this is the likeness of image.

Well then, as we have explained,[4] we take the comings forth of the divine Persons after the model of understanding and willing; the Son issues as the Logos of mind, and the Holy Ghost as the Love of will. So that in rational creatures, endowed with mind and will, we find a likeness of the Trinity in the manner of an image when they conceive an idea and love springs from it.

In all creatures, however, we find a likeness of the Trinity by way of trace in that there is something in all of them that has to be taken back to the divine Persons as its cause. For each created thing subsists in its own existence, has a form which makes it the kind of thing it is, and bears on something other than itself. Because it is a definite and created substance it tells of its principle and cause, and so indicates the Person of the Father, who is the beginning from no beginning. Because it has a certain form and species it tells of the Logos, for form in a work of art is from the artist's conception. Because it goes out from itself it tells of the Holy Ghost as Love, for wanting another comes from the will of him who created it so.

On this account St Augustine writes of a trace of the Trinity being discoverable in every creature, for each is a definite thing shaped to a meaning and holding within itself a bearing on others.[5] All this is implied in the three terms, *number, weight, and measure*, put forward by *Wisdom*.[6] For measure refers to a thing's substance limited by its inner principles, number to its species, weight to the field in which it moves. Equivalent terms are the three used by St Augustine,[7] namely *mode, species, and order*. Also another three of his,[8] namely *that which a thing consists in, makes it distinct*, and *answers to it*; for it consists in its substance, is distinctive through form, and fits in by its ordered setting.[d] Other similar triads too can be resolved in the same fashion.

Hence: 1. The likeness of trace concerns those essential attributes of divinity especially accented when we think of one of the Persons; it is by

---

ruler according to the grand design of juridico-theology. Yet much more is implied, for instance a thing's appetite, its teleological direction, its instinct to find its completion in another, its gravitational tendency (note its being likened to *pondus*, and to what fits it, cf art. 6 ad 2). *Species* is used in a sense wider than in the classification of things by genera and species, and applies here to things not composed of matter and form. The comparison of species to numbers goes back at least as far as Aristotle; cf *Metaphysics* VII, 3. 1043b34. *Species* also signifies the notion of beauty. cf 1a. 5, 5.

secundum appropriata; per quem modum ex creaturis in Trinitatem divinarum Personarum veniri potest, ut dictum est.[9]

2. Ad secundum dicendum quod creatura est res proprie subsistens, in qua est prædicta tria invenire. Neque oportet quod in quolibet eorum quæ ei insunt hæc tria inveniantur, sed secundum ea vestigium rei subsistenti attribuitur.

3. Ad tertium dicendum quod etiam processiones Personarum sunt causa et ratio creationis aliquo modo, ut dictum est.[10]

articulus 8. utrum creatio admisceatur in operibus naturæ et artis

AD OCTAVUM sic proceditur:[1] Videtur quod creatio admisceatur in operibus naturæ et artis. In qualibet enim operatione naturæ et artis producitur aliqua forma. Sed non producitur ex aliquo, cum non habeat materiam partem sui. Ergo producitur ex nihilo. Et sic in qualibet operatione naturæ et artis est creatio.

2. Præterea, effectus non est potior* sua causa. Sed in rebus naturalibus non invenitur aliquid agens nisi forma accidentalis, quæ est forma activa vel passiva. Non ergo per operationem naturæ producitur forma substantialis. Relinquitur igitur quod sit per creationem.

3. Præterea, natura facit sibi simile. Sed quædam inveniuntur generata in natura non ab aliquo sibi simili, sicut patet in animalibus generatis per putrefactionem. Ergo eorum forma non est a natura, sed a creatione. Et eadem ratio est de aliis.

4. Præterea, quod non creatur non est creatura. Si igitur in his quæ sunt a natura non adjungatur creatio, sequitur quod ea quæ sunt a natura non sunt creaturæ. Quod est hæreticum.

SED CONTRA est quod Augustinus[2] distinguit opus propagationis, quod est opus naturæ, ab opere creationis.

---

*Piana: *non est prior*, holds no priority over

[9]In the body of the article. cf 1a. 32, 1 ad 1

[10]art. 6

[1]cf 1a. 65, 4. II *Sent.* 1, 1, 3 ad 5; 4 ad 4. *CG* III, 69. *De potentia* III, 8.*Quodl.* IX, 5, 1. *In Meta.* VII, *lect.* 7

[2]*Super Genesim ad litteram* V, 11 & 20. PL 34, 330 & 335

[e]Pursuing this line, that is in the light of faith. We can assent to the mystery of the Trinity only because it is revealed by God. But, *fides quærens intellectum*, we can meditate on it and perceive the consonances in our experience. cf 1a. 32, 1.

[f]The thought is cognate to that of art. 3 ad 2 above. There an infinite series of relations was rejected, for a relation goes immediately to its term, *ad aliquid, pros ti*,

pursuing this line that we can arrive at the Trinity of divine Persons from creatures, as we have already remarked.[9e]

2. The creature in which we discover the threefold distinctions alluded to is a thing which subsists in the proper sense of the term.[f] It is not required that in each of its parts all three notes are found, but that because of these in a single subsisting thing a trace of the Trinity is recognized.

3. We have seen[10] that, without denying the essential causality proper to the divine nature, the comings forth of the divine Persons are modulating causes and reasons in the doctrine of creation.

article 8. *does creation mingle in the workings of nature and art?*

THE EIGHTH POINT:[1] I. It would seem so.[a] For whenever nature or art are at work some form is produced. However it is not produced from something, since matter is not part of it. Therefore it is produced from nothing. Thus creation always enters into the working of nature and art.

2. Again, no effect surpasses its cause. Yet we discover that the things of nature are agents only because of their accessory forms, which are active or passive.[b] A substantial form, then, is not produced by their agency. We are forced to conclude that it comes from creation.

3. Then also, a nature reproduces its like. However observation shows that some things generated in nature are not from something like them, this being evident when decomposition breeds worms.[c] Their form, then, arises by creation, not natural agency. The same argument applies in other cases.

4. In addition, what is not created is not a creature. If, then, creation did not enter into the products of nature it would follow they were not creatures. Which is heretical.

ON THE OTHER HAND St Augustine draws a distinction between a work of propagation, which is of nature, and a work of creation.[2]

---

a real subsistent; here an infinite expanse of likenesses is avoided by rooting each one in its subject, namely one single subsisting thing.

[a]Where do substantial forms come from? First, it is urged they are not drawn out of matter. Secondly, how can substantial reality be sufficiently explained as a result of a modification or accident, namely the action, of a producing cause.

[b]Accessory form, *forma accidentalis*, active, i.e. the action of the agent, and passive, i.e. the capacity of the thing acted on to undergo the action. Thus the active form of fire which can burn, the passive form of wood, or disposition, to be burned.

[c]In the days before Pasteur it was commonly held that some low forms of life could be produced by spontaneous generation.

RESPONSIO: Dicendum quod hæc dubitatio inducitur propter formas. Quas quidam posuerunt non incipere per actionem naturæ, sed prius in materia extitisse, ponentes latitationem formarum. Et hoc accidit eis ex ignorantia materiæ, quia nesciebant distinguere inter potentiam et actum; quia enim formæ præexistunt in materia in potentia, posuerunt eas simpliciter præexistere.

Alii vero posuerunt formas dari vel causari ab agente separato per modum creationis. Et secundum hoc cuilibet operationi naturæ adjungitur creatio. Sed hoc accidit eis ex ignorantia formæ. Non enim considerabant quod forma naturalis corporis non est subsistens, sed quo aliquid est; et ideo, cum fieri et creari non conveniat proprie nisi rei subsistenti, sicut supra dictum est,[3] formarum non est fieri neque creari, sed concreata esse. Quod autem proprie fit ab agente naturali est compositum, quod fit ex materia. Unde in operibus naturæ non admiscetur creatio, sed præsupponitur aliquid* ad operationem naturæ.

1. Ad primum ergo dicendum quod formæ incipiunt esse in actu compositis factis, non quod ipsæ fiant per se, sed per accidens tantum.

2. Ad secundum dicendum quod qualitates activæ in natura agunt in virtute formarum substantialium. Et ideo agens naturale non solum producit sibi simile secundum qualitatem, sed secundum speciem.

3. Ad tertium dicendum quod ad generationem animalium imperfectorum sufficit agens universale, quod est virtus cælestis, cui assimilantur non secundum speciem, sed secundum analogiam quamdam; neque oportet dicere quod eorum formæ creantur ab agente separato. Ad generationem vero animalium perfectorum non sufficit agens universale, sed requiritur agens proprium, quod est generans univocum.

---

*Leonine: omits *aliquid*, but is presupposed to
[3]art. 4
[d]*Latito*, to lie low. The abstract, *latitatio*, occurs in Quintilian.
[e]*De potentia* III, 8, credits Anaxagoras with this teaching on the testimony of the *Physics* I, 4 (187a12–b7) that he postulated undifferentiated primitive stuff from which the constitutents of things are sifted out; teaching also that can be associated with Empedocles. In the same place Aristotle speaks of Anaximander extracting the contrasts of things out of indeterminate prime substance. cf *Metaphysics* XII, 2 (1069b20). Chalcidius, in his commentary on the *Timæus* (309) refers to the Stoics holding this view.
[f]Aristotle introduced and developed the notion of the potential as real. Before and after him, not reaching to his refinement or failing to conceive what he meant, many have held what was not actual was unreal. The imagination assists with this conclusion, picturing what is real only as a concrete thing, and the world of matter as a kind of storehouse from which forms can be drawn.

REPLY: The problem arises because of forms. Some, holding they were latent in matter,[d] reckoned that they existed there beforehand and did not arise through natural agency.[e] It struck them so because they did not grasp what matter is, owing to their inability to distinguish between potentiality and actuality:[f] because forms pre-existed in matter potentially they concluded that they already actually existed there.

Others[g] took the position that forms were given or caused by some spiritual force after the manner of creation.[h] And so creation enters into every operation of nature. It struck them so because they did not grasp what form is. For they did not take into account that the natural form of a body is not a subsisting thing but that according to which a thing is. So then, since to come to be and to be created are terms that properly apply only to a subsisting thing, as we have already noted,[3] forms are not made or created, but rather co-created. What is made by natural agency is the composite thing, and this is made from matter. Hence creation does not mingle in the workings of nature, but something is presupposed to them.

Hence: 1. Forms begin to exist actually when the composite is made, and then they do not exist in themselves, but in another.

2. Active qualities in nature act in virtue of the substantial form behind them. For this reason a natural agent produces its like as regards the kind of thing it is, and the resemblance is not merely one of quality.

3. A general agent or some force in the heavens, is enough to account for the genesis of certain low kinds of animal life. They derive from it by some analogy, but not as belonging to the same species; there is no need to invoke a spiritual force for the production of their forms. Such a general force, however, is not sufficient for generation of higher animals; they require a generator of the same kind as themselves.[1]

---

[g]II Sent. 18, 2, 3, lists Plato among those who held that the production of forms arose from creative action. It is unlikely that St Thomas meant the Christian idea of creation, but only, as he says, 'a manner of production that was not generation'.
[h]De potentia III, 8, refers to this spiritual cause as 'a supernatural agent which, Plato held, was the giver of forms, and which to Avicenna was the ultimate intelligence among unembodied substances. And some of the moderns who follow him say this is God.' Among these was an important theologian, William of Auvergne (c. 1249), Bishop of Paris. For Plato see Phædo 101c–104e, and Timæus 50b–51b. The phrase 'dator formarum' seems to have been taken from Averroes in the Latin, In Meta. VII, comm. 31. Themistius and Avicenna credit Plato with this view.
[1]A general agent, agens universale, a notion in natural philosophy, and more limited than the metaphysical causa universalis. A cause of a higher species or order than its effect is called an agens analogum or æquivocum; cause of the same species or order an agens univocum.

4. Ad quartum dicendum quod operatio naturæ non est nisi ex præsuppositione principiorum creatorum, et sic ea quæ per naturam fiunt, creaturæ dicuntur.

ᴶThis article has little direct bearing on the scientific theory of evolution: its purpose is to show that creation, in the sense defined, should not be invoked as working within the action of secondary causes in the production of their proper effects, and that these, precisely as being their products, are not created. The conclusion holds true independently of the particular cosmological system of Aristotle here adopted. The genesis of species is discussed later, 1a. 65–74, Vol. 10 of this series, *Cosmogony*.

The reply scarcely offers a positive contribution to the question of where substantial forms come from, but is mainly content to defend its negative position:

4. The workings of nature always presuppose created elements, and so the things nature makes are called creatures.[j]

---

they are neither, as it were, brought out of the box nor directly produced by the agency of pure Forms or Ideas or substances apart from this world.

An attitude is implied with regard to a philosophical theory of creative evolution. This is a contradiction in terms if Thomist language is used, which is not generally the case with those who see and seek to interpret a life-progress by spurts, each of which arrives at a novel condition. In this connection it may be well to recall, (a) that St Thomas accepted a perennial creation of souls which are also spiritual substances (1a. 90, 2); (b) that a higher form of life includes, completes, and goes beyond a lower (1a. 76, 3 & 4); (c) that creation is continued by God's preserving action (1a. 104, 1 & 2); (d) that his activity is in all activity (1a. 105, 5); and (e) that grace first and glory afterwards take rational life to heights surpassing its powers and claims.

Quæstio 46. de principio durationis rerum creaturarum

Consequenter considerandum est de principio durationis rerum. Et circa hod quæruntur tria:

1. utrum creatura semper fuerit;
2. utrum eas incœpisse sit articulus fidei;
3. quomodo Deus dicatur in principium caelum et terram creasse.

articulus 1. utrum universitas creaturarum semper fuerit

AD PRIMUM sic proceditur:[1] 1. Videtur quod universitas creaturarum, quæ mundi nomine* nuncupatur, non incœperit, sed fuerit ab æterno. Omne enim quod incœpit esse, antequam fuerit possibile fuit ipsum esse; alioquin impossibile fuisset ipsum fieri. Si ergo mundus incœpit esse, antequam inciperet possibile fuit ipsum esse. Sed quod possibile est esse est materia, quæ est in potentia ad esse, quod est per formam, et ad non esse, quod est per privationem. Si ergo mundus incœpit esse, ante mundum fuit materia. Sed non potest esse materia sine forma; materia autem mundi cum forma est mundus. Fuit ergo mundus antequam esse inciperet, quod est impossibile.

2. Præterea, nihil quod habet virtutem ut sit semper quandoque est et quandoque non est, quia ad quantum se extendit virtus alicuius rei, tandiu Sed omne incorruptibile habet virtutem ut sit semper; non enim virtutem

---

*Piana: inserts *nunc*, which now we name

[1]cf II *Sent.* 1, 1, 5. *CG* II, 31–8. *De potentia* III, 17. *In Physic.* VIII, *lect.* 2. *In Meta.* XII, *lect.* 5. *In De cælo* II, *lect.* 6 & 29. *Compend. theol.* 98

aAppendix 2 translates the *opusculum*, *De æternitate mundi*.

Two main theological points are the distinction between God's eternity (cf Ia. 10) and the kind of everlasting duration creature's might be conceived to possess, and that some problems of fact can be met only by the assent of faith. The cosmological setting is that of Aristotle, and the purpose of the Question in the contemporary debate was to show that it provides no decisive arguments against Revelation. It is debated at length in the earlier *De potentia* III, 17. Two key articles are Ia. 2, 3, on an infinite series of causes, and Ia. 7, 4, on actually infinite number; both are in Vol. 2 of this series.

bAs will appear during the course of the discussions, the world's creation is not in dispute. The general subject of inquiry may be translated, On the age of the world. Note that true eternity is a different 'dimension' from perpetual time or agelessness; cf Ia. 10, 1; 11, 2 & 3. A thing may have no beginning or end in time and yet be created.

Question 46. the beginning of the world's duration

We go on to consider the beginning of the duration of created things. Here there are three points of inquiry:

1. whether creatures have always existed;
2. whether it be an article of faith that there was a beginning to them;
3. how we are to understand the statement that in the beginning God created heaven and earth.[a]

article 1. has the universe of creatures always existed?

THE FIRST POINT:[1] 1. It seems that the universe of creatures, which we name the world, never began but always was.[b] Whatever has had a beginning was a possible before it began, otherwise its coming to be would have been impossible. If, therefore, the world had ever begun to be antecedently it would have been a possible. Now this possible to be is matter, in potentiality alike to existence which comes through a form, and non-existence through its absence.[c] If the world had begun to be, then matter existed previously. Matter, however, cannot exist without form, while as for matter together with form, that is what comprises the world. Therefore you would be saying that the world was before it began, which is unthinkable.[d]

2. Moreover, nothing possessing the strength of always existing sometimes is and sometimes is not, for so far as its force goes so far does it endure. Now every imperishable[e] thing has the strength of always being,

---

The first article assembles ten objections, mostly from Avicenna (d. 1037), Averroes (d. 1198), and Maimonides (d. 1204); the last, a capital source, is accessible in *The Guide for the Perplexed*, edited by M. Friedländer. 2nd edition revised, London, 1956. The objections argue from the notion of 1. possibility, 2. necessity, 3. genesis, 4. space, 5. being set in motion, 6. setting in motion, 7. time, 8. duration, 9. complete, and 10. eternal duration.

[c]*privatio*: here translated 'absence'.

[d]The objection is from Maimonides, II, 14. cf Averroes *In Physic.* VIII, 4.

[e]Imperishable, or immortal thing, *incorruptibile*; a non-material thing, without an intrinsic potentiality for coming to be and ceasing to be, or a heavenly body in which the form so possesses and fulfils that matter that an alternative form is excluded; consequently dissolution of the composite by transformation into something else. The cosmological hypothesis may be neglected, and the argument, which comes from Averroes, *In De cælo* I, 119 (cf Aristotle, 281b18), left at one for the existence of self-permanent and stable realities in the universe.

habet ad determinatum durationis tempus. Nihil ergo incorruptibile quandoque est et quandoque non est. Sed omne quod incipit esse quandoque est et quandoque non est. Nullum ergo incorruptibile incipit esse. Sed multa sunt in mundo incoruptibilia, ut corpora cælestia et omnes substantiæ intellectuales. Ergo mundus non incœpit esse.

3. Præterea, nullum ingenitum incœpit esse. Sed Philosophus probat quod materia est ingenita;[2] et quod cælum est ingenitum.[3] Non ergo universitas rerum incœpit esse.

4. Præterea, vacuum est ubi non est corpus sed possibile est esse. Sed si mundus incoepit esse, ubi nunc est corpus mundi prius non fuit aliquod corpus; et tamen poterat ibi esse, alioquin nunc ibi non esset. Ergo ante mundum fuit vacuum, quod est impossibile.

5. Præterea, nihil de novo incipit moveri nisi per hoc quod movens vel† mobile aliter se habet nunc quam prius. Sed quod aliter se habet nunc quam prius movetur. Ergo ante omnem de novo incipientem fuit aliquis motus. Motus ergo semper fuit. Ergo et mobile, quia motus non est nisi in mobili.

6. Præterea, omne movens aut est naturale aut est voluntarium. Sed neutrum incipit movere nisi aliquo motu præexistente. Natura enim semper eodem modo operatur. Unde nisi præcedat aliqua immutatio vel in natura moventis vel in mobili, non incipit a movente naturali esse motus qui non fuit prius. Voluntas autem absque sui immutatione retardat facere quod proponit; sed hoc non est nisi per aliquam immutationem quam imaginatur, ad minus ex parte ipsius temporis. Sicut qui vult facere domum cras, et non hodie expectat aliquid futurum cras, quod hodie non est; et ad minus expectat quod dies hodiernus transeat et crastinus adveniat; quod sine transmutatione non est, quia tempus est numerus motus. Relinquitur ergo quod ante omnem motum de novo incipientem fuit alius motus. Et sic idem quod prius.

7. Præterea, quidquid est semper in principio et semper in fine nec desinere nec incipere potest, quia quod incipit non est in suo fine, quod autem desinit non est in suo principio. Sed tempus semper est in suo

---

†Piana: *et*
[2]*Physics* I, 9. 192a25–34
[3]*De Cælo* I, 3. 270a12
[f]Maimonides, II, 13.
[g]Averroes, *In De cælo* III, 29.
[h]motion, change, *kinesis.*
[i]Maimonides, II, 14. Averroes, *In Physic*, VIII, 7.
[j]Natural agent, one which acts from a blind necessity so far as it is concerned; voluntary agent, one which acts from knowledge, and often with deliberation. A

and of not lasting for a limited span of time. Hence no imperishable thing sometimes is and sometimes is not. Yet anything that begins to be at one time is and at another time not. Hence no imperishable thing begins to be. Now there are many imperishable things in the world, for example the heavenly bodies and all intellectual substances. Therefore the world did not begin to be.

3. Further, what is ungenerated does not begin to be, Aristotle shows that matter is ungenerated,[2] and likewise the heavens.[3] Hence the universe had no beginning.[f]

4. Besides, a void is where a body is not present, but could be. In the event of the world having begun, where its body is now a body was not previously present, though one could have been there, otherwise there could not be one there now. The consequence would follow that a void preceded the world—which is impossible.[g]

5. Then again, a thing does not start off in motion[h] unless both it and the thing which starts it off become now otherwise from what they were before. Now to be so otherwise is to be set in motion. Hence before the start of any fresh motion there was another motion. Hence motion ever goes back. And because motion is only in what is set in motion, that, too, always was.[i]

6. Or put it like this: a thing that changes another is either a natural or a voluntary agent.[j] Yet neither starts to do this without itself undergoing change beforehand. As for nature, it always operates uniformly, and hence without some preceding physical change in the active or passive things engaged no physical change would be initiated.[k] As for the will, without suffering any interior change, it can delay doing what it proposes, yet this implies some change imagined, at least in the time-series. For instance he who wills to build a house tomorrow and not today, anticipates something tomorrow that is non-existent today, and at least he expects that today will pass and tomorrow will come. Time is the measure of change;[l] and so change is not absent from his proposal. It remains true, therefore, that before any new change begins another change preceded it, which is the conclusion of the fifth objection, namely that change always was.[m]

7. Then also, whatever is always in its beginning and end can neither start nor stop, for whatever starts is not at its end, and whatever stops is

---

complete enumeration, since a thing in motion either sets itself or is set in motion.

[k]The sentence defies literal translation. Possibly the text is defective, or the original dictation was faulty.

[l]Time the measure of change, cf *Physics* IV, 11, 219b1.

[m]Avicenna, *Metaphysics* IX, 1. Averroes, *In Physic.* VIII, comm. 8.

principio et fine, quia nihil est temporis nisi nunc, quod est finis præteriti et principium futuri. Ergo tempus nec incipere nec desinere potest. Et per consequens nec motus, cujus numerus tempus est.

8. Præterea, Deus aut est prior mundo natura tantum aut duratione. Si natura tantum, ergo cum Deus sit ab æterno et mundus est ab æterno. Si autem est prior duratione, prius autem et posterius in duratione constituunt tempus. Ergo ante mundum fuit tempus, quod est impossibile.

9. Præterea, posita causa sufficienti, ponitur effectus; causa enim ad quam non sequitur effectus est causa imperfecta, indigens alio ad hoc quod effectus sequatur. Sed Deus est sufficiens causa mundi, et finalis, ratione suæ bonitatis; et exemplaris, ratione suæ sapientiæ; et effectiva, ratione suæ potentiæ, ut ex superioribus patet.[5] Cum ergo Deus sit ab æterno, et mundus fuit ab æterno.

10. Præterea, cujus actio est æterna et effectus æternus. Sed actio Dei est ejus substantia, quæ est æterna. Ergo et mundus est æternus.

SED CONTRA est quod dicitur *Joann., Clarifica me, Pater, apud temetipsum, claritate quam habui priusquam mundus fieret';*[6]★ et *Prov., Dominus possedit me in initio viarum suarum, antequam quidquam faceret a principio.*[7]

RESPONSIO: Dicendum nihil præter Deum ab æterno fuisse.† Et hoc quidem ponere non est impossibile. Ostensum est enim supra[8] quod voluntas Dei est causa rerum. Sic ergo aliqua necesse est esse sicut necesse est Deum velle illa, cum necessitas effectus ex necessitate causæ dependeat, ut dicitur in *Meta.*[9] Ostensum est autem supra[10] quod, absolute loquendo, non est necesse Deum velle aliquid nisi seipsum. Non est ergo necessarium Deum velle quod mundus fuerit semper. Sed eatenus‡ mundus est

---

★Vulgate: *priusquam mundus esset apud te,* before the world was with thee
†Piana: inserts *potest,* can have been
‡Piana: misprints *æternus* for *eatenus*

[5]Ia. 44, 1, 3 & 4
[6]*John* 17, 5
[7]*Proverbs* 8, 22
[8]Ia. 19, 4
[9]*Metaphysics* V, 5. 1015b9
[10]Ia. 19, 3
[n]Averroes, *In Physic.* VIII, 11. (Aristotle 251b19). Time cannot precede the world, because it is a measure of what happens there.
[o]Priority: a designation attached to various categories of being (and therefore called a *postprædicamentum*), as when we speak of objects being 'opposites' or 'correlatives'. cf *Categoriæ* 10. 11b15 & sqq. An order and precedence are denoted. There are five senses of the word according to which one may be said to be prior to another

not at its beginning. But time is always in its beginning and end, for there is nought in time but the now, which is the end of the past and the beginning of the future. Time, therefore, can neither start nor stop. Nor, therefore, can change, of which time is the measure.[n]

8. Besides, God is before the world by a priority either of nature only or of time.[o] In the first case, since he is from eternity then so is the world. In the second case, since a before and after in duration is what time is, then time will have been before the universe, which is impossible.[p]

9. Further, posit a sufficient cause and you posit its effect: a cause from which an effect does not result is partial and requires another for success. God, however, is the sufficient cause of the world, its final cause by reason of his goodness, its exemplar cause by reason of his wisdom, its efficient cause by reason of his power: this has already been shown.[5] Since he is eternal, then so, too, is the world.[q]

10. To press the point, where the action is eternal so is the effect as well. God's action is his substance, which is eternal, and so, then, is the world.[r]

ON THE OTHER HAND there are the words of our Lord, *And now, Father, glorify thou me in thy own presence with the glory which I had with thee before the world was made.*[6] And in *Proverbs* it is written, *The Lord possessed me in the beginning of his work, the first of his acts of old.*[7]

REPLY: Nothing apart from God has been from all eternity. And this is not to assert the impossible.[8] We have shown that God's will is the cause of things.[8] So then the necessity of their being is that of God's willing them, for, to appeal to Aristotle,[9] the necessity of an effect depends on that of the cause.[t] Next it has been established[10] that, to speak without qualification, there is no need for God to will anything but himself. Hence there is no necessity for God to will an everlasting world. Rather the world exists

---

(*Categoriæ* 12. 14a26 & sqq) of which two are mentioned here. Priority of nature; when one depends on another, like effect on cause or essential property on substance, it is said to be posterior, yet not in duration, for both may be simultaneous. Priority of time; as when one is said to be older than another. cf *Metaphysics* v, 11. 1018b10 & sqq. St Thomas, *lect.* 13.

[p]Avicenna, *Metaphysics* IX, 1.

[q]ibid.

[r]Ibid. Maimonides II, 18. cf St Augustine, *Confessions* XI, 10. PL 32, 814.

[6]The statement is cautious: all the article is going to prove is that the position adopted is philosophically tenable.

[t]Aristotle is speaking of the necessity possessed by an antecedent investing the consequent in a demonstration, but the extension to real cause and effect is warranted by his philosophy: cf 1a. 19, 8; 22, 4.

quatenus Deus vult illum esse, cum esse mundi ex voluntate dependeat, sicut ex sua causa. Non est igitur necessarium mundum semper esse. Unde nec demonstrative probari potest.

Nec rationes quas ad hoc Aristoteles inducit[11] sunt demonstrativæ simpliciter, sed secundum quid, scilicet ad contradicendum rationibus antiquorum, ponentium mundum incipere secundum quosdam modos in veritate impossibiles. Et hoc apparet ex tribus. Primo quidem, quia tam in *Physic.*[12] quam in *De cælo*[13] præmittit quasdam opiniones, ut Anaxagoræ et Empedoclis et Platonis, contra quos rationes contradictorias inducit. Secundo, quia ubicumque de hac materia loquitur, inducit testimonia antiquorum, quod non est demonstratoris, sed probabiliter persuadentis. Tertio, quia expresse dicit in *Topic.*,[14] quod quædam sunt problemata dialectica, de quibus rationes non habemus, ut utrum mundus sit aeternus.

1. Ad primum ergo dicendum quod antequam mundus esset possibile fuit mundum esse, non quidem secundum potentiam passivam, quæ est materia, sed secundum potentiam activam Dei. Et etiam secundum quod dicitur aliquid absolute possibile, non secundum aliquam potentiam, sed ex sola habitudine terminorum, qui sibi non repugnant, secundum quod possibile opponitur impossibili, ut patet per Philosophum, in *Meta.*[15]

2. Ad secundum dicendum quod illud quod habet virtutem ut sit semper: ex quo habet illam virtutem non quandoque est et quandoque non est, sed antequam haberet illam virtutem non fuit. Unde hæc ratio, quæ ponitur ab Aristotele in *De cælo*,[16] non concludit simpliciter quod incorruptibilia non incœperunt esse, sed quod non incœperunt esse per modum naturalem quo generabilia et incorruptibilia incipiunt esse.

3. Ad tertium dicendum quod Aristotles, in I *Physic*,[17] probat materiam

---

[11]*Physics* VIII, I. 250b10 & sqq.
[12]*Physics* VIII, I. 250b24, 251b17
[13]*De cælo* I, 10. 279b4–16, 280a11–30
[14]*Topics* I, 9. 104b16
[15]*Metaphysics* IV, 12. 1019b19
[16]*De cælo* I, 12, 281b & sqq.
[17]*Physics* I, 4. 192a28
[u]The conclusion is carefully stated. The world does not have to be everlasting, and therefore this cannot be demonstrated, i.e. proved from premises that cannot be otherwise. Whether or not it is everlasting *de facto* is another matter, to be settled by ways other than that of demonstration, such as the persuasion of ad 6 and the faith of art. 2 below.
[v]The arguments summarized in the objections.
[w]Enumerated by Maimonides, II, 15.
[x]To recommend: that is by dialectical arguments inducing opinion or belief. *In Meta.* IV, *lect.* 4. They can admit uncertainty or even mistake: cf below, Ia. 48,

just so long as God wills it to, since its existence depends on his will as on its cause. Therefore its existing always is not from inner necessity, and hence cannot be demonstratively proved.[u]

Nor do the arguments advanced by Aristotle[11v] strictly demonstrate the thesis itself; their force is limited to countering the reasons put forward by the ancients for a beginning to the world in ways veritably out of the question.

This reading is justified on three counts.[w] First, in both the eighth book of the *Physics*[12] and the first book of the *De cælo*[13] certain opinions, for example those of Anaxagoras, Empedocles, and Plato, are prefaced to the reasons which rebut them. Second, whenever he is dealing with the subject he brings in the testimony of the ancients, which is the way of one who is out, not to demonstrate, but to recommend according to the probabilities.[x] Third, he explicitly declares in the *Topics*[14] that we do not possess the clear solution for some dialectical problems, among them the question whether the world be eternal.

Hence: 1. Before the world existed it was possible for it to be, not indeed because of the passive potentiality of matter, but because of the active power of God. And the same is true even if we leave out the reference to his might, and we regard a pure possibility just from the association of terms not mutually exclusive:[y] that Aristotle contrasts the possible and the impossible in this sense is evident.[15]

2. Let us look at a thing which has the strength of always being: by that fact it is no longer a contingent, that now is and now is not, all the same it would have been a 'was not' had it not been so endowed.[z] This argument, then, proposed by Aristotle in the *De cælo*[16] does not rigorously conclude that immortal things never began to be, but that they did not begin through the natural process from which things arise which are generable and perishable.

3. Aristotle in the *Physics*[17] proves that matter is ungenerated from its

---

3 ad 3. For Aristotle's distinction between the apodictical and the dialectical see *Topics* I, 1. 100a25. For demonstration, *Posterior Analytics* I, 6. 74b5 & sqq.

Aristotle accepted the world's eternity as a fact, and did not teach that being is created. It may be felt that St Thomas is watering him down, nevertheless notice his sound reasons for not accepting the Aristoteleanism of Averroes.

[y]Possible with reference to a power and possible in itself; for a development of this distinction see 1a. 25, 3.

[z]A free translation, supported by the punctuation of Pègues. A thing may be permanent—if it is. It may stretch permanently into the future without doing so into the past. And if it does it still may not explain itself. Yet note that a 'before' to which creation is 'after' is admittedly imaginary.

esse ingenitam, per hoc quod habet subjectum de quo sit. In 1 autem *De cælo*[18] probat cælum ingenitum, quia non habet contrarium ex quo generetur. Unde patet quod per utrumque non concluditur nisi quod materia et cælum non incœperunt per generationem, ut quidam ponebant, præcipue de cælo. Nos autem dicimus quod materia et cælum producta sunt in esse per creationem, ut ex dictis patet.[19]

4. Ad quartum dicendum quod ad rationem vacui non sufficit in quo nihil est, sed requiritur quod sit spatium capax corporis, in quo non sit corpus, ut patet per Aristotlem in IV *Physic.*[20] Nos autem dicimus non fuisse locum aut spatium ante mundum.

5. Ad quintum dicendum quod primus motor semper eodem modo se habuit; primum autem mobile non semper eodem modo se habuit, quia incoepit esse cum prius non fuisset. Sed hoc non fuit per mutationem, sed per creationem, quæ non est mutatio, ut supra dictum est.[21] Unde patet quod hæc ratio, quam ponit Aristoteles in VIII *Physic.*,[22] procedit contra eos qui ponebant mobilia æterna sed motum non æternum, ut patet ex opinionibus Anaxagoræ et Empedoclis.[23] Nos autem ponimus ex quo mobilia incœperunt semper fuisse motum.

6. Ad sextum dicendum quod primum agens est agens voluntarium. Et quamvis habuit voluntatem æternam producendi aliquem effectum, non tamen produxit æternum effectum. Nec est necesse quod præsupponatur aliqua mutatio, nec etiam propter imaginationem temporis. Aliter enim est intelligendum de agente particulari, quod præsupponit aliquid et causat alterum, et aliter de agente universali, quod producit totum.Sicut agens particulare producit formam, et præsupponit materiam: unde oportet quod formam inducat secundum proportionem ad debitam materiam. Unde rationabiliter in ipso consideratur quod inducit formam in talem materiam et non in aliam, ex differentia materiæ ad materiam. Sed hoc non rationabiliter videtur in Deo, qui simul producit formam et materiam; sed consideratur rationabiliter in eo quod ipse producit materiam congruam formæ et fini.

---

[18]*De cælo* I, 3. 270a13–22   [19]1a. 45, 2
[20]*Physics* IV, I. 208b26   [21]1a. 45, 2 ad 2
[22]*Physics* VIII, I. 251a8–28   [23]ibid. 250b24–30

[a]The reference, from *De cælo* I, 10. 279b15, is to Empedocles and Heraclitus who believed in periodic changes in the constitution of the universe.
[b]No empty space. Place and space, according to Aristotle and St Thomas, have no reality without relation to the real quantity of existing bodies.
[c]*Primus motor*: cf 1a. 2, 3, *Primum movens immobile*, Vol. 2.
[d]There is no reconstruction of a picture of a creator making things at first immobile and then launched on their ways.
[e]Particular and universal cause, cf above 1a. 44, 2; 45, 1.

not having a subject from which it can come about, and in the *De cælo*[18] that the heavens are not generated from their not having a contrary from which their production can start. Hence it is clear that in both cases the only justified conclusion is that matter and the heavens, do not arise through generation, and particularly the latter, as some have maintained.[a] Whereas we have shown[19] why we hold that both are produced in existence by creation.

4. It is not enough to conceive the void as that in which nothing is; you have to define it, as Aristotle does,[20] as a space capable of yet not holding a body. Our contention is that before the world existed there was no place nor space.[b]

5. The prime mover[c] was ever changeless; not so, however, the primary subject of motion, because it began to be whereas hitherto it had not been. Yet this was not done through mutation, but through creation, which is not a change, as we have explained.[21] It is clear, then, that Aristotle's reasoning in the eighth book of the *Physics*,[22] is directed against those who held that the subject of motion was eternal, but not motion itself; apparently Anaxagoras and Empedocles were of this opinion.[23] For our part we assert that motion was always from the moment subjects of motion began.[d]

6. The first cause is a voluntary agent. Yet though his is an eternal will to produce an effect nevertheless he did not produce an eternal effect. This does not imply there was a change, before and after the effect, not even in terms of imaginary time. A particular cause, which works on one thing to make another, is to be conceived of differently from the universal cause, which makes the whole.[e] The first produces a form, but presupposes matter; accordingly the form it introduces should be proportionate to the appropriate matter. Hence quite rightly you expect the form to be induced into such and and not other matter, in order to match the difference there is between them.[f] To expect this of God, however, is not reasonable, for he produces at once both matter and form, except in this sense, that he should produce the matter that fits the form and purpose of the thing he creates.[g]

---

[f]This matter and that. Bare matter, *materia prima*, never exists as such, but always with a form which makes it this bodily being. So qualified and quantified, it is called *materia secunda*, also *materia signata*, a principle of individuation: cf *In Meta.* v, lect. 8. *In Boët. De Trin.* iv, 2.

It is such matter, i.e. not as purely potential but as possessed by a form contrary to the one a particular agent acts to produce that sets up a resistance, not present to the universal cause. cf above 1a. 45. 5 ad 2.

[g]As in the creation of the human soul, which quickens matter prepared or 'disposed' to receive it.

It is not that God's willing of this is because of his willing of that, but that he wills this to be for the sake of that; 1a. 19, 5.

Agens autem particulare præsupponit tempus sicut et materiam. Unde rationabiliter consideratur in eo quod agit in tempore posteriori et non priori, secundum imaginationem successionis temporis post tempus. Sed in agente universali, quod producit rem et tempus, non est considerare quod agat nunc et non prius secundum imaginationem temporis post tempus, quasi tempus præsupponatur ejus actioni; sed considerandum est, quod dedit effectui suo tempus quantum voluit, et secundum quod conveniens fuit ad suam potentiam demonstrandam. Manifestius enim mundus ducit in cognitionem divinæ potentiæ creantis si mundus non semper fuit quam si semper fuisset; omne enim quod non semper fuit manifestum est habere causam, sed non ita manifestum est de eo quod semper fuit.

7. Ad septimum dicendum quod sicut dicitur in *Physic.*,[24] prius et posterius est in tempore secundum quod prius et posterius est in motu. Unde principium et finis accipienda sunt in tempore sicut et in motu. Supposita autem æternitate motus, necesse est quod quodlibet momentum in motu acceptum sit principium et terminus motus; quod non oportet si motus incipiat. Et eadem ratio est de nunc temporis. Et sic patet quod ratio illa instantis *nunc*, quod semper sit principium et finis temporis, præsupponit æternitatem temporis et motus. Unde Aristoteles hanc rationem inducit, in VIII *Physic.*,[25] contra eos qui ponebant æternitatem temporis, sed negabant æternitatem motus.

8. Ad octavum dicendum quod Deus est prior mundo duratione. Sed *ly* 'prius' non designat prioritatem temporis, sed æternitatis. Vel dicendum quod designat æternitatem temporis imaginati et non realiter existentis. Sicut, cum dicitur, supra cælum nihil est, *ly* 'supra' designat locum imaginatum tantum, secundum quod possibile est imaginari dimensionibus cælestis corporis dimensiones alias superaddi.

9. Ad nonum dicendum quod sicut effectus sequitur a causa agente naturaliter secundum modum suæ formæ, ita sequitur ab agente per voluntatem secundum formam ab eo præconceptam et definitam, ut ex superioribus patet.[26] Licet igitur Deus ab æterno fuerit sufficiens causa mundi, non tamen oportet quod ponatur mundus ab eo productus nisi secundum quod est in prædefinitione suæ voluntatis, ut scilicet habeat esse post non esse ut manifestius declaret suum Auctorem.

---

[24]*Physics* IV, 11. 219a16–25
[25]*Physics* VIII, 1. 251b10–28
[26]Ia. 19, 4; 41, 2
hLiterally, he gave to his effect the amount of time he willed for it. Not that there was a moment before God's timeless action, but there are moments after his effect from which its beginning may be retrospectively timed.
iThe drift of the argument is as follows: within a given system a change or motion

Again, a particular cause presupposes time as well as matter. With good reason it is observed acting in time after and not in time before, according to the image of one period succeeding another. The universal cause, however, which produces both the thing and time, is not to be regarded as acting now and not before by imagining a succession of periods, as though time were presupposed to its action; though it is to be considered that he dated the effect[h] according to his good pleasure and the fitting manifestation of his power. We are led to the knowledge of divine creative power more evidently from a world that began once upon a time than from a world that never did. For having a cause is not so manifest for a thing that was always as for one that was not always.

7. According to Aristotle the before and after in time depends on the before and after in motion.[24] Hence a first and last limit is to be taken in one as in the other. Granted the eternity of motion, then each moment taken in time would have to be a beginning and an end in motion; this, however, is not required on hypothesis that motion has a beginning. It is the same with time; to think of the instant *now* as ever being the beginning and the end of time presupposes the eternity of time and motion.[1] That is why Aristotle brings forward this argument,[25] against those who asserted the eternity of time, but denied the eternity of motion.

8. God is before the world by duration. The term 'before' here means the priority of eternity,[j] not of time. Or you might say that it betokens an everlasting imaginary time, not time as really existing, rather as when we speak of nothing being beyond the heavens, the term 'beyond' betokens merely an imaginary place in a picture we can form of other dimensions stretching beyond those of the body of the heavens.

9. As an effect of a cause that acts by nature follows from it according to the mode of its form so an effect of a cause that acts through will follows from it according to a form that is preconceived and defined: earlier discussion brought this out.[26] Well then, although God from eternity was the sufficient cause of the world, this does not demand our postulating that the world made by him is any other than as it is in the predetermination of his will, namely as having existence after non-existence, and thus the more clearly to tell of its author.[k]

---

has a start and a stop, the terms *a quo* and *ad quem*. As such it is between them, beginning what is to be and finishing what has been. Were it eternal no moment could be pointed to as a start or a stop. If, however, it has had a beginning then the first moment, preceded by non-being, simply represents a start, not a continuation.

[j]1a. 10, 1–4. Vol. 2, Appendix 16.

[k]As in ad 6, a conscious *ex post-facto* rationalization of what is given by Revelation, or argument *ex convenientia* showing that a conclusion is fitting, not that it has to be.

10. Ad decimum dicendum quod, posita actione, sequitur effectus secundum exigentiam formæ quæ est principium actionis. In agentibus autem per voluntatem, quod conceptum est et prædefinitum accipitur ut forma quæ est principium actionis. Ex actione igitur Dei æterna non sequitur effectus æternus, sed qualem Deus voluit, ut scilicet haberet esse post non esse.

articulus 2. utrum mundum incœpisse sit articulus fidei

AD SECUNDUM sic proceditur:[1] 1. Videtur quod mundum incœpisse non sit articulus fidei, sed conclusio demonstrabilis. Omne enim factum habet principium suæ durationis. Sed demonstrative probari potest quod Deus sit causa effectiva mundi; et hoc etiam probabiliores philosophi posuerunt. Ergo demonstrative probari potest quod mundus incœperit.

2. Præterea, si necesse est dicere quod mundus factus est a Deo, aut ergo ex nihilo aut ex aliquo. Sed non ex aliquo, quia sic materia mundi præcessisset mundum; contra quod procedunt rationes Aristotelis ponentis cælum ingenitum. Ergo oportet dicere quod mundus factus sit ex nihilo. Et sic habet esse post non esse. Ergo oportet quod esse incœperit.

3. Præterea, omne quod operatur per intellectum, a quodam principio operatur, ut patet in omnibus artificibus. Sed Deus est agens per intellectum. Ergo a quodam principio operatur. Mundus igitur, qui est ejus effectus, non fuit semper.

4. Præterea, manifeste apparet artes aliquas et habitationes regionum ex determinatis temporibus incœpisse. Sed hoc non esset si mundus semper fuisset. Mundus igitur non semper fuisse manifestum est.

5. Præterea, certum est nihil Deo æquari posse. Sed si mundus semper fuisset æquiparetur Deo in duratione. Ergo certum est non semper mundum fuisse.

6. Præterea, si mundus semper fuit infiniti dies præcesserunt diem

---

[1]cf *CG* II, 38. *De potentia* III, 14. *De æternitate mundi. Quodl.* III, 14, 2; XII, 6, 1. *Sent.* II, 1, 1, 5
[1]The practical form in the mind and will of the maker; cf 1a. 19, 4 & 7.
[a]The purpose of this article which carries on from the one before, is to show that the arguments for the eternity of the world, while not themselves demonstrative, cannot be demonstratively disproved. The objections come mainly from St Thomas's contemporaries and friends, not from *Aristoteles Arabicus*. Appendix 2.
That creation implies a temporal beginning was the view of Alexander of Hales, of St Thomas's friend, St Bonaventure, and of his master, St Albert the Great. For the more approved philosophers, cf 1a. 44, 2. The inference is that the temporal beginning of the world is among the reasonable preambles to faith.
[c]cf above, *art.* 1.

10. Given the action, the effect follows according to the thrust of the form which is the principle of the action. In causes that act through will the concept and predetermination enter as such an operative form.[1] Therefore an eternal effect does not result from God's eternal action, but only such a one as God has willed, namely an effect possessing existence after non-existence.

article 2. is it an article of faith that the world began?

THE SECOND POINT:[1a] 1. No, for it appears to be a demonstrable conclusion, not a matter of faith, that the world began. For everything that is made has a beginning to its duration. Now that God is the cause producing the world can be demonstrated; indeed the more approved philosophers draw this conclusion. Accordingly it is demonstrable that the world began.[b]

2. Moreover, we cannot but admit that the world was made by God, and therefore either from nothing or from something. But not from something, for in that event its material would have preceded the world, and Aristotle's arguments are against this when maintaining that the heavens are not produced by generation.[c] Hence we have to subscribe to the alternative, that the world was made from nothing. This implies that it had existence after non-existence. Which means that it began to exist.

3. Besides, anything at work through intelligence sets a start for its action, as is shown by the procedure of human art.[d] God produces things through intelligence, and therefore marks a beginning for his action. The world is his work, and therefore was not always.

4. Besides, it would clearly appear that human cultures and their geographical settlement arise at definite periods of time. This would not have happened had the world always existed.[e]

5. That nothing can be God's equal is certain. Yet an eternal world would be his equal in duration. Hence it is certainly not eternal.[f]

6. Moreover, if the world had always existed an infinity of days would

---

[d]An echo of *Physics* III, 4. 203a31. The passage is picking up the thread from Anaxagoras: there must have been a point in time when Intelligence brought things out of the unlimited into separate existence. The argument is used by St Albert, *In Physic.* VIII, 1, 12.

[e]The argument from a correspondence between the patterns of parts and wholes, and inspired by an Augustinian world-view of history congenial to the thought of the twelfth and thirteenth centuries, e.g. John of Salisbury and Vincent of Beauvais, will receive less sympathetic treatment than it seems to deserve.

[f]Alexander of Hales, *Summa Theologica* I, 64.

istum. Sed infinita non est pertransire. Ergo nunquam fuisset perventum ad hunc diem: quod est manifeste falsum.

7. Præterea, si mundus fuit æternus et generatio fuit ab æterno. Ergo unus homo genitus est ab alio in infinitum. Sed pater est causa efficiens filii, ut dicitur in *Physic*.[2] Ergo in causis efficientibus est procedere in infinitum: quod improbatur in *Meta*.[3]

8. Præterea, si mundus et generatio semper fuit infiniti homines præcesserunt. Sed anima hominis est immortalis. Ergo infinitæ animæ humanæ nunc essent actu: quod est impossibile. Ergo ex necessitate sciri potest quod mundus incœperit, et non sola fide tenetur.

SED CONTRA, fidei articuli demonstrative probari non possunt, quia fides de *non apparentibus est*.[4] Sed Deum esse Creatorem mundi, sic quod mundus incœperit esse est articulus fidei; dicimus enim, *Credo in unum Deum* etc.[5] Et iterum Gregorius dicit.[6] quod Moyses prophetizavit de præterito dicens, *In principio creavit Deus cælum et terram*, in quo novitas mundi trahitur.* Ergo novitas mundi habetur tantum per revelationem. Et ideo non potest probari demonstrative.

RESPONSIO: Dicendum quod mundum non semper fuisse sola fide tenetur, et demonstrative probari non potest; sicut et supra de mysterio Trinitatis dictum est.[7]

Et hujus ratio est, quia novitas mundi non potest demonstrationem recipere ex parte ipsius mundi. Demonstrationis enim principium est *quod quid est*. Unumquodque autem secundum rationem suæ speciei abstrahit ab hic et nunc; propter quod dicitur quod *universalia sunt ubique et semper*.[8] Unde demonstrari non potest quod homo, aut cælum, aut lapis non semper fuit.

Similiter etiam neque ex parte causæ agentis, quæ agit per voluntatem.

---

*Leonine: *traditur*, is taught
[2]*Physics* II, 3. 194b30. St Thomas, *lect*. 5   [3]*Metaphysics* II, 2. 994a1. *lect*. 3
[4]*Hebrews* II, I
[5]*Nicene Creed*. Denz. 125
[6]St Gregory the Great. *In Ezechiam*, homily I, I. PL 76, 786
[7]1a. 32, I
[8]*Posterior Analytics* I, 31. 87b33. St Thomas, *lect*. 42
gGiven as Algazel's argument by Averroes; as among those of the Mutakallemin by Maimonides, I, 74. cf St Bonaventure, II *Sent*. I, I, I, ii. For Zeno's fallacy, cf *Physics* VI, 9. 239b8. Time is not composed of indivisible moments, nor is any other magnitiude composed of indivisibles.
hInfinite causal series: cf 1a. 2, 3. Vol. 2.
[1]Sources as in the sixth objection.

have preceded today. An infinity of points, however, cannot be traversed. And so we would never have arrived at today, which is patently untrue.[g]

7. Further, were the world eternal so also would be the generation of things, and one man would be generated by another *ad infinitum*, for, according to the *Physics*,[2] the parent is the efficient cause of the child. On this supposition you would have an infinite series of efficient causes,[h] which is disproved in the *Metaphysics*.[3]

8. Further, if the world and generation have been going on for ever then an infinite number of human beings have come before us. Now the human soul is immortal. Consequently an infinite number of human souls would now exist, which is impossible. Therefore we can cogently argue that the world began; and the conclusion is not held by faith alone.[i]

ON THE OTHER HAND the article of faith[j] cannot be demonstratively proved, for faith is about things *that appear not*.[4] That God is the creator of a world that began to be is an article of faith; we profess it in the Creed.[5k] For his part Gregory teaches[6] that Moses prophesied of the past[l] when he declared that in the beginning God created heaven and earth, for his implication was that the world was new. This therefore is held through revelation alone, and cannot be demonstrated.

REPLY: That the world has not always existed cannot be demonstratively proved but is held by faith alone. We make the same stand here as with regard to the mystery of the Trinity.[7]

The reason is this: the world considered in itself offers no grounds for demonstrating that it was once all new. For the principle for demonstrating an object is its definition.[m] Now the specific nature of each and every object abstracts from the here and now, which is why universals are described as being *everywhere and always*.[8n] Hence it cannot be demonstrated that man or the heavens or stone did not always exist.

Nor is demonstration open to us through the efficient cause.[o] Here this

---

[j]Articles of faith: cf 2a2æ. 1, 2, 6 & 7.

[k]Merely a gambit which offers no threat to the position of St Albert or St Bonaventure.

[l]Prophecy is of the distant in space or time, 2a2æ. 171, 1. From the nature of the case there are no historical records for the Hexaëmeron.

[m]Definition, *quod quid est, to ti ten einai*. The verification of a Predicate about a Subject (the conclusion of an apodictic or demonstrative syllogism) comes through a Middle Term linking the two. In a proof that establishes the very reason, *demonstratio propter quid*, this is the real definition of the Subject. cf 1a. 2, 2. *In Anal. post.* I, lect. 23.

[n]cf 1a. 16, 7 ad 2. *In Anal. post.* I, lect. 42.

[o]cf 1a. 2, 2.

Voluntas enim Dei ratione investigari non potest, nisi circa ea quæ absolute necesse est Deum velle; talia autem non sunt quæ circa creaturas vult, ut dictum est.[9]

Potest autem voluntas divina homini manifestari per revelationem, cui fides innititur. Unde mundum incœpisse est credibile, non autem demonstrabile vel scibile.

Et hoc utile est ut consideretur, ne forte aliquis quod fidei est demonstrare præsumens rationes non necessarias inducat, quæ præbeant materiam irridendi infidelibus, existimantibus nos propter hujusmodi rationes credere quæ fidei sunt.

1. Ad primum ergo dicendum quod, sicut dicit Augustinus,[10] philosophorum ponentium æternitatem mundi, duplex fuit opinio. Quidam enim posuerunt quod substantia mundi non sit a Deo. Et horum est intolerabilis error, et ideo ex necessitate refellitur. Quidam autem sic posuerunt mundum æternum, quod tamen mundum a Deo factum dixerunt. *Non enim mundum temporis* volunt habere, sed suæ creationis initium, ut quodam modo vix intelligibili semper sit factus.* Id autem quomodo intelligant invenerunt, ut idem dicit,[11] *Sicut enim, inquiunt, si pes ex æternitate semper fuisset in pulvere, semper subesset vestigium, quod a calcante factum nemo dubitaret, sic et mundus semper fuit, semper existente qui fecit.*

Et ad hoc intelligendum considerandum est quod causa efficiens quæ agit per motum de necessitate præcedit tempore suum effectum; quia effectus non est nisi in termino actionis, agens autem omne oportet esse principium actionis. Sed si actio sit instantanea et non successiva, non est necessarium faciens esse prius facto duratione, sicut patet in illuminatione. Unde dicunt quod non sequitur ex necessitate, si Deus est causa activa mundi, quod sit prior mundo duratione; quia creatio, qua mundum produxit, non est mutatio successiva, ut supra dictum est.[12]

2. Ad secundum dicendum quod illi qui ponerent mundum æternum dicerent mundum factum a Deo ex nihilo, non quod factus sit post nihilum, secundum quod nos intelligimus per nomen creationis, sed quia non est factus de aliquo. Et sic etiam non recusant aliqui eorum creationis nomen, ut patet ex Avicenna.[13]

---

*Piana: *tempus*

[9]Ia. 19, 3
[10]*De civitate Dei* XI, 4. PL 41, 319
[11]Op. cit. x, 31. PL 41, 311
[12]Ia. 45, 2 ad 3
[13]*Metaphysics* IX, 4 (104va)

[p]Choices cannot be forecast from a necessary principle of meaning.

[q]*Credible*, a more urgent word in Latin than in English. It is *credendum*, to be assented to despite the absence of inner evidence. An object offering inner evidence is called an *intelligibile* when this is immediate, a *scibile* when this is mediate through demonstration.

is a voluntary agent. God's will is unsearchable, except as regards what he cannot but will, and his willing about creatures is not necessarily bound up with that, as we have seen.[9p]

His will, however, can be manifested to man through Revelation, the ground of faith. That the world had a beginning, therefore, is credible,[q] but not scientifically demonstrable.

And it is well to take warning here, to forestall rash attempts at demonstration by arguments that are not cogent, and so provide unbelievers with the occasion for laughing at us and thinking that these are our reasons for believing the things of faith.[r]

Hence: 1. According to St Augustine[10] there were two opinions among philosophers who held the world was eternal. To some the world's substance did not come from God, an error not to be borne and to be convincingly refuted. To others, however, it existed from all ages yet all the same was produced by God. *For they hold that the world has a beginning, not of time, but of creation, which means that, in some scarely intelligible fashion, it ever was made.* He tells us also[11] that they try to explain themselves as follows. *Were a foot, they say, in the dust from eternity there would always be a footprint there and nobody could doubt that it had been imprinted by him who trod there, so likewise the world always was because he who made it always existed.*

For the explanation: we agree that an efficient cause which works through change must precede its effect in time, for the effect enters as the term of the action whereas the agent is its start. Yet in the event of the action being instantaneous and not successive, it is not required for the maker to be prior in duration to the thing made, as appears in the case of illumination.[s] Hence they point out[t] that because God is the active cause of the world it does not necessarily follow that he is prior to it in duration, for, as we have seen[12] creation, whereby he produced the world, is not a successive change.

2. Those who hold the eternity of the world would agree that it was made by God from nothing, in the sense that it was not made from anything, not that it was made after nothing, which is what we understand.[u] Accordingly some of them, Avicenna for instance,[13] do not even reject the word 'creation'.

---

[r] 1a. 1, 8, on the place of proof in theology.
[s] Illumination, see above 1a. 45, 2 ad 3. The reply is a development of the argument in the body of the article, which shows that a temporal beginning does not emerge from an analysis of what it means to be created. Now it is argued that nor does it emerge from the notion of active creation.
[t] Thus Averroes, *Destruct. destruct.* 1.
[u] cf above, 1a. 45, 1 ad 3.

3. Ad tertium dicendum quod illa est ratio Anaxagoræ quæ ponitur in III *Physic.*[14] Sed non de necessitate concludit, nisi de intellectu qui deliberando investigat quid agendum sit, quod est simile motui. Talis autem est intellectus humanus, sed non divinus, ut supra patet.[15]

4. Ad quartum dicendum est quod ponentes æternitatem mundi ponunt aliquam regionem infinities esse mutatam de inhabitabila in habitabile, et e converso. Et similiter ponunt quod artes propter diversas corruptiones et accidentia infinities fuerunt inventæ, et iterum corruptæ. Unde Aristoteles dicit[16] quod ridiculum est ex hujusmodi particularibus mutationibus opinionem accipere de novitate mundi totius.

5. Ad quintum dicendum quod, etsi mundus semper fuisset, non tamen parificaretur Deo in æternitate, ut dicit Boëtius, in fine de *Consol.*[17], quia esse divinum est esse totum simul absque successione; non autem sic est de mundo.

6. Ad sextum dicendum quod transitus semper intelligitur a termino in terminum. Quæcumque autem præterita dies signetur ab illa usque ad istam sunt finiti dies, qui pertransiri poterunt. Objectio autem procedit ac si, positis extremis, sint media infinita.

7. Ad septimum dicendum quod in causis efficientibus impossibile est procedere in infinitum per se; ut puta si causæ quæ per se requiruntur ad aliquem effectum multiplicarentur in infinitum, sicut si lapis moveretur a baculo, et baculus a manu, et hoc in infinitum. Sed per accidens in infinitum procedere in causis efficientibus non reputatur impossibile; ut puta si omnes causæ quæ in infinitum multiplicantur non teneant ordinem nisi unius causæ, sed earum multiplicatio sit per accidens, sicut artifex agit multis martellis per accidens, quia unus post unum frangitur. Accidit ergo huic martello quod agat post actionem alterius martelli. Et similiter accidit huic homini, inquantum generat, quod sit generatus ab alio; generat enim inquantum homo, et non inquantum est filius alterius hominis: omnes enim homines generantes habent gradum unum in causis efficientibus, scilicet gradum particularis generantis. Unde non est impossibile quod

---

[14]*Physics* III, 4. 203a31
[15]1a. 14, 7
[16]*Meteorologica* I, 14. 352a26. cf 351a19 & b8. St Augustine, *De civitate Dei* XII, 10. PL 41, 358
[17]*De consolatione philosophiæ* V, 6. PL 63, 859
vIt will be noticed that the replies to the objections content themselves with showing that these do not demonstrate the contrary of position taken up in the article.
wHere, as in ad 8, no difficulty is felt about showing the temporal beginning of some particular creature.
xThe relation between days in the progression of days does not depend on an

3. This is the argument of Anaxagoras reported in the *Physics*.[14] Yet it is conclusive only with regard to a mind which deliberates according to a procedure like change. Such is the human mind, but not, as we have shown,[15] the divine mind.[v]

4. Those who teach that world is everlasting also think that a particular region has undergone an indefinite number of changes from being uninhabitable to being habitable, and vice versa, and also that the arts because of various decadences and events are endlessly being discovered and lost. On this matter we may quote Aristotle, it is absurd to base our opinion about the newness of the whole world on such provincial changes.[16][w]

5. Even if it were everlasting the world would not be God's equal, as Boëthius points out towards the end of his *De consolatione*,[17] for the divine being is existence whole and all at once without succession, while it is not so with the world's being.

6. The objection proceeds on the assumption that given two extremes there is an infinity of intermediate points between them. Now a passage is always from one term to another, and whichever day from the past we pick on, there is only a limited number between then and today, and this span can be traversed.[x]

7. An infinite series of efficient causes essentially subordinate to one another is impossible, that is causes that are *per se* required for the effect, as when a stone is moved by a stick, a stick by a hand, and so forth: such a series cannot be prolonged indefinitely. All the same an infinite series of efficient causes incidentally subordinate to one another is not counted impossible, as when they are all ranged under causal heading and how many there are is quite incidental.[y] For example, when a smith picks up many hammers because one after another has broken in his hand, it is accidental to one particular hammer that it is employed after another particular hammer. So is the fact that another has procreated him to the procreating act of a particular man, for he does this as a man, and not as the son of a father. For all men in begetting hold the same rank in the order of efficient causes, namely that of being a particular parent.[z] Hence it is not out of the question for a man to be begotten by a man and so on

---

endless series, but on the particular series or system of reference adopted for dating. Thus today depends on yesterday, and to take a long view many days before, but to look at it narrowly as today, it merely depends on yesterday in order to dawn; in this respect the length of the series of days before it is by the way.

[y]Essential and incidental subordination of causes, cf 1a. 2, 3; 7, 4. Vol. 2.

[z]The collectivity does not directly enter into the individual causation. The thought is different in the theology of Original Sin, the fault of Everyman inherited from our first parents, and of its atonement through Christ, the head of mankind. cf 1a2æ. 81, 1, Vol. 26. 3a. 8, 1 & 6, Vol. 49.

homo generetur ab homine in infinitum. Esset autem impossibile si generatio hujus hominis dependeret ab hoc homine, et a corpore elementari, et a sole, et sic in infinitum.

8. Ad octavum dicendum quod hanc rationem ponentes æternitatem mundi multipliciter effugiunt. Quidam enim non reputant impossibile esse infinitas animas actu, ut patet in *Meta*. Algazelis, dicentis hoc esse infinitum per accidens.[18] Sed hoc improbatum est superius.[19] Quidam vero dicunt animam corrumpi cum corpore. Quidam vero quod ex omnibus animabus remanet una tantum. Alii vero, ut Augustinus dicit,[20] posuerunt propter hoc circuitum animarum, ut scilicet animæ separatæ a corporibus post determinata temporum curricula iterum redirent ad corpora. De quibus omnibus in sequentibus est agendum.[21]

Considerandum tamen quod hæc ratio particularis est. Unde posset dicere aliquis quod mundus fuit æternus, vel saltem aliqua creatura ut angelus, non autem homo. Nos autem intendimus universaliter in aliqua creatura fuerit ab æterno.

articulus 3. *utrum creatio rerum fuerit in principio temporis*

AD TERTIUM sic proceditur:[1] 1. Videtur quod creatio rerum non fuit in principio temporis. Quod enim non est in tempore non est in aliquo temporis. Sed creatio rerum non fuit in tempore; per creationem enim rerum substantia in esse producta est. Tempus autem non mensurat

---

[18]*Algazel's Metaphysics* I, 1, 6. Ed. J. T. Muckle. Toronto, 1933. (40)

[19]1a. 7, 4

[20]*Sermones ad populum* CCXLI, 4. PL 38, 1135. *De civitate Dei* XII, 13. PL 41, 361

[21]1a. 75, 6; 76, 2; 118, 6   [1]cf II *Sent.* 1, 1, 6

[a]A particular 'generator' is not the cause of the nature according to which it generates, but of its becoming exemplified in an individual, see above 1a. 45, 8.

[b]The sentence can be translated in two ways. The main sense of the original is clear, but the portmanteau sentence does not fit easily into the argument. *Generatio hominis* may refer to a man's being begotten (the usual translation) or to his begetting (as in this translation). St Thomas is saying that if we think, horizontally as it were, along a line of particular factors there is now no reason why it should not be prolonged indefinitely backwards or forwards, yet that this is impossible vertically, as it were, through a series of essentially subordinate factors.

[c]Algazel (*d.c.* 1111), called the *Abbreviator* from his abridgment of Avicenna. He was considered his faithful expositor; in fact he intended to refute him later.

[d]St Thomas seems to have been in two minds about a multitude actually infinite. His doubt about proving its impossibility shown in the early work, the *Contra Gentiles* II, 81, continues with the later works, *In Physic.* IV, *lect.* 8, and *De æternitate mundi contra murmurantes*. 1a. 7, 4, is more decided about its impossibility.

[e]The teaching of Democritus was known from *Physics* VIII, 1. 251b16.

[f]The survival of a single soul: cf the Averroist doctrine of the single active intellect. 1a. 76, 2; 79, 4 & 5. *De unitate intellectus*.

endlessly.[a] This would not be the case were this begetting to depend on another man or on material elements and solar energy and so on; such a series cannot be interminable.[b]

8. The proponents of the world's eternity escape from this objection in various ways. Some reckon that an actual infinity of souls is not impossible; in his *Metaphysics* Algazel[c] holds that this would amount to an accidental infinity.[18] This position, however, we have already disproved.[19d] Others hold that the soul decays with the body.[e] Others again that from many souls one alone survives.[f] Yet others, as Augustine tells us,[20] on this account assert the doctrine of transmigration, namely that disembodied souls return again to bodies after a determinate course of time.[g] We shall deal with these matters later.[21]

Observe, all the same, that the argument in the objection is limited to the particular; it could be answered by saying that the world was eternal, at least in some creatures, such as angels, though not men. Our inquiry, however, is couched in wider terms, and asks whether any creature at all existed from eternity.

article 3. was the creation of things at the beginning of time?

THE THIRD POINT:[1a] 1. Seemingly not. For what is not in time is not in any part of time. Now the creation of things is outside time, for through it their substance was brought into existence.[b] Time, however, is not the

---

[g]Metempsychosis is better called metasomatosis if a change of body rather than of soul is meant.

[a]A beginning, *principium*, here has the sense of a starting, *inchoatio* or *inceptio*, which is an existing in real relation to its efficient cause and in merely conceptual relation to the antecedent non-existing. Continued existence is called duration, *duratio*, which implies the sustaining action, *conservatio*, of the efficient cause, and therefore, properly speaking, is not attributed to God. Yet cf above art. 1 ad 8, and elsewhere, too, St Thomas refers to eternity as a kind of duration. Here, however, we are concerned with the duration of creatures. Some creatures are permanent, spiritual substances, *incorruptibilia*, subject to alteration only in their activity; their duration is called *ævum*, everternity. Others, *corruptibilia*, are subject to substantial change; their duration is successive and temporary. Time is the measure of successive change. cf 1a. 10, 1–6 (Vol. 2). 1a2æ. 113, 7 ad 5. *In Physic.* IV, *lect.* 17 & 23. 1 *Sent.* 19, 2, 1.

[b]The production of substance as such, whether of the whole by creation or by transformation (*generatio et corruptio*), is instantaneous and not in time immediately and directly. The production of a material substance through secondary agents requires a preparation of the material (*dispositio materiæ*), which can be gradual and imply successive changes, as regards place (local movement), quality (alteration), and quantity (growth), and this is measurable by time. cf *In Meta.* XII, *lect.* 2. *In Physic.* III, *lect.* 1.

substantiam rerum, et præcipue incorporalium. Ergo creatio non fuit in principio temporis.

2. Præterea, Philosophus probat quod omne *quod fit fiebat*,[2] et sic omne fieri habet prius et posterius. In principio autem temporis, cum sit indivisibile, non est prius et posterius. Ergo cum creari sit quoddam fieri, videtur quod res non sint creatæ in principio temporis.

3. Præterea, ipsum etiam tempus creatum est. Sed non potest creari in principio temporis, cum tempus sit divisibile, principium autem temporis indivisibile. Non ergo creatio rerum fuit in principio temporis.

SED CONTRA est quod *Gen.*,[3] dicitur, *In principio creavit Deus caelum et terram.*

RESPONSIO: Dicendum quod illud verbum *Gen. In principio creavit Deus cælum et terram*, tripliciter exponitur ad excludendum tres errores.

Quidam enim posuerunt mundum semper fuisse, et tempus non habere principium. Et ad hoc excludendum exponitur *in principio*, scilicet temporis.

Quidam vero posuerunt duo esse creationis principia, unum bonorum, aliud malorum. Et ad hoc excludendum exponitur, *in principio*, idest in Filio. Sicut enim principium effectivum appropriatur Patri propter potentiam, ita principium exemplare appropriatur Filio propter sapientiam; ut sicut dicitur, *Omnia in sapientia fecisti*,[4] ita intelligatur Deum omnia fecisse in principio, idest in Filio; secundum illud Apostoli, *In ipso*, scilicet Filio, *condita sunt universa.*[5]

Alii vero dixerunt corporalia creata a Deo mediantibus creaturis spiritualibus. Et ad hoc excludendum exponitur, *In principio creavit Deus cælum et terram*, idest ante omnia.

---

[2]*Physics* VI, 6. 237b10. St Thomas, *lect.* 8
[3]*Genesis* I, I
[4]*Psalms* 103 (104), 24
[5]*Colossians* I, 15–16
[c]During the course of his close examination of the arguments of Zeno the Eleatic against the possibility of change or motion.
[d]That is, there is no time in its initial instant.
[e]If we admit that a Scriptural passage may have several literal senses, it seems likely that St Thomas treated these three interpretations as exposing the literal, not the spiritual, still less the 'accommodated' sense of *Genesis* I, I. cf 1a. I, 10. Vol. I, Appendix 12.
[f]See above, art. I & 2, ad 2, 4, 8.
[g]The Manicheans, see below 1a. 49, 3.
[h]The theological method of 'appropriation'; see above 1a. 45, 6.

measure of substance, especially not that of bodiless things. Creation, therefore, was not at the beginning of time.

2. Again, Aristotle proves that *everything which has become must previously have been in process of becoming*,[2c] and so to become implies a before and after. When time began, since that was an indivisible moment, there was no before. Because, therefore, to be created is a kind of coming into being, it seems that things were not created when time began.

3. Further, time itself is also created. Yet not in its very start, since time is divisible whereas its starting moment is indivisible.[d] Therefore the creation of things was not at the start of time.

ON THE OTHER HAND *Genesis* declares, *In the beginning God created the heavens and the earth.*[3]

REPLY: This text has been interpreted in three ways in order to dispose of three errors.[e]

First,[f] some have proposed an everlasting universe and a time with no beginning; to counter this the phrase, *In the beginning*, is read to mean that time once started.

Secondly, some have proposed a dual origin to creation, one the principle of good things, the other of evil;[g] to counter this the phrase, *In the beginning*, is read to refer to the Son of God. For as we think especially[h] of the Father as efficient cause by the note of might so we think especially of the Son as exemplar cause by the note of wisdom. Accordingly the verse, *In wisdom hast thou made them all*,[4] is understood to mean that God made all things in the beginning, that is the Son; as St Paul writes, *He is the first-born of creation, for in him all things were created in heaven and on earth.*[5]

Thirdly, others[I] have taught that bodily things were created by God through the intermediary of spiritual creatures; and to counter this the phrase, *in the beginning*, is read to mean before all things.[j]

[I]Gnostics and Avicenna: cf 1a. 45, 5 & 65, 4.

[J]All three interpretations of *In the beginning* are found in the medieval interlinear gloss; the first is after St Basil and St Ambrose; the second after St Basil, St Jerome, St Augustine; for the third see St Augustine, *Confessions* XII, 20. PL 32, 837.

The first interpretation is the one that most suits the philosophical preoccupations of the present treatise, yet in the larger context of the *Summa* the second interpretation is to be preferred: St Thomas's doctrine of creation is Christocentric and Scriptural, heir to the tradition, Hellenic, Alexandrian, and Palestinian, that God created in Wisdom and the 'word'. This does not appear in the foreground of

Footnote j continued on page 88

Quatuor enim ponuntur simul creata, scilicet cælum empyreum, materia corporalis, quæ nomine terræ intelligitur, tempus et natura angelica.

1. Ad primum ergo dicendum quod non dicuntur in principio temporis res esse creatæ, quasi principium temporis creationis sit mensura, sed quia simul cum tempore cælum et terra creata sunt.

2. Ad secundum dicendum quod verbum illud Philosophi intelligitur de fieri quod est per motum, vel quod est terminus motus. Quia cum in quolibet motu sit accipere prius et posterius, ante quodcumque signum in motu signato, dum scilicet aliquid est in moveri et fieri, est accipere prius et etiam aliquid post ipsum: quia quod est in principio motus vel in termino non est in moveri. Creatio autem neque est motus neque terminus motus, ut supra dictum est.[6] Unde sic aliquid creatur quod non prius creabatur.

3. Ad tertium dicendum quod nihil fit nisi secundum quod est. Nihil autem est temporis nisi nunc. Unde non potest fieri nisi secundum aliquod nunc; non quia in ipso primo *nunc* sit tempus, sed quia ab eo incipit tempus.

---

[6]1a. 45, 2 ad 3; 3
most of the discussions he is here conducting, yet, as has already appeared, the final appeal is always to Revelation, and the philosophy of causation is subsumed in the theology of the Trinity: cf above 1a. 45, 6 & 7. In effect the present treatise can be treated as a bridge-passage between the Questions on the Son as Word and Image (1a. 34 & 35) and on Christ as head of the body, in whom the fulness of God was pleased to dwell, and through him to reconcile all things to himself (3a. 8).

The weight St Thomas attached to a topic cannot be judged from the number of words he devoted to it: he had the trick. almost fussy it has been thought, of leaving no stone unturned that lay before him. In the present case, unless the doctrine of *Colossians* I, 15–23 is seen as central to his thought, he is no more than a religious philospher who is the peer of Avicenna and Maimonides. cf Introduction.

kThe four coevals, *coæqua* of the Gloss. The paragraph echoes the declaration of IV Lateran Council, 1215. Denzinger-Umberg 428.

The four following[k] are commonly supposed to have been created at once and together, namely the empyrean heavens,[1] bodily matter (in other words, the earth), time, and angelic natures.

Hence: 1. The phrase about things being created in the beginning of time means that the heavens and earth were created together with time; it does not suggest that the beginning of time was the measure of creation.[m]

2. Aristotle is talking about the sort of coming to be which arises through change or is the term of a change. Whatever the change you take a before and after, and so before any one point in a designated change—that is while something is changing and becoming—there is another point before and also another one after; what is at the start or at the finish of change is not in the condition of being changed. Now, as we have seen,[6] creation implies neither change nor a term of change. Hence a thing is not created in such a way that beforehand it was being created.

3. A thing is a fact just only as it exists.[n] And time exists only as being now. Hence it can become a fact only because of some present moment. This does not mean that time is in the original *now*, but that it begins then.[o]

---

[1]The empyrean heavens: cf 1a. 66, 3 & 4. The term was introduced into Scriptural commentaries on *Genesis* I from the Venerable Bede by Walafrid Strabo. cf Vol. 10 of this series.

[m]The preposition 'in': things were created 'along with' time, not 'during' time.

[n]cf 1a. 45, 4.

[o]Time, a construct of the past and the future, cannot be compressed into the present instant without making both the past and the future into the present, a contradiction absent from the non-successive simultaneousness of eternity. Hence time does not exist in the initial instant, yet this is the moment of creation from which time begins to flow. To be created is to be a new event without antecedent: cf above 1a. 45, 3.

POST PRODUCTIONEM CREATURARUM in esse, considerandum est de distinctionem earum. Erit autem hæc consideratio tripartita.

Nam primo considerabimus de distinctione rerum in communi;
secundo, de distinctione boni et mali;
tertio, de distinctione spiritualis et corporalis creaturæ.

Quæstio 47. de distinctione rerum in communi

Circa primum quæruntur tria:

1. de ipsa rerum multitudine seu distinctione;
2. de earum inæqualitate;
3. de unitate mundi.

articulus 1. utrum rerum multitudo et distinctio sit a Deo

AD PRIMUM sic proceditur:[1] 1. Videtur quod rerum multitudo et distinctio non sit a Deo. Unum enim semper natum est unum facere. Sed Deus est maxime unus, ut ex præmissis patet.[2] Ergo non producit nisi unum effectum.

2. Præterea, exemplatum assimilatur suo exemplari. Sed Deus est causa exemplaris sui effectus, ut supra dictum est.[3] Ergo, cum Deus sit unus, effectus ejus est unus tantum et non distinctus.

3. Præterea, ea quæ sunt ad finem, proportionantur fini. Sed finis creaturæ est unus, scilicet divina bonitas, ut supra ostensum est.[4] Ergo effectus Dei non est nisi unus.

---

[1]cf Ia. 22, 2. *CG* II, 39–45; III, 97. *De potentia* III, 1 ad 9; 16. *Compend. theol.* 71, 72 & 102. *In Meta.* XII, *lect.* 2. *In De causis, lect.* 24
[2]Ia. 11, 4
[3]Ia. 44, 3
[4]Ia. 44, 4
[a]For Questions 50–102 see Vols 9–13 of this series. Pègues inserts a third article before our last, making four for the Question. It is given in Appendix 3.
[b]Distinction is rooted in the notion of *aliquid*, something, which often does duty for *aliquod*. This is used in opposition to nothing or to a definite object. In this last sense it means this one and not another one, a distinction within a plurality or multitude, which for the present discussion, and evident from the discussions

HAVING DISCUSSED HOW THEY COME into existence, the distinction among creatures is now to be looked into. Our examination will fall into three parts.

> First, we shall consider their plurality in general (47);
> next, the distinction between good and evil (48–49);
> last, that between spiritual and corporeal creatures (50–102).[a]

Question 47. the plurality in general of things

Here there are three points of inquiry:

1. multiplicity or distinctiveness in things;
2. the inequality among them;
3. the unity of the world.

article 1. is the multiplicity and distinction of things from God?

THE FIRST POINT:[1] 1. It would not seem so.[b] For always a unity is such as to engender a unity. Now God's unity is supreme, as has been shown.[2] Therefore the effect he produces is one alone and single. Therefore what he engenders is only the one.

2. Again, a thing resembles the exemplar after which it is fashioned. Now it has been said[3] that God is the exemplar cause of his effect. And since he is one his effect is one, and not diversified.

3. Things for an end are proportionate to it. But the creature's end is one, namely the divine goodness; this is agreed.[4] Therefore God's effect is but one.[c]

---

which have led up to it, is a multiplicity of things, not merely of mental concepts or experimental phenomena. The article covers real distinction both in number and in kind—numerical and formal multiplicity, the latter explicitly.

On the metaphysics of being one; cf *In Meta.* IV, *lect.* 2 & 3 (1003b22–4a35); V, *lect.* 7 & 8 (1015b15–1017a8); X, *lect.* 1–6 (1052a15–1057a19). On limit as a principle within being; cf *In Physic,* I, *lect.* 11 (184b15–16a4); *In Meta.* XII, *lect.* 3 (1069b31–70a30). On the principle of number; cf *De potentia* IX, 7.

[c]The three objections are curt summaries, arranged under the headings of efficient, exemplar, and final causality, of the classical doctrine of Gnostics and Neo-Platonists, that a one only can emanate from the One. With this is associated the mysticism that the path of perfection leaves separateness and variety behind and rejoins the One alone. It is the 'alone' that St Thomas does not admit, as will appear in this Question, consonantly with his whole theology of creation and salvation and his philosophy of the reality of finite things.

SED CONTRA est quod dicitur *Gen.*⁵ quod Deus *distinxit* lucem a tenebris* et *divisit aquas ab aquis.* Ergo distinctio et multitudo rerum est a Deo.

RESPONSIO: Dicendum quod causam distinctionis rerum multipliciter aliqui assignaverunt. Quidam enim attribuerunt eam materiæ, vel soli vel simul cum agente. Soli quidem materiæ, sicut Democritus et omnes antiqui naturales ponentes solam causam materialem; secundum quos distinctio rerum provenit a casu secundum motum materiæ. Materiæ vero et agenti simul distinctionem et multitudinem rerum attribuit Anaxagoras, qui posuit intellectum distinguentem res, extrahendo quod erat permixtum in materia. Sed hoc non potest state propter duo. Primo quidem, quia supra ostensum est quod etiam ipsa materia a Deo creata est.⁶ Unde oportet et distinctionem, si qua est a parte materiæ, in altiorem causam reducere. Secundo, quia materia est propter formam, et non e converso. Distinctio autem rerum est per formas proprias. Non ergo distinctio est in rebus propter materiam, sed potius e converso in materia creata est difformitas ut esset diversis formis accommodata.

Quidam vero attribuerunt distinctionem rerum secundis agentibus. Sicut Avicenna, qui dixit quod Deus intelligendo se produxit intelligentiam primam, in qua, quia non est suum esse, ex necessitate incidit compositio potentiæ et actus, ut infra patebit.⁷ Sic igitur prima intelligentia, inquantum intelligit causam primam, produxit secundam intelligentiam; inquantum autem intelligit se secundum quod est in potentia, produxit corpus cæli, quod movet; inquantum intelligit vero se secundum illud quod habet de actu, produxit animam cæli. Sed hoc non potest stare propter duo. Primo quidem, quia supra ostensum est quod creare solius Dei est.⁸ Unde ea quæ non possunt causari nisi per creationem a solo Deo producuntur; et hæc sunt omnia quæ non subjacent generationi et corruptioni. Secundo, quia secundum hanc positionem, non proveniret ex intentione primi agentis universitas

---

*Vulgate: *divisit*
⁵*Genesis* 4, 7
⁷1a. 50, 2 ad 3
⁶1a. 44, 2
⁸1a. 45, 5
ᵈ*Antiqui naturales*: the Ionian *phusikoi.* Democritus (*d.* 361 B.C.), developed the theory of atomism going back to Leucippus. cf *Physics* II, 2; 4: III, 4. 194a20, 195a2t, 203a34. For his teaching that chance caused the distinction of things, and Aristotle's discussion of purpose in nature, cf *Physics* III, 8–9. 198b10–200b9.
ᵉAnaxagoras, the friend and teacher of Euripides and Pericles (*d.* 428 B.C.). To quote Aristotle, he stood out like a sane man by comparison with the random talkers who went before him, *Metaphysics* I, 3. 984b16. However both Plato, *Phædo*

ON THE OTHER HAND *Genesis* tells us that God separated *the light from the darkness* and *the waters that were under the firmament from the waters which were above the firmament*.[5] Therefore the separation and multitude of things come from him.

REPLY: The distinction of things has been put down to various causes. Some ascribed it to matter, either alone or in combination with an agent. Democritus, for instance, and the early natural philosophers,[d] recognizing only the material cause in things, set down diversity to matter alone and treated it as the chance result of matter in motion. Anaxagoras,[e] on the other hand, attributed their distinctiveness and multitude to the concert of an agent with matter, that is an intelligence which sieved things from the mixture of world-material.

But this will not do, and for two reasons. First, because, as already established, even matter itself was created by God.[6] Consequently the distinction in things, even that which comes from matter, has to be traced to a higher cause. Second, matter is for the sake of form, and not conversely. Therefore distinction in things is not there to meet the requirement of matter, but rather the other way round; created matter is formless so that it may be adapted to a variety of forms.

Others, again, have attributed the variegation of things to secondary agents. Avicenna, for instance, taught that by understanding himself God produced the first intelligence, into which the composition of potentiality and actuality necessarily enters, since it is not its own existence: this will be explained later.[7] Then this first intelligence by knowing the first cause produced the second intelligence; then by knowing itself as being in potentiality, produced the body of the heavens, from which motion arises; and by knowing itself as having actuality produced the soul of the heavens.[f]

Yet neither will this do, and for two reasons. First, as already established, because creation is exclusively God's action.[8] What can be produced only by creation is produced by him alone; such are all things not subject to generation and decay. Secondly, it would make out that the universe of things came to pass from the running together of many active factors, not

---

97c–99c, *Laws* 967b, and Aristotle, *Metaphysics* I, 4, 985a18, confess that he dashes their hopes in not making enough use of mind as the cause of what happens.

[f]Avicenna, *Metaphysics* IX, 4; cf I, 7. The first intelligence is not the divine act of understanding, but a reflection of it, and so itself a creature. For the subsequent causation things, cf above Ia. 45, 5.

In the background lies Avicenna's distinction between the 'ideality' of essence and the 'factuality' of existence, cf Appendix I.

'The soul of the heavens', a cosmological conception of Arabic Aristoteleans, doubted but not expressly contradicted by St Thomas.

rerum, sed ex concursu multarum causarum agentium. Tale autem dicimus provenire a casu. Sic igitur complementum universi, quod in diversitate rerum consistit, esset a casu; quod est impossibile.

Unde dicendum est quod distinctio rerum et multitudo est ex intentione primi agentis, quod est Deus. Produxit enim res in esse propter suam bonitatem communicandam creaturis, et per eas repræsentandam. Et quia per unam creaturam sufficienter repræsentari non potest, produxit multas creaturas et diversas, ut quod deest uni ad repræsentandam divinam bonitatem suppleatur ex alia; nam bonitas, quæ in Deo est simpliciter et uniformiter, in creaturis est multipliciter et divisim. Unde perfectius participat divinam bonitatem et repræsentat eam totum universum quam alia quæcumque creatura.

Et quia ex divina sapientia est causa distinctionis rerum, ideo Moyses dicit res esse distinctas verbo Dei, quod est conceptio sapientiæ. Et hoc est quod dicit *Gen., Dixit Deus, Fiat lux. Et divisit lucem a tenebris.*[9]

1. Ad primum ergo dicendum quod agens per naturam agit per formam per quam est, quæ unius tantum est una; et ideo non agit nisi unum. Agens autem voluntarium, quale est Deus, ut supra ostensum est,[10] agit per formam intellectam. Cum igitur Deum multa intelligere non repugnet unitati et simplicitati ipsius, ut supra ostensum est,[11] relinquitur quod, licet sit unus, possit multa facere.

2. Ad secundum dicendum quod ratio illa teneret de exemplato quod perfecte repræsentat exemplar, quod non multiplicatur nisi materialiter. Unde imago increata quæ est perfecta est una tantum. Sed nulla creatura repræsentat perfecte exemplar primum, quod est divina essentia. Et ideo potest per multa repræsentari. Et tamen, secundum quod ideæ dicuntur exemplaria, pluralitati rerum correspondet in mente divina pluralitas idearum.

3. Ad tertium dicendum quod in speculativis medium demonstrationis quod perfecte demonstrat conclusionem, est unum tantum; sed media

---

[9] *Genesis* 1, 3–4
[10] 1a. 19, 4
[11] 1a. 15, 2
g *Uniformis*: strictly speaking God has not a form; the word here signifies the absence of division within the divine being and the complete identity of all there.
h That is, for our point of view; God still infinitely transcends the whole. The reflection comes from St Albert.
i *And God said, and it was done.* The stress on his spoken word has an old history in exegesis. cf Theophilus, PG 6, 1069, 1602. Theodoret, PG 80, 89. The general view is that the word is metaphorical. Thus St Basil, PG 29, 45. St Gregory of Nyssa, 'the word is his work'. PG 49, 72. For created in the Word, see 1a. 34, 3.
j A natural agent has one form, an intelligent agent many; cf 1a. 14, 1; 18, 3; 19,

from the plan of the first cause, and was, in other words, the result of chance. The world's abundance, composed of variety, would be a random effect. And this makes no sense.

Instead we should state that distinctiveness and plurality of things is because the first agent, who is God, intended them. For he brought things into existence so that his goodness might be communicated to creatures and re-enacted through them. And because one single creature was not enough, he produced many and diverse, so that what was wanting in one expression of the divine goodness might be supplied by another, for goodness, which in God is single and all together,[g] in creatures is multiple and scattered. Hence the whole universe less incompletely than one alone shares and represents his goodness.[h]

And because divine wisdom is the cause of variety in things, Moses tells us of God's word—the Word indeed which is the concept of his wisdom; *God said,*[1] *Be light made, and he divided the light from the darkness.*[9]

Hence: 1. A merely natural agent operates through the form by which it is what it is, and for each thing this is one; which is why it produces but one sort of thing. Whereas a voluntary agent which acts through will, and God is such as we have seen,[10] acts through a form as held in the mind. Since, therefore, it is not against God's singleness and simplicity that he should understand many things, as we have also seen,[11] the truth remains that although he is the One he can also make the many.[j]

2. The objection is valid of a full copy of its exemplar; multiplication in that case is only by numerical repetition. Hence the uncreated Image, the full image of God, is single.[k] No single creature, however, is a complete reproduction of the first exemplar, which is the divine essence, though a multitude of things is less inadequate. Note, nevertheless, that if you take ideas as exemplars, then the plurality of things corresponds to a plurality of ideas in the divine mind.[l]

3. In matters of theory, the middle term of a strict proof through which a conclusion is drawn with certainty is single;[m] when we are showing the

---

1 & 2; 75, 2. The degrees of life and knowledge defined by a widening comprehension of forms.

A voluntary agent, one acting through knowledge and specifically with intelligence, 1a2æ. 6, 1 & 2. Acting through will is not necessarily acting through freewill, 1a2æ. 13, 1–3. Yet God's creative activity is free, both as regards acting or not acting (*quoad exercitium*) and as regards acting for this or for that (*quoad specificationem*); 1a2æ. 9, 1. God is not bound to choose what is best, cf 1a. 25, 6: the general view of the Scholastics, with the exception of Durandus and Scotus.

[k]The uncreated Image: cf 1a. 35, 2.

[l]Plurality of divine ideas, cf 1a. 14, 7; 15, 2. Exemplars, 1a. 44, 3.

[m]That is in *a priori* demonstration.

probabilia sunt multa. Et similiter in operativis quando id quod est ad finem adæquat, ut ita dixerim, finem non requiritur quod sit nisi unum tantum. Sed creatura non sic se habet ad finem qui est Deus. Unde oportuit creaturas multiplicari.

articulus 2. utrum inæqualitas rerum sit a Deo

AD SECUNDUM sic proceditur:[1] 1. Videtur quod inæqualitas rerum non sit a Deo. Optimi enim est optima adducere. Sed inter optima unum non est majus altero. Ergo Dei, qui est optimus, est omnia æqualia facere.

2. Præterea, æqualitas est effectus unitatis, ut dicitur in *Meta.*[2] Sed Deus est unus. Ergo fecit omnia æqualia.

3. Præterea, justitiæ est inæqualia inæqualibus dare. Sed Deus est iustus in omnibus operibus suis. Cum ergo operationi ejus qua esse rebus communicat non præsupponatur aliqua inæqualitas rerum, videtur quod fecerat omnia æqualia.

SED CONTRA est quod dicitur *Eccl.*,[3] *Quare dies diem superat, et iterum lux lucem, et annus annum, sol solem?** *A Domini scientia separata sunt.*

RESPONSIO: Dicendum quod Origenes, volens excludere positionem ponentium distinctionem in rebus ex contrarietate principiorum boni et mali, posuit a Deo a principio omnia creata esse æqualia. Dicit enim quod Deus primo creavit creaturas rationales tantum, et omnes æquales; in quibus primo exorta est inæqualitas ex libero arbitrio, quibusdam conversis in Deum secundum magis et minus, quibusdam etiam secundum magis et minus a Deo aversis. Illæ igitur rationales creaturæ quæ ad Deum per liberum arbitrium conversæ sunt promotæ sunt ad diversos ordines angelorum, pro diversitate meritorum. Illæ autem quæ aversæ sunt a Deo sunt corporibus alligatæ diversis, secundum diversitatem peccati, et hanc causam dicit esse creationis et diversitatis corporum.

Sed secundum hoc, universitas corporalium creaturarum non esset propter bonitatem Dei communicandam creaturis, sed ad puniendum peccatum. Quod est contra illud quod dicitur *Gen.*,[4] *Vidit Deus cuncta quæ*

---

*Vulgate: *et annus annum a sole*
[1]cf 1a. 65, 2. *CG* II, 44 & 45. *De potentia* III, 16. *De anima* 7. *Compend. theol.* 73. 102. *In De div, nom.* 4, *lect.* 16
[2]*Metaphysics* IV, 15. 1021a9–14
[3]*Ecclesiasticus* 33, 7–8
[4]*Genesis* I, 31

probabilities, however, it can be manifold.[n] So also in practical matters, when an object chosen for the sake of an end squares exactly, if I may put it so, with that end then another is not required. No one creature, however, matches the end which is God. Better, therefore, to have many of them.

article 2. is the inequality of things from God?

THE SECOND POINT:[1] 1. It would not seem so.[a] For the best comes from the best. Of the best one is not better than another. Therefore you expect God, who is best, to make all things equal.

2. Moreover, according to the *Metaphysics*,[2] equality is an effect of unity. But God is one. Hence he has made all things equal.

3. Furthermore, giving unequally is just when it is to non-equals. And God is just in all his works. Since his giving them existence presupposes no antecedent inequality in things it would seem that he has made them all equal.[b]

ON THE OTHER HAND there is *Ecclesiasticus* saying, *Why doth one day excel another, and one light another, and one year another year, one sun another sun? By the knowledge of the Lord they were distinguished.*[3]

REPLY: Meaning to attack those who held that distinction in things came from the contrary principles of good and evil, Origen took up the position that God created all things equal in the beginning, only rational creatures at first, all of them equal, and that inequality arose from their free choice, some turning to God, some more, some less, others turning away from him, some more, some less. Those who accepted God were lifted up to the various ranks of the angels according to their degree of merit. While those who refused him were bound to different bodies according to degree of fault. This, he said, was the cause why bodies were made and diversified.[c]

Were this true then the punishment of sin, not the imparting of God's goodness to creatures, would have been the purpose of the corporeal universe. This goes against Scripture, where we read, *God saw all the things that he had made, and they were very good.*[4] And, as St Augustine

---

[n]As in argument from a convergence of probabilities.
[a]Inequality: a notion drawn from quantity and applied by analogy.
[b]An objection to predestination is presented in the same form, 1a. 23, 5 obj. 3.
[c]*Peri Archon* I, 6 & 8; II, 9. PG 11, 166, 178, 229.

fecerat, et erant valde bona. Et ut Augustinus dicit,[5] *Quid stultius dici potest, quam istum solem, ut in uno mundo unus esset, non decori pulchritudinis, vel saluti rerum corporalium consuluisse artificem Deum; sed hoc potius evenisse, quia una anima sic peccaverat? Ac per hoc, si centum animæ peccassent, centum soles haberet hic mundus.*

Et ideo dicendum quod, sicut sapientia Dei est causa distinctionis rerum, ita et inæqualitatis. Quod sic patet. Duplex enim distinctio invenitur in rebus: una formalis, in his quæ different specie; alia vero materialis, in his quæ differunt numero tantum. Cum autem materia sit propter formam, distinctio materialis est propter formalem. Unde videmus quod in rebus incorruptibilibus non est nisi unum individuum unius speciei, quia species sufficienter conservatur in uno; in generabilibus autem et corruptibilibus, sunt multa individua unius speciei, ad conservationem speciei. Ex quo patet quod principalior est distinctio formalis quam materialis.

Distinctio autem formalis semper requirit inæqualitatem, quia, ut dicitur in *Meta.*,[6] formæ rerum sunt sicut numeri, in quibus species variantur per additionem vel subtractionem unitatis. Unde in rebus naturalibus gradatim species ordinatæ esse videntur; sicut mixta perfectiora sunt elementis, et plantæ corporibus mineralibus, et animalia plantis, et homines aliis animalibus; et in singulis horum una species perfectior aliis invenitur.

Sicut ergo divina sapientia causa est distinctionis rerum propter perfectionem universi, ita et inæqualitatis. Non enim esset perfectum universum si tantum unus gradus bonitatis inveniretur in rebus.

1. Ad primum ergo dicendum quod optimi agentis est producere totum effectum suum optimum; non tamen quod quamlibet partem totius faciat optimam simpliciter, sed optimam secundum proportionem ad totum: tolleretur enim bonitas animalis si quælibet pars eius oculi haberet dignitatem. Sic igitur et Deus totum universum constituit optimum secundum modum creaturæ, non autem singulas creaturas, sed unam alia meliorem. Et ideo de singulis creaturis dicitur Gen., *Vidit Deus lucem quod esset bona,*[7] et similiter de singulis; sed de omnibus simul dicitur, *Vidit Deus cuncta quæ fecerat, et erant valde bona.*[8]

---

[5]*De civitate Dei* XI, 23. PL 41, 337   [6]*Metaphysics* VII, 3. 1043b34
[7]*Genesis* 1, 4   [8]ibid 1, 31
[d]St Thomas's theology is profoundly against the notion of the soul being imprisoned in the body. Matter is an essential part of us, by God's doing, not our fault.
[e]On the application of numerical terms even to things without quantity, cf Ia. 30, 3. Vol. 6.
[f]cf Ia. 50, 4. This is a supplementary argument from purpose: the root reason is that in spiritual beings the principle of personality can lie only in the form, whereas in material beings quantified matter supplies a principle of individuation; 3a. 77, 2.
[g]Formal distinctness necessarily implies an inequality, for forms which as such

asks, *What could be more nonsensical that God the artist provided this one sun to this one world, not for the light of its beauty, nor for the benefit of bodily things, but rather because one soul had happened to sin? As though a hundred suns would have risen had a hundred souls sinned.*[5]

Hence it is to be said that God's wisdom is the cause of inequality, as it is of distinction.[d] An explanation goes as follows. There is a double distinction in things, one formal, between things different in kind, the other material, between things different only merely numerically.[e] Now since matter is for the sake of form, distinction by number subserves that by form. Among immortal things we see but one individual to a species, one being enough to perpetuate the species, whereas among things that are generated and decay there are many individuals of the same species in order to keep it going.[f] This shows that formal distinction is more capital than material distinction.

Now distinction of form always requires inequality, for, to quote the *Metaphysics*,[6] forms of things are like numbers, which vary by addition or subtraction of units.[g] So among the things of nature an ordered scale is observed; compounds are higher than elements, plants than minerals, animals than plants, and men than other animals, and under each of these headings we find one species more perfect than others.[h]

Consequently divine wisdom causes the distinction and inequality of things for the perfection of the universe, which would be lacking were it to display but one level of goodness.[i]

Hence: 1. Is it for the best cause to produce the best effect? Taken as a whole and in proportion to the whole, yes. Taken in isolation, no. For what good would it be for an animal were every organ to be an eye with the special excellence of sight? To extend the analogy, we may grant that God made the whole universe the best that a created system could be, not, however, that each single creature is superlative, for there are comparatives, and one is better than another. Of one particular thing it is written, *And God saw the light that it was good,*[7j] and the same may be said of each other in particular; but of all together it is written, *God saw all the things he had made, and they were very good.*[8k]

---

express different natures are themselves unequal. Only when they are embodied in matter can they be repeated numerically and constitute things of equal nature—political egalitarianism is not a necessary consequence. But cf 1a. 42, 1.

[h]cf 1a. 23, 5 ad 3.

[i]It is not that God has necessarily willed the unequal finiteness of things, but that from this arises the perfection of the universe and the showing forth of divine goodness.

[j]Is all for the best in the best of all possible worlds? cf 1a. 25, 6.

[k]A characteristic piece of medieval exegesis. cf 1a. 22, 2 ad 2, on Providence.

2. Ad secundum dicendum quod primum quod procedit ab unitate est æqualitas, et deinde procedit multiplicitas. Et ideo a Patre, cui, secundum Augustinum,[9] appropriatur unitas, processit Filius, cui appropriatur æqualitas, et deinde creatura, cui competit inæqualitas. Sed tamen etiam a creaturis participatur quædam æqualitas, scilicet proportionis.

3. Ad tertium dicendum quod ratio illa est quæ movet Origenem,[10] sed non habet locum nisi in retributione præmiorum, quorum inæqualitas debetur inæqualibus meritis. Sed in constitutione rerum non est inæqualitas partium per quamcumque inæqualitatem præcedentem, vel meritorum vel etiam dispositionis materiæ, sed propter perfectionem totius. Ut patet etiam in operibus artis; non enim propter hoc differt tectum a fundamento quia habet diversam materiam, sed ut sit domus perfecta ex diversis partibus, quærit artifex diversam materiam, et faceret eam, si posset.

articulus 3. utrum sit unus mundus tantum

AD TERTIUM sic proceditur.[1] 1. Videtur quod non sit unus mundus tantum, sed plures. Quia, ut Augustinus dicit,[2] inconveniens est dicere quod Deus sine ratione creavit. Sed ea ratione qua creavit unum poterit creare multos; cum ejus potentia non sit limitata ad unius mundi creationem, sed est infinita, ut supra ostensum est.[3] Ergo Deus plures mundos produxit.

2. Præterea, natura facit quod melius est, et multo magis Deus. Sed melius esset esse plures mundos quam unum, quia plura bona paucioribus meliora sunt. Ergo plures mundi facti sunt a Deo.

3. Præterea, omne quod habet formam in materia potest multiplicari secundum numerum, manente eadem specie; quia multiplicatio secundum numerum est ex materia. Sed mundus habet formam in materia; sicut enim cum dico 'homo' significo formam, cum autem dico 'hic homo' significo formam in materia; ita cum dicitur 'mundus' significatur forma, cum autem dicitur 'hic mundus', significatur forma in materia. Ergo nihil prohibet esse plures mundos.

---

[9]De doctrina Christiana I, 5. PL 34, 21
[10]Peri Archon I, 6. PG 11, 166
[1]cf De potentia III, 16 ad 1. In Meta. XII, lect. 10. De cælo I, 16–20
[2]Lib. 83 quæst. 46. PL 40, 30
[3]1a. 25, 2
[1]cf 1a. 42, 4.
[m]The One and the Many; cf 1a. 11, 2.
[n]cf 1a. 6, 3 & 4; 13, 5 & 6.
[a]The Cassino Codex inserts here an additional article, given in Appendix 3.

2. The first to originate from the One is the Equal, multiplicity comes afterwards. Therefore, from the Father, to whom St Augustine especially ascribes unity,[9] the Son proceeds, who is similarly characterized by equality,[1] and thereafter creatures shot with inequality throughout.[m] All the same, they do share in a certain likeness to God, namely by a correspondence proportionate to their purpose.[n]

3. This is the argument that influenced Origen;[10] it is, however, relevant only to the granting of rewards, where inequality is justified by differences of merit, not to the constitution of things; there inequalities arise in order to achieve the perfection of the whole, not because of any preceding inequality either of merits or even of material dispositions. You see this in works of art, for instance the difference between the roof and the foundations of a building does not lie in the materials they are made of, but arises from the purpose, namely a house complete of all its parts; it is in order to achieve this that the builder procures different materials, and would make them if he could.

article 3. *is there only one world?*

THE THIRD POINT:[1a] 1. It seems there are several, not only one.[b] According to St Augustine it is improper to say that God has created things without a reason.[2] For the same reason that he created one he could create many, since his power is infinite, as already acknowledged,[3] and remains unspent after the creation of one world. Therefore he produced several.

2. Further, if nature works for the best, much more does God. Better, it will be admitted, for there to be more worlds than one alone; many good things are better than few. Therefore many worlds were made by God.

3. Again, a thing having a form embodied in matter can be numerically repeated without varying the species, for such multiplication is rooted in matter. But the world has form with matter;[c] when I say 'man' I signify form, whereas when I say 'this man' I signify the form in matter. Well then, when we speak of 'world' the form is signified, and when of 'this world' then form with matter. There is nothing then against the existence of many worlds.

---

[b]One world, that is universe or cosmos, the whole of creation, not just our earth, or heliocentric system. The article imposes no fixed limit on the size or number of created systems, but argues that all enter into one divine order. The thought is theological or theocentric.

[c]The form of the world; not one substantial form, but a design or pattern of many things. Note *e* below.

SED CONTRA est quod dicitur *Ioann.*,⁴ *Mundus per ipsum factus est*; ubi singulariter mundum nominavit, quasi uno solo mundo existente.

RESPONSIO: Dicendum quod ipse ordo in rebus sic a Deo creatis existens unitatem mundi manifestat. Mundus enim iste unus dicitur unitate ordinis, secundum quod quædam ad alia ordinantur. Quæcumque autem a Deo sunt, ordinem habent ad* invicem et ad ipsum Deum, ut supra ostensum est.⁵ Unde necesse est quod omnia ad unum mundum pertineant. Et ideo illi potuerunt ponere plures mundos qui causam mundi non posuerunt aliquam sapientiam ordinantem, sed casum; ut Democritus, qui dixit ex concursu atomorum esse hunc mundum et alios infinitos.

1. Ad primum ergo dicendum quod hæc ratio est quare mundus est unus, quia debent omnia esse ordinata uno ordine, et ad unum. Propter quod Aristoteles in *Meta.*⁶ ex unitate ordinis in rebus existentis concludit unitatem Dei gubernantis. Et Plato ex unitate exemplaris probat unitatem mundi, quasi exemplati.

2. Ad secundum dicendum quod nullum agens intendit pluralitatem materialem ut finem; quia materialis multitudo non habet certum terminum, sed de se tendit in infinitum; infinitum autem repugnat rationi finis. Cum autem dicitur plures mundos esse meliores quam unum, hoc dicitur secundum multitudinem materialem. Tale autem melius non est

---

*Piana: *ab*, from
⁴*John* 1, 10
⁵1a. 11, 3; 21, 1 ad 3
⁶*Metaphysics* XI, 10. 1076a3. St Thomas, *lect.* 12
ᵈForcing the text? Perhaps as it stands, but not in the light of the explanation St Thomas is going to give. cf Westcott, additional notes on *John* 1, 10, in Rashdall. *DB* IV, 938.
ᵉOrder: the word has since acquired a juridical sense in theology, and can be somewhat flatly conceived. Yet the word has its roots in the notion of striving upwards; cf *orior*. See above 1a. 45, 7.
ᶠ*Unitas ordinis*. This engages the notion of a whole, somehow containing a plurality of parts (1a. 76, 8). Leaving aside logical wholes, formed when the mind brackets different objects together, real wholes are divided into substantial and accidental wholes. The first are single things, which may be composed of essential, integral, or functional parts: there is no question of St Thomas regarding the world as one organism in this sense. An accidental whole, so called, but somewhat misleadingly, because it is a group of distinct things or substance in an arrangement or pattern, or relationship (which is an *accidens*), may be a chance aggregation (thus the winners of a lottery or the survivors of an air-disaster), or an artificial assembly of parts (thus a machine), or a combination of things coming together of their nature (thus a family or a political community). cf *In Ethic.* I, *lect.* I. It is in this last sense that

ON THE OTHER HAND the prologue to St John states, *The world was made by him*,[4] speaking in the singular, as much as to suggest that there is only one world.[d]

REPLY: The reigning order in things established by God's creation manifests the unity of the cosmos.[e] This is because of the single plan ordering some things to others.[f] For all things coming from God have a relation to one another and to him, as we have already shown.[5g] Hence all must belong to the same cosmos. In fact those only have been able to propose a plurality of worlds for whom the cause of the world is chance, not governing wisdom; thus Democritus who taught that this world and an infinity of others happened from the clash of atoms.[h]

Hence: 1. The objection provides the reason why the world is one, namely that things should be ranked together in one order and trained to one end. Indeed it is from the planned unity of order that Aristotle[6] infers that God who rules them is one. And Plato proves the unity of the world from unity of the exemplar after which it is fashioned.[i]

2. No agent intends material plurality as a goal,[j] for a numerical multitude has no fixed limit, since its trend is towards indefinite repetition, and to be indefinite is just what an end is not.[k] The claim that many worlds are better than one is obsessed by the value of mere numbers. Such a best is not in the intention of God the maker. Indeed if we adopt this mood of

---

the universe is regarded as forming one whole. For the mystical body of the Church see 3a. 8, 1.

The argument is eased if the singleness of the world be taken theologically, that is by reference to one governing Wisdom. It would find no difficulty in the co-existence of several particular systems apparently unrelated from a merely physical point of view, though this, as appears from ad 3, is not congenial to the cosmology St Thomas adopts.

[g]Internal and external finality, cf 1a. 65, 2. Also 1a. 2, 3, Vol. 2.

[h]St Thomas's sources for Democritus, Aristotle, *De cælo* III, 4. 303a4; *Physics* III, 4. 203b30. *lect.* 7. VIII, 1. 250b14. *lect.* 1. Cicero, *De natura deorum* I, 26. St Ambrose, *Hexaëmeron* I, 1. PL 14, 135.

[i]Is a vicious circle present in proving the unity of God from the unity of the world (1a. 11, 3) and the unity of the world from the unity of God? It is broken by other proofs for God's unity; the one given is addressed only to those who accept the unity of the world. Moreover, once a position has been established, one can argue up and down from it by *a priori* or *a posteriori* deduction to suit the occasion. The appeal to Plato (*Timæus* 31a), however, is more in line with the present article than that to Aristotle (*In De cælo* I, *lect.* 19).

[j]Except in mass-production for profit. The avarice for artificial ends, such as money, is insatiable and unchecked by the limits set by nature. 2a2æ. 118, 2, 5 & 8.

[k]An end, *finis*, is definite.

de intentione Dei agentis, quia eadem ratione dici posset quod si fecisset duos, melius esset quod essent tres, et sic in infinitum.

3. Ad tertium dicendum quod mundus constat ex sua tota materia. Non enim est possibile aliam terram quam istam, quia omnis terra ferretur naturaliter ad hoc medium, ubicumque esset. Et eadem ratio est de aliis corporibus quæ sunt partes mundi.

---

[1]The reply is considering God's *potentia ordinata*, Ia. 25, 5 ad 1. An indefinite numerical repetition is not clearly impossible in itself, cf above Ia. 46, 1 & 2.

looking at things we might argue that had he made two worlds it would have been better had he made three, and so forth indefinitely.[1]

3. The universe stands on the whole of its matter. For there to be an another earth than this one is not possible, for each earth would naturally gravitate towards the same centre, wherever it was. The same applies to other bodies which are parts of the world.[m]

---

[m]The geocentric reference is no longer a commendation of the position St Thomas is defending. Essentially it is that all matter is comprised in God's present actual order of things, whether they be earth-directed or not. cf 1a. 66, 2.

DEINDE CONSIDERANDUM EST de distinctione rerum in speciali. Et primo de distinctione boni et mali; deinde de distinctione spiritualis et corporalis creaturæ. Circa primum quærendum est

> de malo,
> et de causa mali.

Quæstio 48. de malo

Circa malum quæruntur sex:

1. utrum malum sit natura aliqua;
2. utrum malum inveniatur in rebus;
3. utrum bonum sit subjectum mali;
4. utrum malum totaliter corrumpat bonum;
5. de divisione mali per pœnam et culpam;
6. quid habeat plus de ratione mali, utrum pœna vel culpa.

articulus 1. utrum malum sit natura quædam

AD PRIMUM sic proceditur.[1] 1. Videtur quod malum sit natura quædam. Quia omne genus est natura quædam. Sed malum est quoddam genus; dicitur in *Prædicamentis*[2] quod *bonum et malum non sunt in genere, sed sunt genera aliorum*. Ergo malum est natura quædam.

2. Præterea, omnis differentia constitutiva alicuius speciei est natura quædam. Malum autem est differentia constitutiva in moralibus; differt enim specie malus habitus a bono, ut liberalitas ab illiberalitate. Ergo malum significat naturam quamdam.

3. Præterea, utrumque contrariorum est natura quædam. Sed malum et bonum non opponuntur ut privatio et habitus, sed ut contraria, ut probat

---

[1]cf II *Sent.* 34, 2. *CG* III, 7, 8 & 9. *In De div. nom.* 4, lect. 14. *De malo* I, 1. *Compend. theol.* 115   [2]*Categoriæ* 11. 14a23
[a]Vols 9-15.
[b]*Pœna*: pain, or penalization, but see below, art. 5.
[c]*Natura quædam*, a being of real nature, as goodness is.
[d]*Genus*: here taken broadly as a general type of existing, as in *genus humanum*, not narrowly as one of the five manners as of predicating, as when 'generic' is contrasted with 'specific' or 'differential' or 'proper' or 'incidental'.
[e]cf 1a2æ. 18, 1 & 2. Vol. 18.
[f]Privation, a key-term. It is not the simple negation of a good, but the absence of one that could and should be present, often, but not necessarily according to a

NEXT WE HAVE TO CONSIDER the distinction of things in particular. And first that between good and evil, next that between spiritual and bodily creatures.[a] So we begin by investigating

> evil (48),
> and the cause of evil (49).

Question 48. evil

Here there are six points of inquiry:

1. whether evil be a sort of reality;
2. whether it be found in things;
3. whether it be seated in good;
4. whether evil destroys good entirely;
5. the division of evil between penalty[b] and fault;
6. which of the two is the worse?

article 1. is evil some sort of reality?

THE FIRST POINT:[1] 1. Apparently evil is positively real.[c] For every genus is that, and evil is a sort of genus;[d] it is stated in the *Categories* that *good and evil are not in a genus, but are genera for other things*.[2] Therefore evil is a sort of reality

2. Moreover, every difference that serves to constitute a kind of thing is itself of the nature of reality. Evil does this in the field of morals, for a vice is specifically different from a virtue, like avarice from open-handedness.[e] Therefore evil does signify some kind of reality.

3. Besides, of two contraries each is real. Now evil is not contrasted with good as a privation to a possession, but as its contrary;[f] Aristotle shows

---

moral judgment. The discussions that follow involve the logic of opposition. Strict opposites are what cannot co-exist in the same thing in the same way at the same times. The opposition may be of contradictories, namely of a positive and its flat negation, good and not-good; this allows of no half-way position. Or the opposition may be between the having and the suffering deprivation, this last affecting a subject that should possess the quality in question, thus seeing and blind; this allows of an intermediate term, namely non-seeing; yet we do not say that a stone is blind in any privative sense. Or the opposition may be of contraries, namely of two positives each of which excludes the other, thus red and blue, presumption and despair; this allows of intermediate conditions. On relative opposites, e.g. father and son, we need not delay, for the discussion on good and evil will revolve round the second and third type of opposition. cf *Categoriæ* 10–11. 11b15–14a25.

Philosophus, in *Prædicamentis*,[3] per hoc quod inter bonum et malum est aliquid medium, et a malo potest fieri reditus ad bonum. Ergo malum significat naturam quamdam. 4. Præterea, quod non est non agit. Sed malum agit, quia corrumpit bonum. Ergo malum est quoddam ens et natura quædam. 5. Præterea, ad perfectionem universitatis rerum non pertinet nisi quod est ens et natura quædam. Sed malum pertinet ad perfectionem universitatis rerum; dicit enim Augustinus[4] quod *ex omnibus consistit universitatis admirabilis pulchritudo, in qua etiam illud quod malum dicitur, bene ordinatum, et suo loco positum, eminentius commendat bona.* Ergo malum est natura quædam.

SED CONTRA est quod Dionysius dicit,[5] *Malum non est existens neque bonum.*

RESPONSIO: Dicendum quod unum oppositorum cognoscitur per alterum, sicut per lucem tenebræ. Unde et quid sit malum oportet ex ratione boni accipere. Diximus autem supra[6] quod bonum est omne id quod est appetibile: et sic cum omnis natura appetat suum esse et suam perfectionem, necesse est dicere quod esse et perfectio cujuscumque naturæ rationem habeat bonitatis. Unde non potest esse quod malum significet quoddam esse, aut quamdam formam seu naturam. Relinquitur ergo quod nomine mali significetur quædam absentia boni. Et pro tanto dicitur quod malum neque est existens nec bonum; quia cum ens inquantum hujusmodi sit bonum, eadem est remotio utrorumque.

I. Ad primum ergo dicendum quod Aristoteles ibi loquitur secundum opinionem Pythagoricorum, qui malum existimabant esse naturam quandam, et ideo ponebant bonum et malum genera. Consuevit enim Aristoteles, et præcipue in libris logicalibus, ponere exempla quæ probabilia erant suo tempore secundum opinionem aliquorum philosophorum.

Vel dicendum, sicut dicit Philosophus in *Meta.*,[7] quod *prima contrarietas*

---

[3]*Categoriæ* 10. 12a22, 13a15   [4]*Enchiridion* 10. PL 40, 236.
[5]*De divinis nominibus* 4. PG 3, 717. St Thomas, *lect.* 16   [6]Ia. 5, 1
[7]*Metaphysics* IX, 4. 1055a33. *lect.* 6
[g]A nature, that is a source of motion.
[h]The good: a term at once defined and flexible. Since any language is committed, at least in its prose, to a space of shared human experience more confined than that of metaphysical and theological truth, its use as a Predicate is admittedly imprecise according to any one particular system of reference. So also its opposite term, the 'bad'. St Thomas is not daunted, and by his method of analogy is ready to work with 'benign ambiguity' or 'designed equivocation'. The alternatives are a nominalism which can do little more than co-ordinate points of experience in a working plan, though in themselves they are quite disparate, or an ultra-realism which treats

this from the fact that an intermediate position lies between them, and that from evil there can be a return to good.[3] Evil, therefore, means something real.

4. Again, what does not exist does not act. But evil indeed acts, for it destroys good. Hence evil is a being of real nature.[g]

5. Further, only what is real goes to make up the perfection of the universe of things. Yet evil does contribute to this; St Augustine says that *the admirable beauty of the universe is composed of all things; there even what is called evil, well-balanced and in its place, serves to enhance the good.*[4] Hence evil has some sort of real nature.

ON THE OTHER HAND Dionysius writes, *Evil is neither an existent nor a good.*[5]

REPLY: Like night from day, you learn about one opposite from the other. So you take good in order to grasp what evil means.[h] Now we have accepted the definition that good is everything that is desirable.[6] Well then, since each real thing tends to its own existence and completion, we have to say that this fulfils the meaning of good in every case. Therefore evil cannot signify a certain existing being, or a real shaping or positive kind of thing. Consequently, we are left to infer that it signifies a certain absence of a good.[i] That is why Dionysius calls it neither an existent nor a good, for since being as such is good, the taking away of the one or of the other amounts to the same.

Hence: 1. Aristotle is speaking in the style of the Pythagoreans in this passage; they thought of evil as having a real nature, and accordingly proposed that good and evil were classes of things.[j] He was wont, especially in his works on logic, to lay out samples of the opinions of other philosophers current in his day.

Or you might answer quoting from his *Metaphysics*[7] that the positive condition of possessing and the privative condition of lacking a form is the basic

---

universal ideas as subsisting things, and which may well end by treating their exemplifications as virtually univocal.

[i]The argument is treating evil in most general terms as opposed to *bonum transcendentale*. This, properly speaking, is not *malum simpliciter*. For, as will appear, evil is always *secundum quid*, that is, defined by reference to a subject as the absence of a good which is due; CG III, 6. And caused by a good out of place. The *malum metaphysicum* of Leibniz is not entertained by St Thomas; though the existence of created things is brought forth from the divine existence according to a deficient assimilation, *In De div. nom.* 1, lect. 1, and they come forth by a kind of descent, CG IV, 7, the condition of creatureliness is not considered as an evil nor its production as a lapse.

[j]The Pythagorean pairs, thus good-evil, day-night, even-odd, straight-crooked, sweet-bitter, male-female, etc. cf *Metaphysics* I, 5. 986a33.

est habitus et privatio, quia scilicet in omnibus contrariis salvatur, cum semper unum contrariorum sit imperfectum respectu alterius, ut nigrum respectu albi, et amarum respectu dulcis. Et pro tanto bonum et malum dicuntur genera, non simpliciter, sed contrariorum; quia sicut omnis forma habet rationem boni ita omnis privatio, inquantum hujusmodi, habet rationem mali.

2. Ad secundum dicendum quod bonum et malum non sunt differentiæ constitutivæ nisi in moralibus, quæ recipiunt speciem* ex fine, qui est objectum voluntatis, a quo† moralia dependent. Et quia bonum habet rationem finis, ideo bonum et malum sunt differentiæ specificæ in moralibus; bonum per se, sed malum inquantum est remotio debiti finis.‡ Nec tamen remotio debiti finis constituit speciem in moralibus nisi secundum quod adjungitur fini indebito; sicut neque in naturalibus invenitur privatio formæ substantialis nisi adjuncta alteri formæ. Sic igitur malum quod est differentia constitutiva in moralibus, est quoddam bonum adjunctum privationi alterius boni; sicut finis intemperati est non quidem carere bono rationis, sed delectabile sensus absque ordine rationis. Unde malum, inquantum malum, non est differentia constitutiva, sed ratione boni adjuncti.

3. Et per hoc etiam patet responsio ad tertium. Nam ibi Philosophus loquitur de bono et malo secundum quod inveniuntur in moralibus. Sic enim inter bonum et malum invenitur medium; prout bonum dicitur quod est ordinatum, malum autem quod non solum est deordinatum, sed etiam nocivum alteri. Unde dicit Philosophus[8] quod *prodigus vanus quidem est, sed non malus.* Ab hoc etiam malo quod est secundum morem contingit fieri reditum ad bonum, non autem ex quocumque malo. Non enim ex cæcitate fit reditus ad visionem, cum tamen cæcitas sit quoddam malum.

4. Ad quartum dicendum quod aliquid agere dicitur tripliciter. Uno modo formaliter, eo modo loquendi quo dicitur albedo facere album. Et sic malum, etiam ratione ipsius privationis, dicitur corrumpere bonum,

---

*Piana: *species,* plural.
†Leonine: *a qua,* referring to the difference
‡Pègues and most mss: omit final clause
[8]*Ethics* IV, 1. 1121a25. St Thomas, *lect.* 4
[k]*Habitus, hexis* and *privatio, steresis.*
[l]1a2æ. 18, 4 & 5. Vol. 18, Appendices 10, 13 & 14. cf *Metaphysics* X, 4. 1055a33.
[m]Due end: the *debitum* in St Thomas's moral theology does not imply a categoric imperative, duty for duty's sake, but an imperative that is hypothetical, if the agent is to be fulfilled.
[n]The point is dealt with at greater length in the analysis of a sinful act; 1a2æ. 72, 75 & 76, Vol. 25.
[o]1a2æ. 72, 1.

contrast of contraries,[k] observed in every case since one is always found wanting in respect of the other, thus black or bitter with regard to white or sweet. To this extent good and evil are treated as belonging to the same generic class, not in themselves, but in the category of contrary opposition, for as every positive form carries the meaning of being a good, so the being deprived of it carries that of being an evil.

2. Good and evil are not constitutive differences except in the field of morals, where acts get their specific character from the end, the objective of will, on which morality depends.[1] Since good has the character of end, so is it that good and evil are specific differences for morality—good of itself, evil as setting aside the due end.[m] Yet this rejection of the proper purpose does not itself constitute a type of moral action except as conjoined to an undue attachment;[n] as indeed in nature we never find a thing deprived of one substantial form except because another is present. So then the evil which is a specific difference in morality is some good involving being deprived of another good: the end for an intemperate man, for example, is not to be devoid of that value which consists in acting intelligently, but to obtain the sensuously pleasurable outside the order of reason.[o] Hence evil is a differential constitutive, not for its own sake, but by reason of the good with which it is bound.[p]

3. The answer to the third objection works along the same lines. Aristotle is discussing, in the passage cited, good and bad in morals. There an intermediate condition is met with when good is taken for what is ordered, and evil for what is not only disordered but injurious to another as well. So Aristotle writes that to go to excess in giving *is not the mark of a wicked or ignoble man, but only of a foolish one.*[8q] Moreover there can be a return from moral evil to good,[r] but not from any sort of evil: blindness is a sort of evil, and it offers no way back to sight.[s]

4. A thing is said to act in three manners. First, in that of a formal cause, thus we speak of whiteness making a thing white. And so even by reason of the deprivation it denotes, evil is said to destroy good, for the decay

---

[p]Evil as emptiness is without meaning; but as a privation caused by the intrusion of a positive form, we look to this in order to define it, namely as a good out of place: thus a weed as bad can be described as a plant out of place. cf 1a2æ. 18, 5 ad 2; 54, 3 ad 2; 79. 2 ad 3.

[q]Aristotle, characteristically, treats moral evil largely in its social and political setting; a lack of virtue which does nobody any harm is not regarded as wicked. The Christian moralists, however, are more severe in applying a personal standard. cf 1a2æ. 18, 9 ad 2. Vol 18 of this series.

[r]The recognition of an intermediate position between the extremes of moral good and evil finds expression in the delicate examination of 'venial sin'. cf 1a2æ. 72, 5.

[s]On privation as a point of no return to the opposite 'possession', cf *In Meta.* x, *lect.* 5 & 6. Death is perhaps a better example than blindness.

quia est ipsa corruptio vel privatio boni. Alio modo dicitur aliquid agere effective, sicut pictor dicitur facere album parietem. Tertio modo per modum causæ finalis, sicut finis dicitur efficere movendo efficientem. His autem duobus modis malum non agit aliquid per se, idest secundum quod est privatio quædam, sed secundum quod ei bonum adjungitur; nam omnia actio est ab aliqua forma, et omne quod desideratur ut finis est perfectio aliqua. Et ideo, ut Dionysius dicit,[9] malum non agit neque desideratur nisi virtute boni adjuncti; per se autem est infinitum, et præter voluntatem et intentionem.

5. Ad quintum dicendum quod, sicut supra dictum est,[10] partes universi habent ordinem ad invicem secundum quod una agit in alteram, et est finis alterius et exemplar. Hæc autem, ut dictum est,[11] non possunt convenire malo nisi ratione boni adjuncti. Unde malum neque ad perfectionem universi pertinet, neque sub ordine universi concluditur, nisi per accidens, idest ratione boni adjuncti.

articulus 2. utrum malum inveniatur in rebus

AD SECUNDUM sic proceditur.[1] I. Videtur quod malum non inveniatur in rebus. Quidquid enim invenitur in rebus, vel est ens aliquod, vel privatio entis alicuius, quod est non ens. Sed Dionysius dicit[2] quod malum distat ab existente, et adhuc plus distat a non existente. Ergo malum nullo modo invenitur in rebus.

2. Præterea, ens et res convertuntur. Si ergo malum est ens in rebus, sequitur quod malum sit res quaedam. Quod est contra prædicta.[3]

3. Præterea, *albius est quod est nigro impermixtius*, ut dicitur in *Topic.* Aristotelis.[4] Ergo et melius est quod malo impermixtius. Sed Deus facit semper quod melius est, multo magis quam natura. Ergo in rebus a Deo conditis nihil malum invenitur.

SED CONTRA est quod secundum hoc removerentur omnes prohibitiones et pœnæ, quæ non sint nisi malorum.

---

[9] *De divinis nominibus* 4. PG 3, 717. St Thomas, *lect.* 22
[10] Ia. 2, 3; 19, 5; 21, 1 ad 3; 44, 3; 47, 3
[11] Reply to fourth objection
[1] cf Ia. 22, 2 ad 2. I *Sent.* 46, 3; II, 34, 1. *CG* III, 71. *De potentia* III, 6 ad 4. *Compend. theol.* 142. *In De div. nom.* 4, *lect.* 16
[2] *De divinis nominibus* 4. PG 3, 716. St Thomas, *lect.* 16
[3] art. I above
[4] *Topics* III, 5. 119a27

and privation of good is what indeed it is. Second, in that of an efficient cause, thus when a house-painter whitewashes a wall. And third, in that of a final cause, thus when an end is said to effect something by moving its efficient cause. In neither of these two last manners does evil do anything of itself, that is as a certain deprivation, but only because of the good that goes with it, for every action springs from a positive form and everything that is desired as an end is a completion of some sort.[t] Hence, as evil neither acts nor is desired save in virtue of an associated good, Dionysius concludes the passage by remarking that of itself it is without end and aside from will and intention.[9]

5. How the parts of the universe are co-ordinated among themselves has been brought out already;[10] one acts on another, and one is the purpose and pattern of another. An evil, as we have seen,[11] cannot perform these functions except by reason of an associated good. Hence evil belongs neither to the integrity of the universe nor serves its development, except incidentally because of an accompanying good.[u]

article 2. is evil found in things?

THE SECOND POINT:[1a] It would seem not, and for the following reason. Whatever is found in things is either some being or a privation of some being, that is a non-being. Now Dionysius says that evil is far from the existent and farther still from the non-existent.[2] It is not found in things then at all.

2. Again, 'being' and 'thing' are convertible terms. If evil then is a reality it follows that it is also a thing, which denies what has already been decided.[3]

3. Besides, as Aristotle remarks, *the whiter is that which is more unmixed with black.*[4] Therefore the better is that which is less mixed with the bad. Now God always makes what is better, much more than nature does. Therefore the things established by God hold no evil.

ON THE OTHER HAND on this assumption all prohibitions and punishments would be out of place, for they are concerned only with evils.

---

[t] Evil itself is indefinite and shapeless, *informatum*. On the unconnectedness of sins see 1a2æ. 73, 1.
[u] On evil as conspiring to the order of the universe, see above 1a. 19, 9, Vol. 5 of this series. Introduction.
[a] The discussion follows from art. 1, but, as will be seen, concentrates on suggesting why evil is in the world rather than on directly answering the inquiry. The article is not demonstrative. The inquiry, 'is it found', is for St Thomas often a preliminary to inductive argument.

RESPONSIO: Dicendum quod, sicut supra dictum est,[5] perfectio universi requirit inæqualitatem esse in rebus ut omnes bonitatis gradus impleantur. Est autem unus gradus bonitatis ut aliquid ita bonum sit quod nunquam deficere possit. Alius autem gradus bonitatis est ut sic aliquid bonum sit quod a bono deficere possit. Qui etiam gradus in ipso esse inveniuntur; quædam enim sunt quæ suum esse amittere non possunt, ut incorruptibilia; quædam vero sunt quæ amittere possunt, ut corruptibilia.* Sicut igitur perfectio universitatis rerum requirit ut non solum sint incorruptibilia, sed etiam corruptibilia, ita perfectio universi requirit ut sint quædam quæ a bonitate deficere possint, ad quod sequitur ea interdum deficere. In hoc autem consistit ratio mali, ut scilicet aliquid deficiat a bono. Unde manifestum est quod in rebus malum invenitur, sicut et corruptio; nam et ipsa corruptio malum quoddam est.

1. Ad primum ergo dicendum quod malum distat et ab ente simpliciter et non ente simpliciter, quia neque est sicut habitus neque sicut pura negatio, sed sicut privatio.

2. Ad secundum dicendum quod, sicut dicitur in *Meta.*,[6] ens dupliciter dicitur. Uno modo, secundum quod significat entitatem rei prout dividitur per decem prædicamenta, et sic convertitur cum re. Et hoc modo nulla privatio est ens, unde nec malum. Alio modo dicitur ens quod significat veritatem propositionis quæ in compositione consistit, cujus nota est hoc verbum 'est'; et hoc est ens quo respondetur ad quæstionem 'an est'. Et sic cæcitatem dicimus esse in oculo, vel quamcumque aliam privationem. Et hoc modo etiam malum dicitur ens. Propter hujus autem distinctionis ignorantiam aliqui, considerantes quod aliquæ res dicuntur malæ vel quod malum dicitur esse in rebus, crediderunt quod malum esset res quædam.

3. Ad tertium dicendum quod Deus et natura et quodcumque agens facit quod melius est in toto, sed non quod melius est in unaquaque parte, nisi per ordinem ad totum, ut supra dictum est.[7] Ipsum autem totum quod est universitas creaturarum, melius et perfectius est, si in eo sint quædam quæ a bono deficere possunt, quæ interdum deficiunt, Deo hoc non impediente. Tum quia providentiæ non est naturam destruere sed salvare, ut Dionysius dicit:[8] ipsa autem natura rerum hoc habet ut quæ deficere

---

*Piana & Leonine: *incorporalia . . . corporalia.* The text follows Pègues, a better reading since St Thomas thought the heavenly bodies were imperishable

[5]ıa. 47, 2
[6]*Metaphysics* IV, 7. 1017a22–34. *lect.* 3
[7]ıa.47, 2 ad 1
[8]*De divinis nominibus* 4. PG 3, 733. St Thomas, *lect.* 23
[b]*A posse ad esse non valet illatio*? Yet observe that the passage is not apodictic (cf

REPLY: We have already observed how the completeness of the universe requires inequality among things in order to achieve all degrees of goodness.[5] One degree is that a thing should be so good that it can never fall away, another that it should be good yet of such sort that its goodness can run out. These degrees run through the whole range of existence; for some cannot lose it, these are immortal substances, whereas others can, and these are mortal substances. The perfection of the universe requires them both; likewise some that can cease to be good, and in consequence on occasion do.[b] Such a defection from good is precisely what evil is. Clearly, then, evil is found in things just as decay is, which itself is a sort of evil.

Hence: 1. Evil is quite different from being and non-being pure and simple, for it is neither like having a form nor like simply not having it, but like being found wanting.[c]

2. As noted in the *Metaphysics*,[6] the word 'being' is used in two senses.[d] In the first to signify the entity of a thing, and so taken it is divided into the ten categories,[e] and is equivalent to what is real. And in this sense no privation is a being, and consequently no evil either. Second, to signify the truth of a proposition, a uniting of Subject and Predicate marked by the verb 'is'; this is the being that answers to the interrogative, 'is it?' In this sense can we speak of blindness being in the eye, and likewise of any other privation being in its subject. So also can evil be called a being. It was because they did not advert to this distinction, and were influenced by language which calls some objects bad and refers to evil existing in the world, that some have believed that evil was a positive reality.[f]

3. God and nature and any agent do what is better for the whole, and for each part as subserving the whole, yet not in isolation; this we have already pointed out.[7] That whole composed of the universe of creatures is the better and more complete for including some things which can and do on occasion fall from goodness without God preventing it.[g] First, because it befits Providence, as Dionysius reflects,[8] to respect nature, not destroy

---

ad 3), but merely reflecting on the facts. What a choked world it would be if *corruptibilia* never died away.
[c]Simple affirmation—being; simple negation—pure absence of being or nonentity; privation—a non-being in a subject in being caused by the presence of a being.
[d]cf 1a. 3, 4 ad 2. Appendix 1.
[e]Aristotle's ten categories or 'predicaments' of being, substance and the nine types of 'accident'. cf *In Meta.* v, *lect.* 9. *In Physic.* III, *lect.* 5.
[f]Manicheans, at least those so by feeling. 1a. 48, 1 ad 1; 49, 3.
[g]According to the natural cycle of *generatio* and *corruptio*, which should not be interfered with and upset.

possunt quandoque deficiant. Tum quia, ut dicit Augustinus,[9] Deus est adeo potens quod etiam potest bene facere de malis. Unde multa bona tollerentur si Deus nullum malum permitteret esse. Non enim generaretur ignis nisi corrumperetur aër; neque conservaretur vita leonis nisi occideretur asinus; neque etiam laudaretur justitia vindicans et patientia sufferens si non esset iniquitas.

articulus 3. *utrum malum sit in bono sicut in subjecto*

AD TERTIUM sic proceditur.[1] 1. Videtur quod malum non sit in bono sicut in subjecto. Omnia enim bona sunt existentia. Sed Dionysius dicit[2] quod malum *non est existens, nec in existentibus.* Ergo malum non est in bono sicut in subjecto.

2. Præterea, malum non est ens, bonum vero est ens. Sed non ens non requirit ens in quo sit sicut in subjecto. Ergo nec malum requirit bonum in quo sit sicut in subjecto.

3. Præterea, unum contrariorum non est subjectum alterius. Sed bonum et malum sunt contraria. Ergo malum non est in bono sicut in subjecto.

4. Præterea, id in quo est albedo sicut in subjecto dicitur esse album. Ergo et id in quo est malum sicut in subjecto est malum. Si ergo malum sit in bono sicut in subjecto, sequitur quod bonum sit malum; contra id quod dicitur *Isa., Væ, qui dicitis malum bonum, et bonum malum.*[3]

SED CONTRA est quod Augustinus dicit[4] quod malum non est nisi in bono.

RESPONSIO: Dicendum quod, sicut dictum est,[5] malum importat remotionem boni. Non autem quælibet remotio boni malum dicitur. Potest enim accipi remotio boni privative et negative. Remotio igitur boni negative accepta mali rationem non habet, alioquin sequeretur quod ea quæ nullo modo sunt mala essent; et iterum quod quælibet res esset mala ex hoc quod non habet bonum alterius rei, utpote quod homo esset malus quia non habet velocitatem capreæ, vel fortitudinem leonis. Sed remotio boni privative accepta malum dicitur, sicut privatio visus cæcitas dicitur.

---

[9]*Enchiridion* 11. PL 40, 236
[1]cf 1a. 17, 4 ad 2. II *Sent.* 34, 4. *CG* III, 11. *De malo* I, 2. *Compend. theol.* 118
[2]*De divinis nominibus* 4. PG 3, 733. *lect.* 23
[3]*Isaiah* 5, 20
[4]*Enchiridion* 14. PL 40, 238
[5]art. 1
[h]The four elements, air, fire, water, and earth, were regarded as being transmutable one to another.

it; and the nature of things so has it that what can fall away sometimes will. Again, as St Augustine remarks,[9] because God is so very powerful that he can even bring good out of evil. Hence many goods would disappear were he to permit no evil. For example, no fire would be kindled were air not spent,[h] the lion would not survive were the ass not killed, and there would be no vindication of justice nor patient endurance to be praised were there no wickedness.[1]

article 3. is evil seated in good?

THE THIRD POINT:[1] 1. It seems unlikely. For all goods are existing things. Dionysius, however, teaches that *evil is neither an existing thing nor in existing things.*[2] Therefore evil is not seated in good.

2. Again, an evil, unlike a good, is not a being. Yet a non-being does not require a real subject to exist in. Neither, then, does an evil in this manner require a good.

3. Further, one of two contraries does not reside in the other.[a] Now a good and a bad are contraries. Hence evil does not reside in good.

4. Besides, we term white that in which whiteness is, so we term bad that in which evil is. Well then if evil is in good, you will have to say that good is evil, which Isaiah condemns, *Woe to those who call evil good and good evil.*[3]

ON THE OTHER HAND, St Augustine writes that evil is not except in good.[4]

REPLY: As we have seen,[5] an evil means the displacement of a good. Not that every absence of a good is bad, for it can be taken in a negative and in a privative sense. The mere negation of a good does not have the force of evil, otherwise it would follow that wholly non-existents were bad, also that a thing was bad because it did not possess the quality of something else, a man, for instance, who was not swift as a mountain-goat and strong as a lion.[b] The absence of good taken deprivatively is what we call evil, thus blindness which is the privation of sight.

---

[1]4 1a. 25, 6. Good out of evil: the life of the lion from the death of the ass, this give and take, the hunt and be hunted within the balance of nature we are in a position to appreciate, but not the price for moral evil. Is anyone's virtue worth another one's vice? We may make some sort of provisional assessment, yet it is very much from outside. Vol. 5 of this series, Introduction.
[a]Contraries as different successive states in the same subject are mutually exclusive.
[b]A thing with inappropriate endowments is an oddity, not an improvement.

Subjectum autem privationis et formæ est unum et idem, scilicet ens in potentia; sive sit ens in potentia simpliciter, sicut materia prima, quæ est subjectum formæ substantialis et privationis oppositæ, sive sit ens in potentia secundum quid et in actu simpliciter, ut corpus diaphanum quod est subjectum tenebrarum et lucis. Manifestum est autem quod forma per quam aliquid est actu perfectio quædam est, et bonum quoddam; et sic omne ens in actu bonum quoddam est. Et similiter omne ens in potentia, inquantum hujusmodi, bonum quoddam est, secundum quod habet ordinem ad bonum; sicut enim est ens in potentia ita et bonum in potentia. Relinquitur ergo quod subjectum mali sit bonum.

1. Ad primum ergo dicendum quod Dionysius intelligit malum non esse in existentibus sicut partem, aut sicut proprietatem naturalem alicujus existentis.

2. Ad secundum dicendum quod non ens negative acceptum non requirit subjectum. Sed privatio est negatio in subjecto, ut dicitur in *Meta.*,[6] et tale non ens est malum.

3. Ad tertium dicendum quod malum non est sicut in subjecto in bono quod ei opponitur, sed in quodam alio bono; subjectum enim cæcitatis non est visus, sed animal. Videtur tamen, ut Augustinus dicit,[7] hic fallere dialecticorum regula quæ dicit contraria simul esse non posse. Hoc tamen intelligendum est secundum communem acceptionem boni et mali, non autem secundum quod specialiter accipitur hoc bonum et hoc malum. Album autem et nigrum, dulce et amarum, et hujusmodi contraria, non accipiuntur nisi specialiter, quia sunt in quibusdam generibus determinatis. Sed bonum circuit omnia genera; unde unum bonum potest esse simul cum privatione alterius boni.

4. Ad quartum dicendum quod Propheta imprecatur væ illis quid dicunt id quod est bonum, secundum quod est bonum, esse malum. Hoc autem non sequitur ex præmissis, ut per prædicta patet.[7]

articulus 4. utrum malum corrumpat totum bonum

AD QUARTUM sic proceditur:[1] 1. Videtur quod malum corrumpat totum bonum. Unum enim contrariorum totaliter corrumpitur per alterum. Sed bonum et malum sunt contraria. Ergo malum potest corrumpere totum bonum.

---

[1]*Metaphysics* III, 2. 1004a15. *lect.* 3
[6]*Enchiridion* 14. PL 40, 238
[7]cf 1a2æ. 85, 2. II *Sent.* 34, 5. *CG* III, 12. *De malo* II, 12
[c]Matter while actuated by one substantial form still remains potential to another. The stronger the form the more it grips, as it were, and possesses its matter. Thus

Now the subject of a form and of its privation is one and the same, namely a being in potentiality, whether it be a being in pure potentiality, like bare matter which is the subject of both a substantial form and of its opposite privation,c or whether it be a being which is actual in itself but is potential in this or that respect, like a transparent body which can receive both light and darkness.d Clearly a form through which something actually exists is a sort of completion, and therefore a sort of good, and so every actual being is a certain good. And likewise a potential being, even as potential, is a sort of good because of its relation to good, for as capable of being actual so is capable of being good.e We are left with the conclusion that an evil is seated in a good.

Hence: 1. Dionysius means that evil is not in existent things as part of them, nor as a natural property of any existing thing.

2. Non-being as purely negative assuredly requires no subject. Privation, however, is a negation in a subject, as Aristotle says,6 and evil is that kind of non-being.

3. An evil is not seated in the very good opposed to it, but in some other good; the blind subject is not the eyesight, but the animal organism. Would it then not seem that, as Augustine asks,7 a rule of dialectics is here broken, namely that contraries cannot exist simultaneously? No, for it still applies when good and evil are taken in generalized opposition, though not as particularized with respect to this particular good and this particular evil. Black and white, bitter and sweet, and other such contraries as belonging to determinate classes of being can be taken only as locally contrasted. Whereas good encircles all classifications; hence one particular good can exist alongside the privation of another particular good.f

4. The prophet curses those who claim that good as such is bad. Obviously this is not implied in what we have set down.

article 4. does evil destroy good entirely?

THE FOURTH POINT:1 1. It would seem so. For does not one contrary completely destroy its opposite? And good and evil are contraries. Therefore evil completely destroys good.

---

the endowment of immortality in a glorified soul means that its matter is only remotely potential to becoming a corpse. Suppl. 82, 1.
dOr for grass to be transformed into sheep.
eAs actuality and potentiality is a division with respect to being, so good and evil is so with respect to good.
fGood and evil are opposites, and as such and in the abstract they are exclusive. But in the concrete one type of good can co-exist with another type of evil: a good painter can be a cripple.

2. Præterea, Augustinus dicit[2] quod malum nocet inquantum adimit bonum. Sed bonum est sibi simile et uniforme. Ergo totaliter tollitur per malum.

3. Præterea, malum, quamdiu est, nocet et aufert bonum. Sed illud a quo semper aliquid aufertur quandoque consumitur, nisi sit infinitum; quod non potest dici de aliquo bono creato. Ergo malum consumit totaliter bonum.

SED CONTRA est quod Augustinus dicit[3] quod malum non potest totaliter consumere bonum.

RESPONSIO: Dicendum quod malum non potest totaliter consumere bonum. Ad cujus evidentiam considerandum est quod triplex est bonum. Quoddam per malum totaliter tollitur, et hoc est bonum oppositum malo; sicut lumen totaliter per tenebras tollitur, et visus per cæcitatem. Quoddam vero bonum est quod nec totaliter tollitur per malum nec diminuitur, scilicet bonum quod est subjectum mali; non enim per tenebras aliquid de substantia aëris diminuitur. Quoddam vero bonum est quod diminuitur quidem per malum, sed non totaliter tollitur, et hoc bonum est habilitas subjecti ad actum.

Diminutio autem hujus boni non est accipienda per subtractionem, sicut est diminutio in quantitatibus, sed per remissionem, sicut est diminutio in qualitatibus et formis. Remissio autem hujus habilitatis est accipienda e contrario intensioni ipsius. Intenditur enim hujusmodi habilitas per dispositiones quibus materia præparatur ad actum, quæ quanto magis multiplicantur in subjecto tanto habilius est ad recipiendum perfectionem et formam. Et e contrario remittitur per dispositiones contrarias, quæ quanto magis multiplicatæ sunt in materia, et magis intensæ, tanto magis remittitur potentia ad actum.

Si igitur contrariæ dispositiones in infinitum multiplicari et intendi non possunt, sed usque ad certum terminum, neque habilitas prædicta in infinitum diminuitur vel remittitur. Sicut patet in qualitatibus activis et passivis elementorum; frigiditas enim et humiditas, per quæ diminuitur sive remittitur habilitas materiæ ad forman ignis, non possunt multiplicari in infinitum. Si vero dispositiones contrariæ in infinitum multiplicari possunt, et habilitas prædicta in infinitum diminuitur vel remittitur. Non

---

[2]*Enchiridion* 12. PL 40, 237. cf *De moribus Ecclesiæ* II, 3. PL 32, 1347   [3]ibid
[a]Namely the form of good, the material of good, and the active disposition to be good.
[b]i.e. to be active and fully real. The distinction can be compared to that between the root and the fruit: the blossom may be nipped but the tree remains healthy enough.

2. Moreover, St Augustine says that evil is hurtful because it does away with good.[2] But good is all of a piece and uniform, and therefore wholly done away with by evil.

3. Again, evil while it lasts is ever sapping and eating away at good. Now that which is continually being eaten away is at some time entirely consumed, unless it be infinite, which cannot be said of any created good. Therefore evil consumes good entirely.

ON THE OTHER HAND there is St Augustine teaching that evil cannot utterly devour good.[3]

REPLY: Evil cannot destroy good altogether. Consider the evidence. For the present inquiry we can divide good into three classes.[a] First, the good wholly eliminated by the evil, and this is the one which is its opposite; thus light is quite dispelled by darkness, and sight deprived by blindness. Next, the good which is neither entirely destroyed nor lessened by the evil, namely the good which is the subject of evil; air loses nothing of its substance because of darkness. Last, the good which is diminished but not wholly taken away by the evil; this good is the ability of to be actual.[b]

How can this diminish? Not by the subtraction which applies to quantities, but by the slackening which applies to qualities and forms. This weakening of the ability to be actual can be described from the heightening which is the reverse. This is an intensification through dispositions which prepare the matter for actuality; the more these are repeated in the subject the readier it is to receive form and perfection. And conversely the more this readiness abates because of contrary dispositions, and the oftener and more strongly they are repeated in the material, so much the more does the potentiality to be actual grow slack.[c]

If then these contrary dispositions cannot be repeated or grow indefinitely, but only up to a certain point, the ability in question cannot be indefinitely lessened or weakened. This appears in the active and passive qualities of the elements; for coldness and wetness, whereby the aptness of matter to receive the form of fire is lessened or held back, cannot be endlessly increased.[d] If indeed such contrary dispositions could be, the aptness in question would be endlessly diminished or weakened. Nevertheless it would never be taken away, for it would always remain at its root

---

[c]This analysis of the intensifying of dispositions and virtues is pursued in 1a2æ. 52, 1; 53, 2; 66, 1.
[d]There is no absolute cold or absolute wet, but only the last straw, the *ultima dispositio*, the subject will stand. The reification in the examples should not distract from the argument itself.

enim totaliter tollitur, quia semper manet in sua radice, quæ est substantia subjecti. Sicut si in infinitum interponantur corpora opaca inter solem et aërem, in infinitum diminuitur habilitas aëris ad lumen; nunquam tamen, manente aëre, tollitur totaliter, qui secundum naturam suam est diaphanus. Similiter in infinitum potest fieri additio in peccatis, per quæ semper magis et magis minuitur habilitas animæ ad gratiam; quæ quidem peccata sunt quasi obstacula interposita inter nos et Deum, secundum illud Isa.,[4] *Peccata nostra diviserunt inter nos et Deum.** Neque tamen tollitur totaliter ab anima prædicta habilitas, quia consequitur naturam ipsius.

1. Ad primum ergo dicendum quod bonum quod opponitur malo totaliter tollitur; sed alia bona non totaliter tolluntur, ut dictum est.[5]

2. Ad secundum dicendum quod habilitas prædicta est media inter subjectum et actum. Unde ex ea parte qua attingit actum diminuitur per malum, sed ex ea parte qua tenet se cum subjecto remanet. Ergo licet bonum in se sit simile, tamen propter comparationem ejus ad diversa non totaliter tollitur, sed in parte.

3. Ad tertium dicendum quod quidam, imaginantes diminutionem boni praedicti ad similitudinem diminutionis quantitatis, dixerunt quod sicut continuum dividitur in infinitum, facta divisione secundum eamdem proportionem, ut puta quod accipiatur medium medii, vel tertium tertii, sic in proposito accidit. Sed hæc ratio hic locum non habet. Quia in divisione in qua servatur eadem proportio semper subtrahitur minus et minus; minus enim est medium medii quam medium totius. Sed secundum peccatum non de necessitate minus diminuit de habilitate prædicta quam præcedens, sed forte aut æqualiter, aut magis.

Dicendum est ergo quod licet ista habilitas sit quoddam finitum, diminuitur tamen in infinitum, non per se sed per accidens, secundum quod contrariæ dispositiones etiam in infinitum augentur, ut dictum est.[6]

articulus 5. utrum malum sufficienter dividatur per pœnam et culpam

AD QUINTUM sic proceditur:[1] 1. Videtur quod malum insufficienter dividatur per pœnam et culpam. Omnis enim defectus malum quoddam esse videtur. Sed in omnibus creaturis est quidam defectus quod se in esse

---

*Vulgate: *Sed peccata vestra diviserunt inter vos et Deum vestrum*
[4]*Isaiah* 59, 2
[5]In the body of the article
[6]In the body of the article
[1]cf II *Sent.* 35, 1. *De malo* I, 4

which is the substance of the subject. Thus if an infinity of opaque screens were interposed between the sun and the atmosphere, the aptness of the air's capacity to receive light would be indefinitely diminished, but it would never be completely lost, for it is of the nature of air to be translucent. Again sin could be endlessly piled on sin, more and more weakening the soul's readiness for grace, which sins are like obstacles placed between us and God, according to Isaiah's words, *Our iniquities have made a separation between us and God.*[4e] Yet the readiness would remain notwithstanding, for it follows from the soul's very nature.[f]

Hence: 1. The good which is directly opposite to an evil is wholly made away with, as we have said,[5] but not other goods.

2. The preparedness in question lies between a substance and its activity. As looking to activity it is lessened by evil, but as looking to the substance it persists. Hence, even though good in itself is all of a piece, nevertheless because related to diverse elements in a situation it can be taken away partially, though not totally.

3. Some authors,[g] imagining the lessening of good in terms of quantitative decrease, have held that as a continuum is infinitely divisible, providing the division be proportional, for instance subtracting a half of a half or a third of a third and so on. It is thus, they say, in the present case. But without avail. For when a division is continued by the same ratio a less and less amount is ever being progressively subtracted: a half of a half is less than the half of a whole. Yet a subsequent sin does not necessarily rob our readiness for good of less than a preceding sin; it can do as much, perhaps, or even more.

The answer should be that although this readiness is something finite, it can be indefinitely lessened, not of itself but because of other factors, namely, as we have explained,[6] by the endless increase of contrary dispositions.

article 5. is evil adequately divided into pain and fault?

THE FIRST POINT:[1] 1. Is it? For every defect, so it appears, is a kind of evil. Now a defect in all creatures is the inability to keep themselves in being,

---

[e] cf 1a2æ. 85, 1 & 2.
[f] Readiness for grace: later commonly called *potentia obedientialis*. The soul's innate responsiveness to be acted on by divine grace and to surpass its own natural capabilities: cf 1a. 12, 4 ad 3; 30, 11, 1. *CG* II, 37.
[g] e.g. William of Auxerre (*d.* 1231). *Summa Aurea* II, 26, 5. cf 1a2æ. 85, 2.

conservare non possunt, qui tamen nec pœna nec culpa est. Non ergo sufficienter malum dividitur per pœnam et culpam.

2. Præterea, in rebus irrationalibus non invenitur culpa nec pœna. Invenitur autem in eis corruptio et defectus, quæ ad rationem mali pertinent. Ergo non omne malum est pœna vel culpa.

3. Præterea, tentatio quoddam malum est. Nec tamen est culpa, quia *tentatio cui non consentitur, non est peccatum, sed materia exercendae virtutis,* ut dicitur in Glossa.[2] Nec tamen est pœna, quia tentatio præcedat culpam, poena autem subsequitur. Insufficienter ergo malum dividitur per pœnam et culpam.

4. Sed contra videtur quod divisio sit superflua. Ut enim Augustinus dicit,[3] malum dicitur quia nocet. Quod autem nocet pœnale est. Omne ergo malum sub poena continetur.

RESPONSIO: Dicendum quod malum, sicut supra dictum est,[4] est privatio boni, quod in perfectione et actu consistit principaliter et per se. Actus autem est duplex, primus et secundus. Actus quidem primus est forma et integritas rei, actus autem secundus est operatio. Contingit ergo malum esse dupliciter. Uno modo per subtractionem formæ, aut alicuius partis quæ requiritur ad integritatem rei; sicut cæcitas malum est, et carere membro. Alio modo per subtractionem debitæ operationis, vel quia omnino non est vel quia modum et ordinem non habet.

Quia vero bonum simpliciter est objectum voluntatis, malum, quod est privatio boni, secundum specialem rationem invenitur in creaturis habentibus voluntatem. Malum igitur quod est per subtractionem formæ vel integritatis rei habet rationem poenæ; et præcipue supposito quod omnia divinae providentiæ et justitiæ subdantur, ut supra ostensum est:[5] de ratione enim poenæ est quod sit contraria voluntati. Malum autem quod consistit in subtractione debitæ operationis in rebus voluntariis habet rationem culpæ. Hoc enim imputatur alicui in culpam, cum deficit a perfecta actione cujus dominus est secundum voluntatem. Sic igitur omne malum in rebus voluntariis considerandum vel est pœna vel culpa.

---

[2]*Glossa ordinaria* in II *Cor.* 12, 7. VI, 76E. cf PL 192, 84
[3]*Enchiridion* 12. PL 40, 237. cf PL 32, 1347   [4]art. 3   [5]1a. 22,2
[a]*Poena*, pain or penalty, not pain as an affective condition (*tristitia*) though this may be involved, nor penalty as punishment for a breach of law, though this too may be involved, but a condition of lacking an appropriate good. The sense will appear in the discussion. Cajetan says, *in loc.*, moral evil is what we do, penal evil is what we suffer. The division is like that between moral and physical evil, 'physical' being taken in a wide sense, and not restricted to bodily or material nature.
[b]II *Corinthians* 12, 7, *And to keep me from being too elated by the abundance of revelations, a thorn was given me in the flesh.*

yet this is neither their punishment nor their fault. The division, therefore, does not meet the situation.[a]

2. Again, you find neither penalty nor fault in non-rational creatures. All the same you do find defect and decay, which come under the heading of evil. Hence not every evil is a penalty or fault.

3. Besides, temptation is a kind of evil. Yet it is not a fault, for on II *Corinthians*[b] the Gloss comments, *Temptation to which one does not give in is not a sin, but an occasion for the practice of virtue.*[2] Neither is it a penalty, for temptation comes before fault, while penalty comes after. Therefore the division of evil into penalty and fault does not fit.

4. On the contrary[c] it seems that the division is superfluous. For, to quote St Augustine, a thing is called evil because it injures.[3] What does this is penal. So then every evil comes under pain.

REPLY: An evil, as we have said above,[4] is a privation of a good, and good chiefly and of itself lies in perfection and actuality. Actuality is twofold, primary and secondary. The first is the form and integrity of a thing, the second its operation.[d] Consequently an evil that happens also is twofold. The first is an evil consisting in the loss of a form or part required for a thing's integrity; thus to be blind or to lack a member.[e] The second is the evil of withdrawal in activity that is due, either by its omission or by its malfunctioning according to manner and measure.[f]

Now since good pure and simple is the objective of will, evil, which is the privation of good, is found in a special manner in rational creatures possessing will. The evil which comes through the loss of a thing's form and integrity has there the character of pain that is suffered, especially on the supposition which has been justified,[5] that all things are subject to divine Providence and justice. For the point of a penalization is to be against the will of the sufferer.[g] The evil which consists in a failure in due activity about moral matters has the character of fault. For a person is held responsible and to blame for a shortcoming that falls under the control of the will, namely a failure to perform a full action.[h] Thus, then, every evil in voluntary matters is either a penalty or a fault.

---

[c]Instead of the usual *sed contra* supporting the position to be adopted, the argument goes to the other extreme of the objections, and claims that the division is redundant, rather than ineffective.

[d]cf 1a2æ. 3, 2. The distinction comes from Aristotle.

[e]Evil has a wider meaning than sin, 1a2æ. 21, 1.

[f]cf 1a. 5, 5. Malfunction according to objective, circumstance, or motive; 1a2æ. 18, 2, 3 & 4.

[g]cf 1a2æ. 87, 2. 2a2æ. 18, 3.

[h]cf 1a2æ. 21, 2.

1. Ad primum ergo dicendum quod quia malum privatio est boni et non negatio pura, ut dictum est supra,[6] non omnis defectus boni est malum, sed defectus boni quod natum est et debet haberi. Defectus enim visionis non est malum in lapide, sed in animali, quia contra rationem lapidis est quod visum habeat. Similiter etiam contra rationem creaturæ est quod in esse conservetur a seipsa; quia idem dat esse et conservat. Unde iste defectus non est malum creaturæ.

2. Ad secundum dicendum quod pœna et culpa non dividunt malum simpliciter, sed malum in rebus voluntariis.

3. Ad tertium dicendum quod tentatio prout importat provocationem ad malum semper malum culpæ est in tentante. Sed in eo qui tentatur non est proprie, nisi secundum quod aliqualiter immutatur; sic enim actio agentis est in patiente. Secundum autem quod tentatus immutatur ad malum a tentante incidit in culpam.

4. Ad quartum dicendum quod de ratione pœnæ est quod noceat agenti in seipso. Sed de ratione culpæ est quod noceat agenti in sua actione. Et sic utrumque sub malo continetur, secundum quod habeat rationem nocumenti.

articulus 6. utrum habeat plus de ratione mali pœna quam culpa

AD SEXTUM sic proceditur:[1] 1. Videtur quod habeat plus de ratione mali pœna quam culpa. Culpa enim se habet ad pœnam ut meritum ad præmium. Sed præmium habet plus de ratione boni quam meritum, cum sit finis eius. Ergo pœna plus habet de ratione mali quam culpa.

2. Præterea, illud est majus malum quod opponitur majori bono. Sed poena, sicut dictum est,[2] opponitur bono agentis; culpa autem bono actionis. Cum ergo melius sit agens quam actio, videtur quod pejus sit poena quam culpa.

3. Præterea, ipsa privatio finis pœna quædam est, quæ dicitur carentia visionis divinæ. Malum autem culpæ est per privationem ordinis ad finem. Ergo pœna est majus malum quam culpa.

SED CONTRA, sapiens artifex inducit minus malum ad vitandum majus sicut medicus præcidit membrum ne corrumpatur corpus. Sed Dei sapien-

---

[6]art. 3
[1]cf 1a. 19, 9. 2a2æ. 19, 1. *De malo* 1, 5. II *Sent.* 37, 3, 2
[2]art. 2
[1]Can and ought.
[1]The creature is dependent on God's efficient causality throughout the whole course of its existence: 1a. 104, 1. Its own proper inadequacy is no *malum metaphysicum*.

Hence: 1. Since, as we have noted,[6] evil is privative of good and not purely negative, not every absence of good is an evil, but only of that which a thing by nature can have and is expected to have.[1] The lack of sight is an evil in an animal, but not in a stone which is not made to see. Likewise it is not according to the nature of a creature that it should be self-preserving in being; the cause of its existence is the cause of its continuance. Hence it is no evil for a creature to be unable to keep itself in existence.[j]

2. Penalty and fault do not divide evil simply speaking, but the evil found in matters subject to will.

3. When temptation means a provocation to moral evil, then fault always goes with it in the person tempting, not, properly speaking, in the person tempted, unless in some way he yields to it; then the action passes into the one acted on. To the extent that he is moved to evil by the tempter he falls into fault.[k]

4. As for the argument to the other extreme, it is of the essence of penalty to hurt the agent in himself, and it is of the essence of fault to hurt his activity. And so both are contained in the notion of evil as injurious.

article 6. is the quality of evil stronger in penalty or in fault?

THE SIXTH POINT:[1] 1. Penalty seems to share in the meaning of evil more than fault does. For fault is to penalty as merit to reward. But reward, as being its end,[a] means good more than merit does. Correspondingly penalty more than fault.

2. Moreover, that evil is greater which is opposed to the greater good. Yet as stated,[2] penalty is against the agent's integrity, while fault is against the value of his activity. Since what a person is outweighs what he does, it seems that penalty is worse than fault.

3. Again, the condition of being deprived of our end is a penalty, and we agree that this is having forfeited the vision of God,[b] Fault, however, is a deprivation in our bearing towards that end. Therefore penalty is a greater evil than fault.

ON THE OTHER HAND a wise practitioner brings in a lesser evil to exclude a greater, like a surgeon amputating a limb to save the whole body. Divine

---

[k]Temptation: 1a2æ. 80, 1.
[a]St Thomas will not deny this. His moral theory is not Stoic nor Kantian. Vol. 18, Appendix 9.
[b]1a. 12, 1. 1a2æ. 3, 8.

tia infert pœnam ad vitandam culpam. Ergo culpa est majus malum quam poena.

RESPONSIO : Dicendum quod culpa habet plus de ratione mali quam pœna; et non solum quam pœna sensibilis, quæ consistit in privatione corporalium bonorum, cujusmodi pœnas plures intelligunt; sed etiam universaliter accipiendo pœnam, secundum quod privatio gratiæ vel gloriæ pœnæ quædam sunt.

Cujus est duplex ratio. Prima quidem est, quia ex malo culpæ fit aliquis malus, non autem ex malo pœnæ; secundum illud Dionysii,[3] *Puniri non est malum, sed fieri pœnæ dignum.* Et hoc ideo est quia cum bonum simpliciter consistat in actu et non in potentia, ultimus autem actus est operatio, vel usus quarumcumque rerum habitarum, bonum hominis simpliciter consideratur in bona operatione vel bono usu rerum habitarum. Utimur autem rebus omnibus per voluntatem. Unde ex bona voluntate, qua homo bene utitur rebus habitis, dicitur homo bonus; et ex mala malus. Potest enim qui habet malam voluntatem etiam bono quod habet male uti; sicut si grammaticus voluntarie incongrue loquatur. Quia ergo culpa consistit in deordinato actu voluntatis, pœna vero in privatione alicujus eorum quibus utitur voluntas, perfectius habet rationem mali culpa quam pœna.

Secunda ratio sumi potest ex hoc, quod Deus est auctor mali pœnæ, non autem mali culpæ. Cujus ratio est, quia malum pœnæ privat bonum creaturæ, sive accipiatur bonum creaturæ aliquid creatum, sicut cæcitas privat visum, sive sit bonum increatum, sicut per carentiam visionis divinæ tollitur creaturæ bonum increatum. Malum vero culpæ opponitur proprie ipsi bono increato; contrariatur enim impletioni divinæ voluntatis, et divino amori quo bonum divinum in seipso amatur, et non solum secundum quod participatur a creatura. Sic igitur patet quod culpa habet plus de ratione mali quam pœna.

1. Ad primum ergo dicendum quod licet culpa terminetur ad pœnam sicut meritum ad praemium, tamen culpa non intenditur propter pœnam sicut meritum propter præmium, sed potius e converso pœna inducitur ut vitetur culpa. Et sic culpa est pejus quam pœna.

2. Ad secundum dicendum quod ordo actionis, qui tollitur per culpam,

---

[3]*De divinis nominibus* 4. PG 3, 724. St Thomas, *lect.* 18
cBut cf ad 1, below.
dcf above art. 5.
eUsing what we have. For the technical meaning of *usus* cf Ia2æ. 16, 1.
†A good man *simpliciter*, not just *secundum quid*: cf the distinction between intellectual and moral virtue: Ia2æ. 56, 3; 58, 2.

wisdom inflicts pain to prevent fault.[c] Therefore fault is a greater evil than pain.

REPLY: The quality of evil lies more in fault than in pain, not merely more than the sensible pain which lies in the deprivation of bodily endowments —which is what most of us well appreciate—but more than pain in the broadest sense of the term as well, which includes the loss of grace and eternal bliss.

The conclusion has a double reason. The first is that a person becomes bad because of fault, not pain; Dionysius observes, *the evil is not to be penalized, but to deserve it.*[3] And this is true because the good simply speaking consists at last analysis in actuality, not potentiality.[d] Now ultimate actuality is activity or employing our resources.[e] So man's good simply speaking is seen in his good activity profiting from his talents.[f] And this we do through our will. Hence we speak of a man being good because his will is good in turning his gifts to good use, and we speak of him as bad because his will is correspondingly bad. For a man of bad will can misuse his gifts, like a cultivated person who deliberately commits a solecism. Since therefore fault consists in a misdirected act of will and penalty in a deprivation of something employed by the will, the first more fully manifests the quality of evil than the second.

The other argument is to this effect: God is the author of the evil of penalty, but not of the evil of fault. The evil called penalty is the deprivation of a creaturely good, whether that is a matter of created being, thus blindness is a lack of sight, or involves an uncreated good,[g] thus the loss of the vision of God. The evil called fault, however, directly opposes the uncreated good itself; it conflicts with the fulfilment of the divine will, and with the divine love whereby divine goodness is loved for itself, not only as shared in by the creature.[h] On this account the quality of evil is evidently greater in fault than in penalty.

Hence: 1. Though fault culminates in penalty as merit does in reward, still the purpose is different; fault is not bent on penalty as merit on reward,[i] rather the reverse, for penalty is brought in so that fault may be avoided.[j] Hence fault is worse than penalty.

2. Well-ordered activity, which is destroyed by fault, is a more achieved

---

[g]cf 1c. 12, 1; 1a2æ. 3, 1.
[h]On loving God for himself, cf 2a2æ. 25, 1; 26, 2; 44, 4.
[i]cf 1a2æ. 21, 3 & 4; 114, 4. Merit is the result not the purpose of a good action.
[j]Punishment as a deterrent. There are other pragmatic reasons for it, namely to correct the wrongdoer or to remove a danger to the community.

est perfectius bonum agentis, cum sit perfectio secunda, quam bonum quod tollitur per pœnam, quod est perfectio prima.

3. Ad tertium dicendum quod non est comparatio culpæ ad pœnam sicut finis et ordinis ad finem, quia utrumque potest privari aliquo modo et per culpam et per pœnam. Sed per pœnam quidem secundum quod homo removetur a fine et ab ordine ad finem, per culpam vero secundum quod ista privatio pertinet ad actionem, quæ non ordinatur ad finem debitum.

ᵏSecond perfection, first perfection; cf above art. 5. The being of a thing is more perfect than its acting, yet in terms of the good its good acting is a fuller notion and includes its good being; 1a. 5, 1 ad 1.

good for an agent, being a crowning perfection, than the good destroyed by penalty, which is its initial perfection.[k]

3. It is not a fair comparison between penalty and fault in terms of what is the end and what is because of the end, for loss with respect to either can be suffered through both penalty and fault. Through penalty in that a person is displaced from his end and from what bears him to it; through fault indeed that this displacement results from voluntary activity not directed to the right end.[1]

---

[1]These replies should be seen as arguing closely to a point, not as attempting to meet an entire situation. The borderline between sickness and sin is easier to draw in theory than in practice, and balancing them is rather an abstract exercise. Well-being, *salus*, is a complete, and not merely a moral condition. cf Vol. 18.

Quæstio 49. de causa mali

Consequenter quæitur de causa mali. Et circa hoc quæruntur tria:

1. utrum bonum possit esse causa mali;
2. utrum summum bonum, qod est Deus, sit causa mali;
3. utrum sit aliquod summum malum, quod sit prima causa omnium malorum.

articulus 1. utrum bonum possit esse causa mali

AD PRIMUM sic proceditur:[1] 1. Videtur quod bonum non possit esse causa mali. Dicitur enim *Matt.*,[2] *Non potest arbor bona malos fructus facere.*

2. Præterea, unum contrariorum non potest esse causa alterius. Malum autem est contrarium bono. Ergo bonum non potest esse causa mali.

3. Præterea, effectus deficiens non procedit nisi a causa deficiente. Sed malum, si causam habeat, est effectus deficiens. Ergo habet causam deficientem. Sed omne deficiens malum est. Ergo causa mali non est nisi malum.

4. Præterea, Dionysius dicit[3] quod malum non habet causam. Ergo bonum non est causa mali.

SED CONTRA, est quod Augustinus dicit,[4] *Non fuit omnino unde oriri posset malum nisi ex bono.*

RESPONSIO: Dicendum quod necesse est dicere quod omne malum aliqualiter causam habeat. Malum enim est defectus boni quod natum est et debet haberi. Quod autem aliquid deficiat a sua naturali et debita dispositione non potest provenire nisi ex aliqua causa trahente rem extra suam dispositionem; non enim grave movetur sursum nisi ab aliquo impellente, necc agens deficit in sua actione nisi propter aliquod impedimentum.

Esse autem causam non potest convenire nisi bono, quia nihil potest esse causa nisi inquantum est ens; omne autem ens inquantum hujusmodi bonum est. Et si consideremus speciales rationes causarum, agens et forma et finis perfectionem quamdam important, quæ pertinet ad rationem boni; sed et materia, inquantum est potentia ad bonum, habet rationem boni.

Et quidem quod bonum sit causa mali per modum causæ materialis, jam ex præmissis patet; ostensum est enim[5] quod bonum est subjectum mali.

---

[1]cf Ia2æ. 75, 1. *CG* II, 41; III, 10 & 13. *De potentia* III, 6, ad 1, 2 & 3. *De malo* I, 3. *In Div. nom.* 4, *lect.* 22. II *Sent.* I, 1, 1 ad 2
[2]*Matthew* 7, 18
[3]*De divinis nominibus* 4. PG 3, 732. *lect.* 22

Question 49. the cause of evil

And now, addressing ourselves to the question of the cause of evil, there are three points of inquiry:

1. can good be the cause of evil?
2. is God, the supreme good, the cause of evil?
3. is there a supreme evil which is the first cause of all evils?

article 1. can good be the cause of evil?

THE FIRST POINT:[1] 1. It seems not. For in *Matthew* we read, *A good tree cannot bring forth bad fruit.*[2]

2. Again, one contrary cannot be the cause of its opposite. Evil is the contrary of good. And therefore is not caused by it.

3. Besides, a defective effect is the result only of a defective cause. Evil is a defective effect, and any cause it has will also be defective. Whatever is defective is bad. Consequently the cause of evil is only what is evil.

4. Then also, Dionysius declares that evil has no cause.[3] So then something good is not its cause.

ON THE OTHER HAND there is Augustine saying, *Nothing at all was there whence evil could arise except from good.*[4]

REPLY: We cannot but hold that in some way every evil has a cause. For evil is an absence of good from a thing which can and ought naturally to possess it. That something falls short of its natural and due disposition can come only from some cause dragging it away; a weight does not shoot upwards unless propelled, an agent does not fail in its action unless impeded.

Now to be a cause belongs only to a good; nothing can be a cause except in so far as it is a being, and every being as such is a good.[a] And when we consider the special meaning of each of the four causes[b] we come to the same conclusion; to be an efficient cause, a formal cause, and a final cause imply a certain perfection which belongs to the notion of the good; even matter shares it as being in potentiality to good.

That a good is the cause of good after the manner of a material cause has already appeared, when we showed that good is the seat of evil.[5]

---

[4]*Contra Julianum* I, 9. PL 44, 670
[5]1a. 48, 3
[a]*Omne ens bonum*, 1a. 5, 3.
[b]*Metaphysics* v, 2. 1013a24. St Thomas, *lect.* 2.

Causam autem formalem malum non habet, sed est magis privatio formæ.

Et similiter nec causam finalem, sed magis est privatio ordinis ad debitum finem; non solum enim finis habet rationem boni, sed etiam utile quod ordinatur ad finem.

Causam autem per modum agentis habet malum, non autem per se, sed per accidens.

Ad cujus evidentiam, sciendum est quod aliter causatur malum in actione et aliter in effectu. In actione quidem causatur malum propter defectum alicujus principiorum actionis, vel principalis agentis vel instrumentalis; sicut defectus in motu animalis potest contingere vel propter debilitatem virtutis motivæ, ut in pueris, vel propter solam ineptitudinem instrumenti, ut in claudis.

Malum autem in aliqua re—non tamen in proprio effectu agentis—* causatur quandoque ex virtute agentis, quandoque autem ex defectu ipsius vel materiæ. Ex virtute quidem vel perfectione agentis, quando ad formam intentam ab agente sequitur ex necessitate alterius formæ privatio; sicut ad formam ignis sequitur privatio formæ aëris vel aquæ. Sicut ergo quanto ignis fuerit perfectior in virtute tanto perfectius imprimit formam suam, ita etiam tanto perfectius corrumpit contrarium; unde malum et corruptio aëris et aquæ est ex perfectione ignis. Sed hoc est per accidens, quia ignis non intendit privare formam aquæ, sed inducere formam propriam; sed hoc faciendo, causat et illud per accidens. Sed si defectus in proprio effectu ignis, puta quod deficiat a calefaciendo, hoc est vel propter defectum actionis, qui redundat in defectum alicujus principii, ut dictum est, vel ex indispositione materiæ, quæ non recipit actionem ignis agentis. Sed et hoc ipsum quod est esse deficiens accidit bono, cui per se competit agere. Unde verum est quod malum secundum nullum modum habet causam nisi per accidens. Sic autem bonum est causa mali.

1. Ad primum ergo dicendum quod, sicut Augustinus dicit,[6] *Arborem malam appellat Dominus voluntatem malam, et arborem bonam, voluntatem bonam.* Ex voluntate autem bona non producitur actus moralis malus, cum ex ipsa voluntate bona judicetur actus moralis bonus. Sed tamen ipse motus malæ voluntatis causatur a creatura rationali, quæ bona est. Et sic est causa mali.

2. Ad secundum dicendum quod bonum non causat illud malum quod est sibi contrarium, sed quoddam aliud, sicut bonitas ignis causat malum

---

*Piana: omits parenthesis

[6]*Contra Julianum* I, 9. PL 44, 672

[c]Nor is it an exemplar cause. *De veritate* III, 4, 'a thing is called bad by its failure to share in divinity.' Plotinus, *Enneads* I, 8, 2; III, 3, 5.

Evil has no formal cause, rather is it instead a privation of form.[c]

Likewise it has no final cause, rather is it instead a privation of direction to a due end; and the quality of being good is shown not only by an end, but also by a means to it.[d]

Yet evil has an efficient cause, but it is one that acts indirectly, not directly.[e]

Let us explain how evil is caused otherwise in the action and in its effect. In the action it is due to some handicap in one of the active principles, whether the principal or whether the instrumental cause; for instance a failure to walk may come from the power being undeveloped, as in babies, or from a disability of a limb, as in cripples.

In the effect—we are not thinking so much about the proper and immediate effect of the agent[f]—evil is caused sometimes by the very strength of the agent, and sometimes because of something wanting either in it or in the material. From its strength when from the form to which it reaches out there follows of necessity the privation of another form: thus the form of fire expels the form of water or air, and the stronger the fire the more completely it impresses its own form and consumes what is contrary, so that it is from the very force of heat that air or water are exhausted. Yet this is incidental, for the inherent tendency of fire is not to destroy the form of water, but to introduce its own, though in doing the one it incidentally causes the other.[g] As for defect in the proper effect of fire, namely that it fails to heat, then this goes back either to a deficiency in some active principle, and this we have touched on, or is because the material is unprepared and resists the fire's action. That something goes by default is incidental to good, which of its nature is active. The truth is that the only cause evil has is incidental, and in this way a good is the cause of an evil.

Hence: 1. *The Lord calls an evil will a bad tree*, St Augustine says,[6] *and a good will a good tree*. A sound act of will does not produce a morally bad act, for it provides the test for adjudging that an act is morally good.[h] Nevertheless the motion of willing ill is caused by a rational creature, who is good, and so is the cause of evil.

2. A good does not cause the evil which is its contrary, but another sort of evil, as the goodness of fire causes what is bad for air, and a man who is

---

[d]*Bonum honestum et delectabile*—the end: *bonum utile*—the means. 1a. 5, 6.
[e]Or incidentally, not essentially.
[f]For that would argue defect in the agent.
[g]cf 1a. 19, 9.
[h]1a2æ. 19, 8.

aquæ; et homo bonus secundum suam naturam causat malum actum secundum morem. Et hoc ipsum per accidens est, ut dictum est.[7] Invenitur autem quod etiam unum contrariorum causat aliud per accidens, sicut frigidum exterius ambiens calefit, inquantum calor retrahitur ad interiora.

3. Ad tertium dicendum quod malum habet causam deficientem aliter in rebus voluntariis et naturalibus. Agens enim naturale producit effectum suum talem quale ipsum est, nisi impediatur ab aliquo extrinseco; et hoc ipsum est quidam* defectus ejus. Unde nunquam sequitur malum in effectu, nisi præexistat aliquid aliud malum in agente vel materia, sicut dictum est.[8] Sed in rebus voluntariis defectus actionis a voluntate actu deficiente procedit, inquantum non subjicit suæ regulæ. Qui tamen defectus non est culpa, sed sequitur culpa† ex hoc quod cum tali defectu operatur.

4. Ad quartum dicendum quod malum non habet causam per se sed per accidens tantum, ut dictum est.[9]

articulus 2. *utrum summum bonum, quod est Deus, sit causa mali*

AD SECUNDUM sic proceditur:[1] 1. Videtur quod summum bonum, quod est Deus, sit causa mali. Dicitur enim *Isa.*,[2] *Ego Dominus, et non est alter Deus,‡ formans lucem et creans tenebras, faciens pacem et creans malum'.* Et *Amos,*[3] *Si erit malum in civitate quod Dominus non fecerit?*

2. Præterea, effectus causæ secundæ reducitur in causam primam. Bonum autem est causa mali, ut dictum est.[4] Cum igitur omnis boni causa sit Deus, ut supra ostensum est,[5] sequitur quod etiam omne malum sit a Deo.

3. Præterea, sicut dicitur in *Physic.*,[6] idem est causa salutis navis et periculi. Sed Deus est causa salutis omnium rerum. Ergo est ipse causa omnis perditionis et mali.

---

*Piana: *quidem*
†Piana: *et eum sequitor culpa,* and fault follows it
‡Vulgate: omits *Deus*
[7]In the body of the article. cf Ia. 19, 9
[8]In the body of the article
[9]ibid
[1]cf Ia. 19, 9; 48, 6. *CG* II, 41; III, 71. *De malo* I, 5. II *Sent.* 32, 2, 1; 37, 3, 1. *De substantiis separatis* 15. *Compend. thol.* 141. *In Joann.* 9, lect. I. *In Rom.* I, lect. 7
[2]*Isaiah* 45, 6
[3]*Amos* 3, 6
[4]art. I
[5]Ia. 2, 3; 6, 1 & 4
[6]*Physics* II, 3. 195a11

good by nature causes an act which is bad by morals.[1] Yet this is incidental, as we have remarked.[7] Moreover one contrary is sometimes the incidental cause of another, for instance when the outside cold makes a room warmer by keeping in the heat.[j]

e. The deficient cause of evil works differently in natural actions and in voluntary actions.[k] A natural agent produces the sort of effect which corresponds to the sort of thing it is itself, unless it be blocked by something outside itself, which makes for its failure. We have explained how evil never results in the effect unless another sort of evil pre-exists in the agent or material.[8] With voluntary causes, however, the deficient action proceeds from an actually deficient will, that is, a will not submitted to its rule and measure. This deficiency is not itself a fault; fault results from the fact that the will acts with this defect.[1]

4. We have pointed out that evil does not have a direct cause, but only an incidental cause.[9]

article 2. *is the supreme good, which is God, the cause of evil?*

THE SECOND POINT:[1] 1. It seems so.[a] We read in *Isaiah, I am the Lord, and there is no other. I form light and create darkness, I make weal and create woe.*[2b] And again in *Amos, Does evil befall a city unless the Lord has done it?*[3]

2. Again, the effect of a secondary cause goes back to the first cause. Now good is the cause of evil, it has been stated.[4] Therefore, since he is the cause of all good, as has been shown,[5] it follows that all evil is from God.[c]

3. Besides, according to the *Physics*, the cause both of *the safety and of danger for the ship*, is the same.[6d] God is the safeguarding cause of all things. Also, then, of all perdition and evil.

---

[1]1a2æ. 18, 4.
[j]The analogy holds at least in human psychology, if not in thermal mechanics.
[k]Natural action, agent, i.e. without the conscious intention of a voluntary action, agent. cf 1a. 19, 1.
[1]An important point. Fault, *culpa*, is not to be unruled (a *malum pœnæ*), but to act unruled. It is mode, not of being, but of acting.
[a]Divine causality and sin is treated in a special Question, 1a2æ. 79.
[b]*Isaiah*, add, *I am the Lord, who do all these things.*
[c]A secondary cause is dependent on the first cause for its form and its action; 1a. 105, 5.
[d]Aristotle. 'The same cause is often alleged for opposite effects. For if its presence causes one thing the opposite is laid to its account if it be absent. Thus, if the pilot's presence would have brought the ship safe to harbour, we say that he caused its wreck by his absence.'

SED CONTRA, est quod dicit Augustinus[7] quod Deus non est auctor mali, quia non est causa tendendi ad non esse.

RESPONSIO: Dicendum quod, sicut ex dictis patet,[8] malum quod in defectu actionis consistit, semper causatur ex defectu agentis. In Deo autem nullus defectus est, sed summa perfectio, ut supra ostensum est.[9]

Unde malum quod in defectu actionis consistit vel quod ex defectu agentis causatur non reducitur in Deum sicut in causa.

Sed malum quod in corruptione rerum aliquarum consistit reducitur in Deum sicut in causam. Et hoc patet tam in naturalibus quam in voluntariis. Dictum est enim[10] quod aliquod agens, inquantum sua virtute producit aliquam formam ad quam sequitur corruptio et defectus, causat sua virtute illam corruptionem et defectum. Manifestum est autem quod forma quam principaliter Deus intendit in rebus creatis est bonum ordinis universi. Ordo autem universi requirit, ut supra dictum est,[11] quod quædam sint quæ deficere possint, et interdum deficiant. Et sic Deus, in rebus causando bonum ordinis universi, ex consequenti et quasi per accidens, causat corruptiones rerum; secundum illud quod dicitur Reg.,[12] *Dominus mortificat et vivificat*. Sed quod dicitur Sap.[13] quod Deus *mortem non fecit*, intelligitur quasi per se intentam.

Ad ordinem autem universi pertinet ordo justitiæ, qui requirit ut peccatoribus pœna inferatur. Et secundum hoc Deus est auctor mali quod est pœna, non autem mali quod est culpa, ratione supra dicta.[14]

1. Ad primum ergo dicendum quod auctoritates illæ loquuntur de malo pœnæ, non autem de malo culpæ.

2. Ad secundum dicendum quod effectus causæ secundæ deficientis reducitur in causam primam non deficientem quantum ad id quod habet entitatis et perfectionis, non autem quantum ad id quod habet de defectu.

---

[7]*Lib. 83 Quæst.* 21. PL 40, 16
[8]art. 1
[9]Ia. 4, 1
[10]art 1
[11]Ia. 22, 2 ad 2; 48, 2
[12]I *Samuel* 2, 6. From Hannah's song of praise
[13]*Wisdom* 1, 13
[14]In the body of the article. Also Ia. 48, 6
eGod creates in order to share and communicate his goodness, see above Ia. 19, 2. Nothingness does not serve, and as such is not caused directly by God; cf Ia. 104, 4, on annihilation. Nor is relative nothingness of evil, cf above Ia. 48, 6.
fCajetan, *in loc.*, 'Let it be said briefly that God is not the defective cause of defect in action, though he is of the defectible thing from which action flows.' And Ia2æ. 79, 2, 'An act of sin is and is an act, and on both counts comes from God. All being in whatsoever manner it is must derive from the first being, and every act

ON THE OTHER HAND there is St Augustine saying that God is not the author of evil for he is not the cause of a trend towards to non-being.[7e]

REPLY: It is clear from earlier discussions that the evil which consists in defective action is always caused from a defect in the agent.[8] We have shown that in God there is no defect, but consummate perfection.[9] Hence the evil which lies in defective activity or which is caused by a defective agent does not flow from God as its cause.[f]

Nevertheless that evil which consists in a decay of some things is traced back to God as its cause. And this appears in respect both to natural and to voluntary things. We have seen[10] that in so far that from its strength it produces a form which expels another form an agent of its power causes this loss. God's principal purpose in created things is clearly that form or good which consists in the order of the universe. This requires, as we have noticed,[11] that there should be some things that can, and sometimes do fall away. So then, in causing the common good of the ordered universe, he causes loss in particular things as a consequence and, as it were, indirectly, according to the words, *The Lord kills and brings to life*.[12g] But we read also, *God has not made death*,[13] and the meaning is that he does not will death for its own sake.

The course of justice, which belongs to the universal order, requires that punishment be visited on sinners. On this count God is the author of the evil which is called penalty, but not of that which is fault, and for the reason already given.[14h]

Hence: 1. The authorities appealed to are speaking of the evil of penalty, not of fault.

2. The effect of a deficient secondary cause is derived from a non-deficient first cause with respect to what is real and complete there, not to what is defective. For example, all the motion in the act of limping

---

must derive from God who is act by his essence. He is therefore the cause of every action. But sin signifies a being and an acting with a certain defect. That defect is from a created cause, namely freewill falling from the order of the first cause, and therefore is not to be taken back to the first cause.' cf art. 1 ad 3.

gThis is an argument from the common good considered as the community-good of the universe. The full common good, in the theological sense of the word, is God himself, sharing his good in a society constituted by knowledge and love without suppression of subordinate parts. cf T. Gilby, *Between Community and Society*, London, New York, 1951.

hThe evil of fault rises from a will not conformed in action to its rule and measure: 1a. 49 ad 3. It is not possible that God causes this either *per se* or *per accidens*. For he cannot be in conflict with himself, and his will is the supreme rule: cf 1a2æ. 79, 1 & 2. Also 1a. 48, 6.

Sicut quidquid est motus in claudicatione causatur a virtute motiva; sed quod est obliquitatis in ea, non est ex virtute motiva, sed ex curvitate cruris. Et similiter quidquid est entitatis et actionis in actione mala reducitur in Deum sicut in causam; sed quod est ibi defectus non causatur a Deo, sed ex causa secunda deficiente.

3. Ad tertium dicendum quod submersio navis attribuitur nautæ ut causæ, ex eo quod non agit quod requiritur ad salutem navis. Sed Deus non deficit ab agendo quod est necessarium ad salutem. Unde non est similis.

articulus 3. *utrum sit unum summum malum, quod sit causa omnis mali*

AD TERTIUM sic proceditur:[1] 1. Videtur quod sit unum summum malum, quod sit causa omnis mali. Contrariorum enim effectuum contrariæ sunt causæ. Sed in rebus invenitur contrarietas, secundum illud *Eccl.*,[2] *Contra malum bonum est, et contra vitam mors;* * *sic et contra virum justum peccator.* Ergo sunt contraria principia, unum boni et aliud mali.

2. Præterea, si unum contrariorum est in rerum natura et reliquum, ut dicitur in *De cælo.*[3] Sed summum bonum est in rerum natura, quod est causa omnis boni, ut supra ostensum est.[4] Ergo est et summum malum ei oppositum, causa omnis mali.

3. Præterea, sicut in rebus invenitur bonum et melius ita malum et pejus. Sed bonum et melius dicuntur per respectum ad optimum. Ergo malum et pejus dicuntur per respectum ad aliquod summum malum.

4. Præterea, omne quod est per participationem reducitur ad illud quod est per essentiam. Sed res quæ sunt malæ apud nos non sunt malæ per essentiam, sed per participationem. Ergo est invenire aliquod summum malum per essentiam,† quod est causa omnis mali.

5. Præterea, omne quod est per accidens reducitur ad illud quod est per se. Sed bonum est causa mali per accidens. Ergo oportet ponere aliquod summum malum, quod sit causa malorum per se. Nec dici potest quod malum non habeat causam per se, sed per accidens tantum; quia sequeretur quod malum non esset in pluribus, sed in paucioribus.

6. Præterea, malum effectus reducitur ad malum causæ, quia effectus deficiens est a causa deficiente, sicut supra dictum est.[5] Sed hoc non est

---

*Vulgate: *et contra mortem vita,* and life against death
†Piana: omits *per essentiam*
[1]cf *CG* II, 41; III, 15. *De potentia* III, 6. II *Sent.* I, 1, 1 ad 1; 34, 1 ad 4. *De substantiis separatis* 16. *Compound. theol.* 117. *In De div. nom.* 4, lect. 22
[2]*Ecclesiasticus* 33, 15

comes from a person's vitality, but not the ungainliness which comes from the crooked leg. Likewise all that real and active in a bad action comes from God as its cause, yet the defect there arises from a deficient secondary cause.

3. The sinking of the ship may be blamed on the pilot for not taking all reasonable precautions for her safety. God, however, does not fail in providing everything for salvation.[1] Hence there is no parallel.

article 3. is there one sovereign evil which is the cause of every evil?

THE THIRD POINT:[1] 1. So it would seem.[a] For of contrary effects there are contrary causes. Now we find in things the contrast of contraries; *Ecclesiasticus* tells us, *Good is set against evil, and life against death; so also the sinner against the just man.*[2] Therefore there are contrary principles, good on one side, evil on the other.

2. Again, if one among contraries belongs to the nature of things so too do the remainder, as Aristotle observes.[3] Now the supreme good is real, and is the cause of every good, so it has been stated.[4] Opposed to it, then, a supreme evil exists, the cause of every evil.

3. Besides, we meet with things good and better, so also with things bad and worse. But the comparative of good, the better, supposes the superlative, namely the best. Likewise bad and worse suppose the very worst.

4. Moreover, whatever is such by participation originates in what is such by essence. But the evil things in our environment are bad by participation, not by essence. Hence a sovereign and essential evil which is the cause of every evil can be discovered.

5. Further, all that exists of another comes back to what exists of itself. Now a good is the cause of an evil through the influence of something else.[b] So we should postulate some supreme evil which of itself is the cause of evils. Nor can you allege that evil has an indirect cause merely, not a direct cause, for then it would follow that evil would crop up rarely, not frequently, as it does in fact.

6. Again, bad in an effect derives from bad in the cause, for as stated,[5] a deficient effect is from a deficient cause. An infinite causal regression,

---

[3]*De cælo* II, 3. 286a33. St Thomas, *lect.* 4
[4]1a. 2, 3; 6, 2 & 4
[5]art. 1 & 2
[1]1a2æ. 109, 1–6.
[a]Is there a kind of kingdom of evil? cf 3a. 8, 7 & 8. Or an interconnection of sins? cf 1a2æ. 73, 1.
[b]*Per accidens,* here *per aliud,* of another, not of itself. Cf above art. 1.

procedere in infinitum. Ergo oportet ponere unum primum malum, quod sit causa omnis mali.

SED CONTRA est quod summum bonum est causa omnis entis, ut supra ostensum est.[6] Ergo non potest esse aliquod principium ei oppositum, quod sit causa malorum.

RESPONSIO: Dicendum quod ex prædictis patet non esse unum primum principiorum malorum, sicut est unum primum principium bonorum. primo quidem, quia primum principium bonorum est per essentiam bonum, ut supra ostensum est.[7] Nihil autem potest esse per suam essentiam malum; ostensum est enim quod omne ens, inquantum ens, bonum est;[8] et quod malum non est nisi in bono ut in subjecto.

Secundo, quia primum bonorum principium est summum et perfectum bonum, quod præhabet in se omnem bonitatem, ut supra ostensum est.[9] Summum autem malum esse non potest, quia, sicut ostensum est,[10] etsi malum semper diminuat bonum, nunquam tamen illud potest totaliter consumere; et sic, semper remanente bono, non potest esse aliquid integre et perfecte malum. Propter quod Philosophus dicit[11] quod *si malum integrum sit, seipsum destruet,* quia destructo omni bono—quod requiritur ad integritatem mali—* subtrahitur etiam ipsum malum, cujus subjectum es bonum.

Tertio, quia ratio mali repugnat rationi primi principii. Tum quia omne malum causatur ex bono, ut supra ostensum est.[12] Tum quia malum non potest esse causa nisi per accidens; et sic non potest esse prima causa, quia causa per accidens est posterior ea quae est per se, ut patet in *Physic.*[13]

Qui autem posuerunt duo prima principia, unum bonum et alterum malum, ex eadem radice in hunc errorem inciderunt, ex qua et aliæ extraneæ positiones antiquorum ortum habuerunt, quia scilicet non consideraverunt causam universalem totius entis, sed particulares tantum causas particularium effectuum. Propter hoc enim, si aliquid invenerunt esse nocivum alicui rei per virtutem suæ naturæ, æstimaverunt naturam illius rei esse malam; puta si quis dicat naturam ignis esse malam, quia combussit domum alicuius pauperis.

---

*Piana: omits phrase in parenthesis
[6]Ia. 2, 3; 6, 4
[7]Ia. 6, 3 & 4
[8]Ia. 5, 3; 48, 3
[9]Ia. 6, 2
[10]Ia. 48, 4
[11]*Ethics* IV, 5. 1126a12. St Thomas, *lect.* 13
[12]art, I

however, is out of the question, and therefore we must arrive at one ultimate evil one upon which every evil depends.

ON THE OTHER HAND we have shown that the sovereign good is the cause of the whole of being.[6] There just cannot be a contrasting principle which is the cause of evils.

REPLY: From the preceding discussions it is evident that there cannot be a first principle of everything evil as there is of everything good.

First, because the first source of good things, as we have shown,[7] is good by essence. Whereas there is nothing that can be evil by essence; as we have also shown,[8] every being as such is good, and evil does not exist save as seated in a good.

Second, and this too we have seen,[9] the first source of good things is the supreme and perfect good anticipating all goodness within itself. But a supreme evil cannot be, for, as we have shown,[10] even though evil may indefinitely diminish good it can never entirely consume it, and so, while good remains, there cannot be anything wholly and completely evil. The thought prompts Aristotle to remark that were evil total it would destroy itself,[11c] for the demolition of all good—a necessary condition for evil to be whole and entire—would cut out from under evil its very basis.

Third, the meaning of being an evil is inconsistent with that of being a first principle. Both because every evil is caused by good, in the sense explained,[12] and because the causality it engages is indirect, so that it cannot be a first cause, for an incidental cause is subsequent to an essential cause, as appears in the *Physics*.[13]

As for those who upheld there were two first principles, one good and another evil,[d] their mistake sprang from the same root as that of other strange beliefs of the ancient philosophers, namely they did not consider the universal cause of the whole of being, but only the particular causes of particular effects.[e] On this account when they discovered that by the strength of its own nature one thing was damaging to another they reckoned that the nature of that thing was evil; for example, that fire's nature was bad for burning down some poor man's home.

---

[13]*Physics* II, 6. 198a8. St Thomas, *lect.* 13

[c]The point is magnified somewhat out of its context. Aristotle is discussing the excess of anger which can be self-stultifying. 'One can be angry with the wrong persons, at the wrong things, more than is right, too quickly, and too long—yet all these excesses are not to be found in the same person. Indeed they could not, for evil destroys even itself, and if it is complete becomes unbearable.'

[d]Dualism: cf *CG* II, 41.

[e]Long views and short views, cf above 1a. 44, 2.

Judicium autem de bonitate alicujus rei non est accipiendum secundum ordinem ad aliquid particulare, sed secundum seipsum et secundum ordinem ad totum universum, in quo quælibet res suum ordinem ordinatissime tenet, ut ex dictis patet.[14]

Similiter etiam, qui* invenerunt duorum particularium effectuum contrariorum duas causas particulares contrarias, nesciverunt reducere causas particulares contrarias in causam universalem communem. Et ideo usque ad prima principia contrarietatem in causis judicaverunt. Sed cum omnia contraria conveniant in uno communi, necesse est in eis, supra causas contrarias proprias, inveniri unam causam communem; sicut supra qualitates contrarias elementorum invenitur virtus corporis cælestis. Et similiter supra omnia quæ quocumque modo sunt invenitur unum primum principium essendi, ut supra ostensum est.[15]

1. Ad primum ergo dicendum quod contraria conveniunt in genere uno; et etiam conveniunt in ratione essendi. Et ideo licet habeant causas particulares contrarias, tamen oportet devenire ad unam primam causam communem.

2. Ad secundum dicendum quod privatio et habitus nata sunt fieri circa idem. Subjectum autem privationis est ens in potentia, ut dictum est.[16] Unde, cum malum sit privatio boni, ut ex dictis patet,[17] illi bono opponitur cui adjungitur potentia, non autem summo bono, quod est actus purus.

3. Ad tertium dicendum quod unumquodque intenditur secundum propriam rationem. Sicut autem forma est perfectio quædam ita privatio est quædam remotio. Unde omnis forma et perfectio et bonum per accessum ad terminum perfectum intenditur; privatio autem et malum per recessum a termino. Unde non dicitur malum et pejus per accessum ad symmum malum, sicut dicitur bonum et melius per accessum ad summum bonum.

4. Ad quartum dicendum quod nullum ens dicitur malum per participationem, sed per privationem participationis. Unde non oportet fieri reductionem ad aliquid quod sit per essentiam malum.

---

*Leonine: *quia*
[14]Ia. 47, 2 ad 1
[15]Ia. 2, 3
[16]Ia. 48, 3
[17]ibid
[f]A theologian, instructed by Revelation, holds a position about the order and purpose of the universe less tentative than that of a philosophical scientist. Yet he can offer no substitute for purely rational investigation, and should be careful not to intrude on or interrupt the show of evidence.
[g]cf above Ia. 48, 3.
[h]We do not stop at blue or red, but look for the cause of colour. The argument

The goodness, however, of a thing should not be assessed from its reference to another particular thing, but on its own worth according to the universal scheme of things, wherein each, as we have seen,[14] most admirably holds an appointed place.[f]

So also it was that some, when faced with two contrary causes for two contrary effects, were at a loss how to resolve them into a common universal cause; in consequence they read this causal opposition into ultimate world-principles. What we should do instead is this: since all contraries agree in having something in common,[g] to discover one common cause beneath what is peculiar to the particular contrary causes in question, analogous to a cosmic power underlying the contrary qualities of the elements.[h] This was the way we pursued[15] to reach an original and unique source of reality behind all things that exist, no matter how.

Hence: 1. Contraries come together in the same common class; they also agree in sharing in the nature of reality. Their particular causes are contraries, nevertheless all should be traced back to one common first cause.

2. To possess a form and to be deprived of it belongs to the same subject, that is in the nature of things. Now the subject of a privation, as we have seen,[16] is a being in potentiality, and hence, since evil is a privation, as we have also seen,[17] it is the opposite of that particular good which answers to the potentiality in question, not to the supreme good which is pure actuality.

3. A thing becomes more intensified in conformity to its proper nature. Now as its form spells a certain achievement so does its privation spell a corresponding failure. Hence any form and perfection grows more intense by advancing towards a point of completion, while privation and evil come by retreating from it.[i] That is why we do not speak of bad becoming worse by approaching some supreme evil in the same manner that we speak of good becoming better by approaching to the supreme good.[j]

4. Never is a being called evil because it shares in evil, but because it suffers deprivation by failing to share in the good. Hence there is no need to resolve an evil into a reality which is essential evil.

---

echoes Aristotle on the common principle at work behind the contrasting effects in particular changes; e.g. *De cælo* I, 2. 269a30. It does not depend, however, on the hypothesis that a *corpus cæleste* exercises universal physical causality or that there is a fifth element behind the play of earth, water, fire, and air.

[i]On growth by intensification, cf 1a2æ. 52 & 53. For the background theory see L. B. Geiger, *La Participation dans la philosophie de S. Thomas d'Aquin*, Paris, 1953.

[j]There is no *summum malum* or absolute evil contrary to the *summum bonum*. Only in morals can things, or acts rather, be against God, and then the root of the opposition, as has been suggested, lies in being contradictory, not contrary.

5. Ad quintum dicendum quod malum non potest habere causam nisi per accidens, ut supra ostensum est.[18] Unde impossibile est fieri reductionem ad aliquid quod sit per se causa mali. Quod autem dicitur quod malum est ut in pluribus, simpliciter falsum est. Nam generabilia et corruptibilia, in quibus solum contingit esse malum naturæ, sunt modica pars totius universi. Et iterum in unaquaque specie defectus naturæ accidit ut in paucioribus. In solis autem hominibus malum videtur esse ut in pluribus; quia bonum hominis secundum sensum non est hominis inquantum homo, idest secundum rationem;* plures autem sequuntur sensum quam rationem.

6. Ad sextum dicendum quod in causis mali non est procedere in infinitum, sed est reducere omnia mala in aliquam causam bonam, ex qua sequitur malum per accidens.

---

*Piana: *secundum sensum corporis . . . sed secundum rationem*

[18]art. I

kPhysical evil, *malum naturæ*, here taken as belonging to the world of the *Physics*. The spiritual world is regarded also as a world of nature more extensive than the

5. As we have shown,[18] an evil admits of an indirect cause merely. And so it is impossible to take it back to anything that is the direct cause of evil. As for the reference to evil being present in the majority of cases, it is simply untrue. For things subject to generation and decay, in which alone we experience physical evil,[k] compose but a small part of the whole universe, and besides defects of nature are minority occurrences in any species.

They seem to be in a majority only among human beings. For what appears good for them as creatures of sense is not simply good for them as human, that is as reasonable beings; in fact most of them follow after sense, rather than intelligence.[1]

6. There is no going back indefinitely in the series of causes of evil. Instead all evils are to be resolved into some cause which is good, and from which evil results indirectly.

---

bodily world. cf 1a. 50, 3. For *malum pœnæ* as an evil of nature, cf above 1a. 48, 5.

[1]The fact is registered, why it should be so is left until later: cf 1a2æ. 77 & 85.

Appendix 1

DERIVED EXISTENCE
(1a. 45)

1. ROOTED IN a common tradition, the religions of the Bible and the Koran are alike in uncompromisingly affirming one God, the maker of heaven and earth; so it was from the first, and so it remained after the refinements of Greek thought had been grafted into their religious philosophy: St Thomas's developed doctrine of creation was heir to the speculations of the great Jewish and Moslem philosophers. The Scriptural *yoser*, *poietes*, *factor* soon became *creator*, from *creo*, to bring forth, and was given the special sense of calling into being from a complete blank.[1] Precision came from the mass of catechetical, apologetic, and polemical writings occasioned by pantheism, polytheism, and dualism; the names of St Hippolytus, Tertullian, and Origen may be singled out in the process. The patristic period culminates with St Augustine: he attacked theories of one single emanation from God and the production of all else through a descending series of intermediaries; he examined and decided against the eternity of the world; and he remains the classical author on the attribution of creative activity to the Persons of the Trinity.[2] St Anselm cleared up the semantics of the question, but it seems fair to say that until the teachings of Neo-Platonists and Aristoteleans had been thoroughly assimilated by thirteenth-century theologians a rigorously metaphysical account of creation was not established. The present treatise is its greatest monument.

Though the debate is perennial, the notion of creation falls rather flat when metaphysical philosophy goes to ground during periods engrossed with positivism. It springs from Plotinus and Proclus, to cast back no earlier and reflect only on Western philosophies of religion; it exercised John Scotus Eruigena, Avicenna, Maimonides, and Averroes; it was not settled in the *Summa*, for it was raised fifty years later by the Dominican Meister Eckhart who loved the writings of St Thomas and found himself condemned; it runs through Spinoza onwards to the great German systematic ideologies on the structure of thought and reality. How can there be beings? How can *is* be repeated at depth and not merely in outward appearance? How can the changeless create and not be changed? These, and many more, are the questions that cluster round the issue. This appendix entertains no ambition to answer them, and attempts no more than a sketch of some of the features of the salient occupied by St Thomas.

2. First as to his terminology. Repeating the language of Dionysius, in the translation of John Scotus Eruigena, he speaks equably of *eductio, emanatio, exitus, effluxus ab ente primo*, without fear of suggesting pantheism; his own

---

[1]cf the Hebrew *bara*, always reserved to God. Also *qanah*, Greek *ktisis*
[2]cf 1a. 45, 6 & 7

proper usage hardens in favour of *productio totius esse a causa universali omnium entium.*[3] The fundamental principle of his explanation is the real distinction between essence and existence in created things.[4] This entitative composition, as it is sometimes called, is an application of Aristotle's distinction between potentiality and actuality, and is carried from bodily things (the essential composition of primary matter and substantial form) to all finite things.[5] His first discussions, which go back to his early days before he was made Master of Theology, are found in the *De ente et essentia.*[6]

We use 'existence' to translate *'esse'*, but in his days *exsistere*, to come forth, to be manifest, had not acquired its present meaning, and it may be that he refrained from using it in the present question in order to keep the common filiation of *'ens'*, *'essentia'*, and *'esse'*. The first is the most flexible term of the three, and can cover anything that is not nothing, thus possible being, potential being, and actual being. The second has two main and related meanings, namely a thing's meaning, *ratio*, intelligibility, specific being, the reply to the question 'what is it?' and also its substance or its being irreducible to any other subject; confusion of these two meanings has produced misunderstanding of St Thomas's argument. The third almost always should be read with what may be called a full existential impact.

3. We have referred to a confusion between ideal essence and real essence. Avicenna, who was a major influence on the thirteenth-century scholastics, had drawn from Alfarabi a distinction between the intelligibility (or possibility) of a thing and the fact of its being real (or actual). What a thing is does not include the fact that it is. It was concluded that existence is adventitious, or a kind of accident, to essence. On this head Avicenna was criticized by Averroes, a closer Aristotelean and a less welcome figure to most of the Latin thinkers. St Thomas himself began from Avicenna under St Albert the Great, but escaped from the fallacy. Nevertheless echoes of ontological thought remain, notably in the contrast between the necessity of a meaning and the contingency of its being an event,[7] and this, combined with the views of an 'essentialist' as opposed to experiential or 'existentialist' wing among his followers, provides some excuse for those who in attacking his distinction between essence and existence have fallen into *ignorantia elenchi.*

---

[3]e.g. Ia. 45, 3
[4]cf N. del Prado, *De veritate fundamentali philosophiæ Christianæ*, Fribourg, 1911. D. Bañez, *Scholastica commentaria in* Iam. 3, 4, reprinted Madrid, 1934. Bañez stands second to none as a commentator on the *Prima Pars*. J. Maritain, *Seven Lectures on Being*, New York, 1956. E. Gilson, *Being and Some Philosophers*, Toronto, 1952; *The Christian Philosophy of St Thomas Aquinas*, London, New York, 1957
[5]cf *In Meta.* XII. lect. 2
[6]Also entitled *De quidditate et esse*. Written before 1256; the early date of 1252 has been conjectured. Edited from 8 Paris texts by M. D. Roland-Gosselin, Paris, 1926. From 11 additional Italian and German texts by C. Bauer, Münster, 1926. Translation by A. Maurer, Toronto, 1949.
[7]cf Ia. 46, 2

The dispute is not just an affair of Scholastics, with Thomists on one side and Scotist and Suarezians on the other; it enters into the post-Bergsonian protest against the philosophisms of Descartes, Wolff, and Hegel. When speaking to the present point, St Thomas does not picture a world of essences outcropping into the world of fact, and makes it clear that his position is not that of Avicenna. 'The existence of a thing, though other than its essence, is not nevertheless to be understood as something superadded in the manner of an accident, but as though constituted by the principles of the essence.'[8] In other words, real existence is not conceived as a new predicate of a real subject; it is the actuality which makes real what is potential there, and consequently cannot be elicited from that potentiality, namely the essence.[9] The two are not contrasted as ideal and real, or on parallel lines, for both are in the same line; existence is the causally actualized continuation and culmination of essence, as actually light or white is of potentially light or white. 'Existence is more intimately and profoundly interior to everything than whatever else, since it informs all that is real.'[10]

4. Were a creature's essence identical with its existence it would exist of itself, and therefore would not need to be created. Moreover, were simple existence a common predicate of every reality, it would follow that creatures were not diversified among themselves as beings, that is at the level of metaphysics, but only at some other level, for instance, of commonsense philosophy or ethics.[11] A potentiality is not self-actuating, and therefore is distinct from its actuality. A potentiality to existence as such is not, of course, separable from its actuality, as though it really could exist before it did, nevertheless the two are really distinct in the actualized potentiality.[12] This is the guiding principle of St Thomas's explanation of what creatureliness is and how there can be many created beings distinct in kind and degree.

---

[8]*In Meta.* IV, *lect.* 2
[9]*De ente et essentia* 5. Ia. 3, 4
[10]Ia. 8, 1
[11]cf Introduction (10)
[12]cf Ia. 46, 1 ad 2; 3 ad 1 & 2. for a similar turn of argument

Appendix 2

AN EVERLASTING WORLD
(1a. 46)

THE *Prima Pars* was completed in 1268 at Viterbo where St Thomas was lecturing to the Papal Court; it had been started in 1265 at Rome, so that the treatise from it translated in this volume can be placed between these dates, and probably nearer to the earlier than the later. It could have been composed in Rome, Anagni, Orvieto, or Viterbo, for the government was then conducted from mobile headquarters, not from a sort of Whitehall— a fact not without significance for the temper of thought in high places. In 1269 he was suddenly recalled to Paris, partly to maintain the position of the Dominicans in the University, mainly to defend an object of belief, namely that the world once began. In both respects his intervention was decisive.

The tide of Aristoteleanism was flowing strongly and bearing with it the teachings of Averroism. This is not the place to determine who more faithfully rendered the thought of Aristotle, the Latin Averroists who took him from the Arabic, or the Albertino-Thomists who were beginning to work from the Greek: a friend of St Thomas's, and his colleague at the Papal Court, the Dominican William of Moerbeke, Archbishop of Corinth, was a famous Hellenist. The Christian doctrine of creation cannot find explicit support in Aristotle, and the impact of his teaching at Paris, notably its picture of a world based on the eternal principles of imperishable forms and ungenerable matter, seemed to oppose traditional doctrines in its dependence on creative freewill. That was how it struck men as rationalists; there is no reason to doubt that most of them were believers who accepted Christian teaching on morality and human destiny. But, like many philosophers and scientists since, they were prepared to work with a divided mind, and hold a double-truth theory, that what is true in reason could be false in faith, and vice versa.

It was St Thomas's effort to get below the surface of Aristotle's thought, and though perhaps over-ready to see Aristotle as more of a Christian than he really was, and to read some texts accordingly, his interpretations are not strained in relation to the general tenor of the *Physics* and *Metaphysics*; thus, for example, his appreciation of the difference between a demonstrative and a probable argument.[1] Indeed, if he erred as a commentator, it was in failing to recapture the period flavour of Aristotle, not his thinking: that was a mark of most medieval literary criticism. That he felt strongly about vindicating Aristotle as a support for Christians is evident from the first of his works

---

[1] cf 1a. 46, 1

against the Paris Averroists which dates from this period (1270), the *De unitate intellectus*, which ends with unwonted warmth:

'So in order to wreck an error these are the points I have put together, from the reasonings and sayings of philosophers, not from the documents of faith. It anybody who would glory in science so-called wants to reply to what I have written, let him not mutter in corners with undergraduates who are unable to discriminate on such difficult matters, but let him come out if he dare, and meet, not me alone who am the least, but many others jealous for the truth who can withstand his error and advise on his ignorance.

These words are usually taken to refer to Siger of Brabant, still somewhat of an enigmatic figure, who was a leader, perhaps the most distinguished, of the Latin Averroists. But they are not characteristic of the personal relations of St Thomas with this group; many of the *artistæ* belonged to it who wrote to the Master General of the Dominicans lamenting his death (1274), while some of the divines were soon to get him condemned. In fact the grumblers, or *murmurantes*, to whom the following *opusculum* is addressed were mainly the theologians of the Establishment, with many of whom St Thomas was also on terms of close friendship. His own master, St Albert the Great, began by preferring the non-eternity to the eternity of the universe as representing the more probable position, but hardened in the end against the latter, holding that *factus* and *æternus* are not in truth compatible. The group stood for the traditional teaching; hence St Thomas's appeal to St Augustine and other received authorities. Yet it was not obscurantist, quite the reverse, for it was prepared to argue that a beginning to the world was a matter of proof, not just of faith.

The work which is closely argued, shows him fighting on two fronts, on one to maintain that a beginning to the world is not impossible to reason, not even to Aristotelean reason, and on the other that it cannot be demonstrated to have been the case. Written in 1270-1, shortly after the *De unitate intellectus*, it develops the position taken up several years before in the *Summa*.[2]

On the Eternity of the World[3]

Granting, in accordance with Catholic belief, that the world's duration had a beginning, the doubt still remains whether it could always have existed. To open out the truth of the matter let us draw the line between where we agree with our opponents and where we differ.

1. If crediting something other than God with eternity means that it was

---

[2]1a. 46, 1 & 2

[3]*De æternitate mundi contra murmurantes*. *Opusc.* XXVII, Piana; XXIII, Parma & Vivès; IV, Mandonnet. The translation is usually from the text edited by J. Perrier, Paris, 1949. There are many mss variants on points of detail. The work bears the marks of hurried composition, and the translator has not hesitated to ease the style here and there

not made by him, this would be an intolerable error, not against faith only, but for philosophers as well who profess and prove that all that has existence in any way whatever cannot be unless caused by that which exists in the highest and truest sense. If what is meant, however, is that a thing always was though entirely caused by God, then this is a position to be looked into to see whether it be tenable.

2. Were it judged impossible this would be on the grounds, either that God could not make a thing that always has been, or that it could not be done, even taking into account his omnipotence.[4]

As for the first all of us are in agreement, that is to say, if we just look at his limitless power, God could have made something that endlessly was. It is the second that remains to be seen.

3. You cannot urge that it is just not feasible for something to come into being yet always to have existed unless you do so because of two conditions or reasons, namely because it would deny the presence of passive potentiality or because it would be a contradiction in terms.

As for the first, remark that before a pure spirit or angel was made, it was not capable of coming to be, for within it there was no antecedent passive potentiality or capacity for existence. All the same God can make an angel and bring it into existence, for so he has done and there it is. In this connection let us accept without reservation the orthodox line that a thing caused by God cannot have existed always, that is to say we rule out the heterodox postulate of an eternally existing passive principle. This, however, is not entailed in the statement that God could make a reality that always was.

4. As for the second, we speak of an impossibility when the notions involved are incompatible, for instance that contradictories should be simultaneously true. Some indeed hold that God can do the impossible, while others deny that he can because of its non-entity. Of course he cannot, for the power to do so would be self-destructive, for it is the power to do what is real. Nevertheless to assert that God has this power is not heretical, though I am convinced that it is false.[5] That what has happened has not happened, for instance, is a contradiction in terms. St Augustine writes,[6] *Anybody declaring that if God is omnipotent he may cause what has been done not to have been done does not notice that he is making out that God can cause things to be true as such from the fact that they are false.* Some masters have devoutly professed, notwithstanding, that God can wipe out the past in this manner; and they were not deemed heretical.

Consequently we should look into these two notions, namely 'created by God' and 'having always existed', and see whether they are incompatible. Whatever the upshot, I repeat that you cannot level a charge of heresy against the statement that God can create an everlasting effect, though I hold it would be false were the notions mutually exclusive. If they are not, then the statement not only is not false but also about what possibly could be true;

---

[4]cf 1a. 25, 3   [5]cf the analysis of omnipotence, 1a. 25, 2–5
[6]*Contra Faustum* XXVI, 5. PL 42, 481

and to dissent from this judgment would be a mistake. It would be a disparagement in effect of God's omnipotence, which surpasses all our understanding and our power, to claim that we might conceive of a creature God could not produce. Nor is the fact of sin at all to the point, for that as such is a hollowness. The whole question boils down to this, Are the notions 'to be created according to entire substance' and 'to have no beginning in duration' mutually irreconcilable or not?

5. That they are not may be shown as follows. One would cancel out the other on one or both of these two postulates; first, that a cause must precede its effect in duration, second, that non-being must precede being in duration, this, so it is said, being our underlying assumption when we talk about a thing caused by God coming into being from nothing.[7]

6. So first let us show there is no need for an efficient cause, which in this case is God, to precede his effects in duration unless he has so willed it.

To start with, no cause producing an instantaneous effect necessarily precedes it in duration. And God is such a cause, not working through change. Therefore he does not have to precede his effects in duration.

The major appears by induction from sudden effects, such as radiation and the like,[8] yet, none the less, may be proved deductively as follows. Posit that a thing exists and you can posit that at the same instant the action of which it is the principle also exists; this appears in things which are generated, for at the very moment that fire begins so does heating. Now when action is instantaneous then the beginning and the end are simultaneous, indeed identical, as is the case with all objects that cannot be split. Therefore on the supposition of an agent instantaneously producing its effect, whatever the moment of its action, you can set down then the term of the action. That term and the finished product are simultaneous. So then it is not unthinkable for a cause producing an instantaneous effect not to precede it in duration, though it would be for a cause producing its effect through change, since the start of change precedes its finish.

It is because they are accustomed to causality at work through change that people grasp with difficulty that an efficient cause is not necessarily prior in duration to its effect. So it is also that those who have not tested the many are inclined to jump to conclusions about the few.

7. Nor can it be objected to our argument that God is an efficient cause through will, since even willing does not necessarily precede its effect in duration, nor yet does a voluntary agent, unless acting from deliberation, and far be it from us to attribute this to God.[9]

8. Further, a cause producing the whole substance of an effect is no less, indeed much more potent than a cause producing a form only by drawing it from the potentiality of the material. Yet such a merely transforming cause may so operate that as soon as it acts the form is produced, as with the

---

[7]cf 1a. 45, 1. Par. 12 picks up this second thread
[8]cf 1a. 45, 2 ad 3   [9]cf 1a. 19, 3-5

light of the sun. With all the more reason then may God, who produces a thing's entire substance, so act that whenever he is so also is his effect.

9. Moreover an effect is complementary to a cause, and this fact is wanting at the instant when a cause has no effect. A complete cause and its effect are simultaneous. But no completion is wanting to God's causality. Hence, given that he is, he can always have had an effect, and therefore there is no must about his having to precede it in duration.[10]

10. Then again, the will to do something takes nothing away from the natural power of the person willing, and with God least of all. Those who dismiss Aristotle's reasons—proving that creatures have always existed from God because like makes like[11]—would be prepared to accept the conclusion were God a non-voluntary agent. Yet they should ask themselves whether it really alters the case. Could he not have willed that what he has willed always was and never was not?

11. Clearly then the statement that an efficient cause may not precede its effect in duration offers no violence to the mind, nor anything belonging to the realm of impossibility, which God cannot bring about.

12. It now remains to be seen whether an effect that never was not is conceivable despite its being defined as made out of nothing.

In support of this not involving a contradiction there is St Anselm in his *Monologion*[12] when he explains what we mean in saying that a creature is made out of nothing. A third reading is this, he points out, that we conceive of something being made, but not out of anything. We employ a similar turn of phrase when we speak of a person being sad about nothing, and mean that his sadness is groundless. This is no awkward construction, for we are simply saying, that apart from the supreme being, all things are made out of nothing, that is, not made out of anything. Clearly no precedence is implied, as though there were nothing once and then something afterwards.

13. Even were a relation to a preceding nothingness to remain affirmed, so that when you say that the creature was made from nothing you mean that it was made after nothing, the term 'after' indicates priority in the most abstract of its several senses. Priority may be of nature or of duration as well.[13] Now you cannot infer what is particular and proper from the general and universal; no more can you necessarily conclude that because a creature is said to be after nothing a precedence in duration is implied, which is tantamount to saying there was nothing beforehand and something thereafter. A priority of meaning is quite enough: that is all you have committed yourself to. For what belongs to an object of itself is prior in thought to what is combined with it only from another. Now a creature has no existence

---

[10]An argument St Thomas will not press beyond what could be possible
[11]*Physics* III, 4. 203b27
[12]8. PL 158, 156
[13]Priority of nature, that is of meaning. A conceptual or notional priority, thus of father before son. Priority of duration, thus of Abraham before Isaac

except from another. Left to itself it is nothing, and in this sense non-existence is the sooner its own by nature than existence.

14. All the same we are not suggesting on this account that nothingness and being are simultaneous, as though nothingness had a duration.[14] For we are not proposing that an everlasting creature once upon a time was as nothing, but that such is its nature that left alone by itself nothing would remain. It is rather as when we speak of air having been illumined by the sun, instead of speaking of its having been made luminous by the sun. Anything that becomes so comes from what does not happen to be so, that is from what was not identical with what it now is; we mean therefore that air is made light from the non-luminous or dark, not that it was ever non-luminous or dark, but that it would be without the sun. The point we are making is better exemplified by constellations and spheres on which the sun never sets.

15. Clearly, then, there is no contradiction in the assertion that an object both has been created by God and has ever existed. If there were it is certainly strange that St Augustine did not notice it, for this would have been a most decisive disproof of the world's eternity, which he attacked on several scores but not on this.[15] Instead he hints that it is not unthinkable, for he sees a meaning in the contention of the Platonists that creatures hold a secondary place but do not come second in time.[16] For, say they, even as a foot, if it had eternally stood in the dust, the footprint would have been eternal also, though nobody would doubt that some foot had trod it there, nor would the one have been before the other, though one would have been made by the other. So also, they conclude, the world and the gods themselves have ever been, co-eternal with the Creator's eternity, though by him created. St Augustine's criticism is on other grounds, never that the position makes no sense. He thinks that those who profess that the world is made by God, but nevertheless not that it had a beginning in time, are saying something, though explaining the origination of creation in a way we can scarcely understand.[17] Our first argument has touched on how and why this is the case.[18]

16. Strange also that renowned natural philosophers have spotted no contradiction, for St Augustine recognizes that he is dealing with writers who agree with us that God is incorporeal and the creator of all natures which but for him do not exist, and goes on to praise them as outstanding in fame and credit.[19] That this is deserved will be evident to a careful student of writers who held that the world always was yet nevertheless was always made by God, and perceived here no contradiction.

17. What of those who do with such subtlety of discernment? Are they

---

[14]There is no combination of *nihil* and *ens*
[15]*De civitate Dei* XI, 4 & 5; XII, 15. PL 41, 319; 364
[16]ibid. X, 31. PL 41, 311. *Substitutio*, a laying under, setting in second place
[17]ibid. XI, 4. PL 41, 319
[18]Par. 6 above
[19]ibid. XI, 5. PL 41, 320–1

founts of wisdom or just ordinary men?[20] Let us look at the authorities they appeal to, and indicate what slight support they afford. Take St John Damascene, for instance, who says that ill-born would be a thing that was brought forth from non-existence yet was co-eternal in existence with him who is without principle and always is.[21] Take also Hugh of St Victor saying that the ineffable power of omnipotence could not have alongside itself another co-eternal whereby its operation could be assisted.[22]

18. Boëthius at the end of his *Consolation* throws light on how we should interpret these and like authorities. He speaks of the mistake made by those who, hearing of Plato's vision of this world as not having had a beginning in time nor as ever going to decay, concluded therefrom that the established world accordingly is co-eternal with its author. For it is one thing, Boethius observed, to be led through endless life, which Plato attributed to the world, and another to enjoy the presence of endless life wholly and equally embraced, which manifestly is proper to the divine mind.[23]

19. Hence what some object to does not follow, namely that an eternal creature would be God's equal in duration. The thought is that nothing can be co-eternal with God, since only he is unchanging. As St Augustine puts it, time runs though a mutability, and cannot be co-eternal to immutable eternity, and therefore the immortality of angels does not pass over into time; nor is their past as though it is not and their future as though it is not yet, nevertheless their motions go through seasons and by thrusting into the future fall back into the past. And therefore they can never be co-eternal with the Creator in whose activity there is nothing past that is still not present, or future than is not there already.[24] So also he says that the nature of the Trinity is wholly eternal, and in such a way that nothing else can be co-eternal with it.[25] And he writes to the same effect in the *Confessions*.[26]

20. They also introduce arguments which Aristotle has handled and solved; among them the difficult one is about the infinity of souls, for if the world is eternal there must now be an unlimited number of souls. Yet it is not to the present point, for God could have made the world without men and their souls, or have made men when he willed although the world had been going on from all ages, in which case there would be no infinity of souls surviving the body. And furthermore it has yet to be demonstrated that God cannot make an actually infinite multitude.

There are other objections which I skip for the present, partly because they are dealt with elsewhere, partly because their very weakness seems to lend force to the probability of the position they attack.

---

[20]An uncharacteristic fling at opponents, here St Thomas's fellow-theologians. Compare the similar touch of temper at the Averroists from *De unitate intellectus* quoted above

[21]*De fide orthodoxa* I, 8. PG 94, 814   [22]*De sacramentis* I, I. PL 176, 187

[23]*De consolatione philosophiæ* V, 6. PL 63, 859. cf Ia. 10, 3

[24]*De civitate Dei* XII, 15. PL 41, 364

[25]*De Genesi ad litteram* VIII, 23. PL 34, 389   [26]*Confessions* XI, 30. PL 32, 826

Appendix 3

CAUSALITY WITHIN THE UNIVERSE
(1a. 47)

A CODEX in the Library of Monte Cassino (no. 138) introduces the Question by promising four points of inquiry. *Primo . . . secundo . . . tertio, de earum ordine, quarto, de unitate mundi.* The third article is inserted with the note that it is not found in the Paris exemplar of Brother Thomas's *Summa.* Pègues takes it into the text, the Leonine includes it as a footnote. Though not found in other extant mss and having a slight flavour not characteristic of the *Summa* 'ordinary', we translate it here as a link between the discussions on Providence and on the divine government of the universe.[1] The subject-matter is dealt with in greater detail later.[a]

article 3. *is there an order of agents among creatures?*

THE THIRD POINT: 1. No, it would seem. To act without is mightier than to act through an intermediary. Of all agents God is the most powerful. Hence he acts without intermediary, and so one creature does not act on another.

2. Moreover, to reproduce its like is of an agent's nature. Now that to the likeness of which it is made is a thing's exemplar. Were one creature to be the efficient cause of another it would follow that the higher were exemplars of the lower. This Dionysius rejects.[2]

3. Furthermore, agent and end coincide in some specific thing, so the *Physics* teach us.[3] If then one creature is the active cause of another one will be its final cause of another. Which seems to be against *Proverbs, The Lord has made all things for himself.*[4]

ON THE OTHER HAND St Paul speaks of the things that are ordained by God.[5] And Dionysius tells us that the law of divinity is to bring back to itself the lower through the higher.[6]

REPLY: Some, speaking after the manner of the Moors,[7] have held that no

---

[1] 1a. 22 & 103. Vols 5 & 14   [2] *De divinis nominibus* 5. St Thomas, *lect.* 2
[3] From *Physics* II, 3. 195b21. *lect.* 5   [4] *Proverbs* 16, 4
[5] *Douay: be subject to the higher powers* (RSV, *governing authorities*) *and those that are ordained* by God (RSV *have been instituted by God*). Romans 13, 1.
[6] *De ecclesiastica hierarchia* 5
[7] The thought of Aristotle first reached the Latin West from across the marches of Moorish Spain
[a] 1a. 103, 6; 105, 5. The article is printed by the Ottawa Piana as an appendix to the *Prima Pars.*

creature has any action on another; what heats it is not fire, but God in the fire. Groundless, then, on this view the attribution of active powers, and qualities, and forms to things.

Instead we should hold that the very inequality constituted in things by divine wisdom requires one creature to act on another.[8] For the inequality of creatures means that one is more complete than another. Now the more compares to the less as actuality to potentiality. And bound up with the meaning of actually existing is acting on what is potential. So then one creature needs must act on another. All the same as a creature draws from God, who is pure actuality, its actual existence, so does it draw its power of acting from God and actually acts in his power, as a secondary cause in virtue of the first cause.[9]

Hence: 1. All things done by the action of creatures God can do without them. It is not, therefore, from any defect of power that he acts through the intermediary of a creature, but from the abundance of his goodness, which grants to a creature not only its own inherent goodness, but also the dignity of being to others the cause of goodness.

2. Because the first exemplar of all things is God, Dionysius rejects the opinion that unembodied intelligences were first exemplars. However, there is nothing to forbid one creature being the secondary exemplar of another.

3. The ultimate end of all things is God. Nevertheless it embraces other ends, in that one creature is ordained to another as to its end, the less to the more perfect, for instance matter to form, elements to compounds, plants to animals, animals to men, as *Genesis* puts it.[10] So is the order of the universe respected, by the acting of one creature on another, by one being made to the likeness of another, and by one being the purpose of another.

---

[8]Ia. 47, 2
[9]cf Ia. 105, 5
[10]*Genesis* I, 26–30

Appendix 4

EVIL

(1a. 48–9)

ST DOMINIC'S Order had been founded in the Midi to counter the persuasion that matter was the principle of evil, and that the way of perfection for the spirit lay in shaking off the body and then, invulnerable, letting it do what it liked. St Thomas steadily refused to reduce the dramatic and ethical confrontation of good and bad to these terms or to elevate it into a philosophical or theological dualism. Bernard Gui tells of him seated in deep abstraction, though at dinner with St Louis, King of France, then suddenly recovering himself, smiting the table, exclaiming 'that settles the Manichees', and calling for his secretary.[1] There is more temper in the story than in the two Questions we are noticing. They offer a diagnosis in most general terms, dispassionate in mood, intended neither to protest against nor reconcile us to our lot, not even to set forth a solution for sensitive or believing minds. They merely set the problem in proportion.

Accordingly it is important to appreciate the limits within which they work. The general discussion is about the distinctions running through creation, and the first type that comes up for theological consideration is that between good and evil. Remembering that the interest here is largely in the philosophical groundwork of theology,[2] it will come as little surprise if not much more seems provided than a preliminary assessment of the problem as it stands for a Christian view of the universe, a *status quæstionis*, or grammar of thought to aid an approach to the mystery of sin and its resolution in the Passion of Christ, to be meditated on later at length.[3]

Next, a distinction should be drawn between the passages meant to be convincing explanations and those meant merely to call in some of the probabilities bearing on the situation, the *argumenta ex convenientia*, recommendations at various strength, and never to be pushed beyond their strength.[4] St Thomas, always respectful towards received authorities, even when in effect he was opposing them, thus with respect to the Augustinian identification of sin with lust,[5] sometimes rehearses special pleadings not closely to the point and likely to fall flatter to our vogue than to his. At first sight it may strike us that he shows too easy and sweeping an approval of the

---

[1]K. Foster, *The Life of St Thomas Aquinas*, biographical documents, London, Baltimore, 1959
[2]cf Introduction
[3]1a2æ. 71–89. Vols 25 & 27 of this series. 3a. 1 & 46–52. Vols 48 & 54
[4]Vol. 1, Appendix 2 (6)
[5]1a. 82, 3

reflection that things which can fail sometimes will,[6] or that he presumes too much in repeating that a martyr's courage counterbalances a tyrant's cruelty.[7] Yet he is expecting his reader's discrimination between a discourse that proceeds *ex propriis*, that is from the very nature of the subject, often in terms in internal finality, and one that makes a pattern by assembling interacting things in terms of external finality.[8] His style is to keep a poker face, though he is not always arguing in deadly earnest.

His argumentation in these two Questions is clear enough to call for no paraphrase. It picks up the conclusions of St Augustine and carries on some of the issues raised in the early eleventh-century polemics of Rupert of Deutz with Anselm of Laon and William of Champeaux. Some main points may be noted. Creatureliness or limited being is not recognized as bad. In this sense there is no *malum metaphysicum*, and no lapse, as was thought by the Gnostics and Manicheans, in the descent from the infinite to the finite, or from the spiritual to the material. The statement that men are not angels carries with it no philosophical regret; 'men' are there merely as the logical Subject of a Predicate, not as a real subject or potentiality for wholly spiritual being. Evil, then, is not simple negation, but the privation of a good that can be and should be present.[9] Hence the material cause which, so to say, supports it is a good; moreover the privation itself follows the extrusion of one contrary by its opposite, which itself is good in its own place, though not there; hence the indirect efficient and final causes of evil are also good.[10] The analysis is more closely pursued with respect to *malum culpæ* or voluntary and moral evil in later discussions on sin and the divine premotion of human acts.[11]

There are sound biological reasons why living things should suffer and die, yet it may be thought that the examination is conducted without much compassion with respect to *malum pœnæ* or physical evil—'physical' here having a wider meaning than 'bodily'. We can see the reason for eating and being eaten, even for old age in human beings, but are less resigned about Dutch disease in elms, rindepest in cattle, or meningitis, and less content to tolerate pain, even as a warning signal or salutary corrective. At once more informed about pathology and more tender to our immediate environment, our protest against many physical evils, and especially the atrocious ones, is so much the more effective and worthy. Yet, to return to the caution already sounded, the treatise offers little more than a detached appreciation of the general problem. This may not be a constituent of our own personal involvement, but is a condition for theological thinking about it.

---

[6]e.g. Ia. 48, 2   [7]e.g. ibid ad 3. cf Vol. 5, Introduction
[8]Vol. 2, Appendix 10
[9]Ia. 48, 1 & 2
[10]Ia. 49, 1
[11]Ia. 105. Vol. 16. Ia2æ. 10 & 13. Vol. 17. Ia2æ. 75 & 78. Vol. 25. Ia2æ. 109 & 112. Vol. 30

Glossary

(A list of the meanings given to some technical terms in the treatise. Variations appear in the footnotes)

abstract: absolute, pure and simple; an object considered apart from the composition involved in concrete existence, by an isolation of its meaning, *ratio*.

accidens: often translated 'modification' or even 'quality'. In general the word has two main senses. 1. In logic, a Predicate that happens to go with a Subject, *per accidens*, that is as a matter of fact, not necessity; called a 'predicable accident'. 2. In natural and metaphysical philosophy, a category of being which is not a thing, but accessory to a thing, not *ens* but *entis*; called a 'predicamental accident'. Nine types are enumerated by Aristotle, of which only three concern us here, namely quantity, quality, and relation.

act, actuality: the Aristotelean entelechy, in terrestial creatures the form and perfection of a material and determinable subject, or being in potentiality. First act renders a thing in being; second act renders it acting. *Operatio* and *actio* are often synonymous; strictly speaking, however, the first can remain within its principle, thus the immanent activities of knowing and loving, while the second, a making rather than a doing, is transitive and produces an outside effect.

agent: an efficient cause.

alteration: change affecting qualities.

analogy: agreement or correspondence between diverse objects which are neither univocal, that is exhibiting the same specific meaning, nor equivocal, that is possessing merely the same name in common, but which are really like. Either by a causal relationship to the first analogate, analogy of attribution, thus all that derives from the Good is itself somehow good; or by a parallel, analogy of proportionality, thus sight is to colour as mind is to being.

appetite, appetitus, inclinatio, orexis: the bent of a thing towards a good. Natural appetite is non-conscious; animal or voluntary appetite is through knowledge; sensory orexis or sensitive appetite is through sensation, rational appetite or will through intelligence.

being, ens: that which is. The notion cannot be analysed into components, and therefore is indefinable, yet it can be extended into various analogical meanings, thus the being of a purely mental construction, *ens rationis*, of a possibility, *ens possibile*, of an appearance or modification, *ens entis*, of a real potentiality, *ens in potentia*, and of an existing thing. All senses revolve round being-a-substance, *ens*.

cause: a positive principle on which real being depends. When used without qualification an efficient cause is usually meant, but there are three other main classes of cause, namely final, formal, and material causes.

chance, casus: applied to an effect produced by the intersection of the causation of two or more unrelated agents.

change, motus, mutatio: the passing from one to another condition or mode of existing. Substantial change or transformation, in primary matter from one kind of thing to another, called corruption with respect to the first, generation to the second: in strict usage this is not called *motus.* 'Accidental' change or modification in a material substance is called alteration for quality, growth and shrinking for quality, and local motion for place.

co-created is used of components of things which are created, namely whole things entirely caused from nothing.

common good: 1. The collective well-being of a group. 2. The divine order within the universe as embraced by mind and will. 3. God's own universal good, apart from though sustaining all created goods.

concrete: existing as or in a real substance.

contingent: possible to be, possible not to be.

contradictories: completely exclusive terms allowing no common agreement or intermediate condition. All men either support Aston Villa or they do not.

contraries: exclusive terms on a common basis which can allow of an intermediate condition, thus virtue and vice. An opposition capital for the problem of evil.

demonstration: a deduction to a conclusion which is certain. Contrasted with an argument from probability or a recommendation, *argumentum ex convenientia.*

disposition: here taken passively for the aptness of a subject to be acted on. A *dispositive cause* with regard to an effect is reckoned under the heading of a material cause.

distinction: any type of non-identity between objects and things. Often called diversity or difference, yet to be precise *diversity* is used for the complete otherness of things, while *specific difference* implies that objects agree in their genus.

duration: continuous existence, called eternity of pure actuality, *ævum* of actuality in underlying potentiality, time of actuality expecting a succeeding actuality.

efficient cause, agens: an executive principle producing what is other than itself, called the *effect,* to which it is prior in nature though not necessarily in time. *Principal cause,* one that acts from its own resources; *instrumental cause,* one that transmits and modifies the causality of a principal cause to produce an effect higher than itself. Yet a *secondary cause* can be principal cause within the range of its own proper activity, thus creatures. The *first cause* may refer to a particular system, but ordinarily it means the first universal cause of the whole universe; this is not the initial cause within the series, but from without communicates causality to the whole.

end, finis: that for the sake of which an agent acts. A good end is worthy in itself, *honestum*, and enjoyable, *delectabile*. Contrast with what is useful for an end, *bonum utile*. An end may be ultimate, God's goodness, or penultimate and intermediate, goodness in creatures, which though from and to God are not for God in the sense of being mere utilities: the analogy here between efficient and final causes is essential to St Thomas's theology. *Objective end*, the thing acted for; *subjective end*, the act of securing it.

ens, essentia, esse, existence: see p. 149.

equivocal: ambiguous, the same in name but not in meaning or reality, whence the fallacy of equivocation or double meaning. Apart from the accidentally equivocal, the *æquivocum a casu*, ambiguity may be designed, *æquivocum a consilio* or analogical, to bring out the likeness between objects while respecting their diversity.

equivocal cause: one not within the species of the effect it produces, which effect is nevertheless like it by analogy.

eternity: the complete, unchanging, and all at once possession of eternal life. Duration beyond that of everlasting time.

evil: the absence of a good that should be present in a subject that is good and effected by an anomalous good. In rational beings divided into penalty, *malum pœnæ*, and fault, *malum culpæ*.

exemplar cause: the idea of a thing in the mind of the maker.

faith: in this treatise the theological virtue committing us to God's truth in revealing himself.

fault, culpa: the misdirection of a free act.

final cause: the end for which a thing is made, and more especially why an action is done, the reason for the acting of the efficient cause. *Internal finality*, the relation of activity to its proper causal objective; *external finality*, purpose within a design of other purposes.

form: 1. The meaning of a thing, its intelligible form. 2. Its inner shaping principle: *substantial form*, the actual principle united with the potential principle of primary matter (essential composition) determines what kind of being a thing has; '*accidental form*' modifies this being and its acting.

formal cause: correlative to material cause; any actuality as received in potentiality, though usually an exemplar as embodied.

genus: a class, and more pointedly one that can be divided into species. Hence *general*, common to many; a notion of extension rather than of intension.

good, bonum: the objective of love and especially of intelligent love which takes in the *ratio bonitatis*. All things are good in so far as they are actual. Moral good is not an ultimate good, but is applied to objects that come under man's loving activity in relation to his last end.

habitus: the condition of possessing and not lacking a form; not used here in its psychological sense, the steady bent towards a type of activity.

heaven, cælum: not used here in its theological sense, but as a term of natural philosophy to refer to the empyreal and sidereal spheres credited by medieval science with some kind of general cosmic causality.

idea: the exemplar of a thing in the mind of its maker.

image: a likeness in kind to an original, or at least according to a characteristic quality, usually its shape.

indirect cause: translates *causa per accidens*, one from which an effect, or better an event, supervenes in fact, not from the proper intention of the cause.

individual, individum: the equivalent of *singulare*, thus Jane Austen, not *particulare*, thus a woman novelist. Strictly speaking, a unit within a quantified field, or a thing numerically distinct from others in the same class.

intensification: increase in quality by deepening in a substance. Thus knowledge can grow intensively as well as extensively.

intentio: 1. In general belongs to the order of knowledge and love, hence *esse intentionale*, in contrast with *executio* which belongs to order of efficient causality. 2. The intent of will towards an end, the *velle* as opposed to the choice, *electio*, of objects furthering that end.

justice, justitia: a fair balance between parts, and especially the virtue of rendering to others what is their due. General justice, for the sake of the common good. Particular justice, for the sake of personal rights: called commutative justice when it lies between person and person; a breach incurs the obligation of making restitution.

material cause: that out of which a thing is made and which continues to remain in its composition.

matter, materia: the potential substantial principle in all coming to be and dying away. Bare matter, *materia prima*, is an abstraction and inference from body in the concrete, *materia secunda*; or this piece of matter, *materia signata*.

metaphysics: the study of being as such in abstraction from sensible being and quantified being.

motion, motus: usually translated change; the progressive actualization still going on of a potential subject, that is not yet having reached its culmination. *Movens*, the agent setting in motion; *mobile*, the subject set in motion.

natural agent, agens naturale: used in this treatise for a purely physical efficient cause, not a voluntary agent. It acts from its inborn dynamism, thus trees and animals, not from an intention of mind and will.

nature: 1. The principle of spontaneous motion from within a thing, in contrast with imposed or 'violent' motion. 2. The type to which a thing belongs. 3. The complexus of interacting creatures within the universe.

nothing, nihil, nullum ens: no-being-at-all, a more unconditional term than non-being, which may refer just to one sort of being.

objective, objectum: the correlative of an active subject, the formal interest engaging it. Material objective, the general context.

participation: the sharing in a note of being which of itself belongs elsewhere.
particular: a restricted general nature, a man, some men, most men. *Particular cause,* one that produces an effect as belonging to a class in things, not in its total being.
passio: the undergoing of *actio.*
penalization, malum pœnæ: a deprivation affecting the condition of a being, usually a rational being, by contrast with fault, malum culpæ, in responsible activity. Roughly equivalent to 'physical' evil as opposed to moral evil. Punishment is the non-voluntary suffering of this effect in consequence of wrongdoing.
place, locus: the immediate surface of the medium surrounding a body, providing its location or *ubi.*
principle, principium: that from which an object starts in any way at all, even nominally or in mere logic; thus a point with respect to a line, a premiss to a conclusion. A real principle is a cause with respect to what proceeds from it when there is dependence of existence.

quality: sometimes any modification or property of a thing, sometimes its special characteristic or *ratio.* Properly speaking, the third of Aristotle's categories, the accessory modification of a thing in itself according to its substantial form, thus an ability, activity, effect undergone, or shape, which though, resulting from quantity, stamps a thing with a certain style.
quantity: the modification of material substance whereby it has parts outside parts within itself and in relation to place, or physical dimensions.

ratio: 1. The objective meaning of a thing, its *logos,* and sometimes its especial point of characteristic. 2. The subjective power of grasping this, the mind, and sometimes by reasoning from premises to conclusion.
relation: the 'towardness' of one object to another. Predicamental relation, *relatio secundum esse,* a modification accessory to the thing or substance, thus 'thing-which-has-been-created'; transcendental relation, *relatio secundum dici,* thus 'creature'.

scientia: 1. Knowledge; 2. which is certain and not just opinion; 3. from internal evidence; 4. arrived at by reasoning; and 5. most properly, reasoning by demonstrative deduction.
soul, anima: the substantial form in a living body; vegetable, animal, human.
space: a relationship of distance between quantities. Imaginary space is a purely mental construction.
species: 1. The kind of being a thing is, and answering to some kind of

definition, which for bodily substance is by proximate genus and specific difference. 2. In psychology and the theory of knowledge, the likeness in a cognitive power relating it to an object. *Species sensibilis* in sensation, *species intelligibilis* in intellection.

spiritual substance: being not composed from matter.

subject: 1. A term of which another is predicated. 2. The thing presupposed to our thoughts about it. 3. A potential being which receives actuality. 4. Rarely, and rather confusingly, the objective of an operation.

substance, substantia: 1. Sometimes translated *ousia*, nature or essence. 2. More often, a being as existing in itself and not in another as in a subject.

time, tempus: the numbered measure of a duration according to a relationship of before and after; the succession of past, present, and future.

total cause, causa totius esse: take both extensively and comprehensively, and refer to each and every being and to all that is there.

trace, vestigium: a likeness that does not amount to an image.

unity: a negative concept, the indivision of a being in itself and its division from other beings.

universal: 1. A general idea that can be exemplified in many instances. 2. *Universal cause,* the first cause of all members of a class, and therefore standing outside it as an equivocal cause. God is the universal cause of the whole of being, and therefore transcends all things.

univocal: is used of different objects which exhibit a common meaning which is exactly the same in every case. *Univocal cause,* one which reproduces its specific nature in another individual.

violentia: the suffering, *passio,* of action from another against the proper tendency of the subject.

virtual, virtute: refers usually to the pre-existence of an effect in the power of a cause able to produce it.

will, voluntas: the power and act of loving an object known through mind, and especially when that object is an end. *Cause through will,* voluntary agent, produces an effect from a form conceived and loved (intended), not from a physical form, as when like breeds like. *Agens per naturam* and *agens per voluntatem* are contrasted in this treatise, but it is not implied that the last is unnatural, but that its activity is not from a necessary and purely physical impulse.

INDEX

(Italic numbers refer to passages not in St Thomas's text)

A

D

defectible being 115, 117, 137, 139
defective cause 133, 135, 137
definiteness of form 17
definition 8, *15*, 79
deliberate action 83, 154
Democritus *84, 92*, 93, 103
demonstration xxvii, 9, 71, 77, 79, 81, 95
  by efficient cause 5, 79, 81
Descartes, R. 150
design, argument from 103, 113, 159
desire for God 23
dialectical argument xxvi, 71, 97
diminution 121, 123
Dionysius, the Pseudo- 17, 19, 49, 51, 109, 113, 115, 117, 119, 129, 133, 148, 158, 159

dispositions 164
  contrary 121
  of subject 49, *85*, 121, 135
  to good 123
distinction *39*, 90, 99, 164
  formal & material 99
  in number and kind 99
  in things 17, *39*
division of quantities 123
Dominic, St *160*
Donne, John *16*
double-truth theory xx, xxv, *151*
dualism of good and evil 87, 97, 143
Durand of St Pourçain 95
duration 64–89, 154, 155, 164
duty *111*

E

Ecclesiasticus, Book of 97, 141
Eckhart, Meister *148*
effect like cause 55, 57
efficient cause 4, 5, 7, 9, *46*, 79, 81, 83, 113, 133, 135, 154, 158, 159, 164
egalitarianism 99
Eleatics 11
emanation *24, 26, 148, 149*
emotion *23*
Empedocles *11, 60*, 71, 73
empyrean heaven 89
end 21, 111, 164
  as principle of motion 55
  definite 103
ens 5, 113, 115, 119, 133, *149*
ente et essentia, Opusc. De 149
Ephesians, Epistle to 49
epistemology 19
equality 77, 97
error & heresy xxv, 153, 154
esse 8, 45, 41, *149*
  and *percipi* 19
  subsistens 6, 41
essence, realm of xxv, *150*
essence and existence *39, 43, 149*
essendi, natura 46, 47
eternal motion 73, 75
eternity *64*, 75, 83, 152, 153, 157
Euripides *92*

everlasting xxv, 65, 69, *70*, 151–9
evil xxii, xxiii, xxvi, 107–47, *160, 161*
  activity of 111, 113
  as conflicting with good 121, 123
  cause of 113, 133–47
  defined by good 109, 111, 113
  desired as good 111, 113
  destructive power of 119, 121, 123, 143
  division of in rational beings 123–31
  for good of whole 139
  in cause & in effect 135
  majority incidence of 147
  moral and physical 111, *124*, 139
  no supreme principle of 141, 143, 145
  permission for 115, 117
  relative not absolute *109*
  seated in good 117, 119
  total 143
evolution xxii, *62*, 63
ex 25, 27, 29
exemplar cause 15, 17, 19, 91, 95, 103, *134*
exemplarism *14, 19*
exemplars 95
existence 6, 7, 8, 9, 39, 41, 47, *93*
  proper effect of God *31, 37*, 45
  universal 45

F

faith xxii, xxiii, xxv, 55, *58*, 77, 79, 81, 152, 165
Father, God the 51, 53, 57, 87
fathering 49
fault 123, 125, 127, 129, 131, 137, 139
feasible, the 53
Ferrariensis, Sylvester *38*
final cause 4, *14*, *20*, 21, 23, 101, 113, 133, 135, 165
finality *103*
finiteness 43
first cause 5–23, 45, 69, 73, 137, 153
  voluntary 73
first intelligence 93
first setter in motion 73
form 165
  accessory 13, 27, 35, 41, 59
  and matter 13, 31, 65, 75, 93, 119

form—*continued*
  as perfection 119
  as principle of definition 17, 75
  as principle of distinction 99, 101
  as purpose 21, 23
  in conception and nature 75, 77, 95
  in universe 57, 61
  mental, for action 75, 77
  production of 23, 35, 59, 61
  substantial 11, 27, 35, 41, 59, 61, *101*
formal cause 4, *14*, 111, 113, 133, 135, 165
formal objective xix, xxii, 41
Forms, Platonic *12*, *15*, *19*, *63*
Foster, K. *160*
freewill 95
Friedländer, M. *65*

G

Gabirol, Ibn *42*
Galatians, Epistle to xxiii
Geiger, L. B. 145
generation *26*, 61, *84*
  human *46*
  of forms 23, 61
generosity, sheer 23, 55
Genesis, Book of 25, 31, 87, 93, 95, 97, 99, 159
geocentric physics *105*
geo-cultural periods 77, 83
Gerard of Cremona *39*
Ghost, God the Holy 51, 53, 55
Gilbert de la Porrée *19*
Gilby, T. *139*
Gilson, E. *149*
gloss, a 25, 87
Gloss, the 25, *88*, 125
Gnosticism xxiv, 87, *91*, *161*
God
  alone or above all xix, *91*
  and nature xix, xxii, *63*
  and responsibility for evil 129, 139, 141
  as creator 25, 27, 29, 31, 43, 45, 47, 49, 53, 55
  as efficient cause 9, 11, 13, 69

God—*continued*
  as exemplar cause 15, 17, 19, 69
  as final cause 21, 69
  as sole creator 43, 45, 47, 49
  as subsisting existence 7
  as universal cause 31
  attributes of 23, 51
  government of world by *158*, *159*
  nature & Persons 53
  of philosophy and theology xix
  perfection of *23*
  will of 69, 71, 73, 75, 81, 93, 95, 139
Good, the 55, *108*, *109*, 129, 165
  and end *54*, 55, *108*, *109*, 111, 133
  as actuality 129
  as cause of evil 133, 135, 137, 139
  attacked by evil 121
  causality of 133
  classes of 121, 123
  degrees of 115
  lessening of 123
  the sovereign 143
good man *128*, 129
grace *123*, 129
  and nature xix, xxii, *63*, 123
Gredt, J. *39*

O

P

Q

R

S

T